ALL ABOUT THELMA AND EVE

JUDITH ROOF

All about Thelma and Eve

Sidekicks and Third Wheels

UNIVERSITY OF ILLINOIS PRESS

URBANA AND CHICAGO

Library of Congress Cataloging-in-Publication Data
Roof, Judith, 1951–
All about Thelma and Eve : sidekicks and third wheels /
Judith Roof.
p.   cm.
Includes bibliographical references and index.
ISBN 0-252-02728-0 (cloth : alk. paper)
ISBN 0-252-07047-X (paper : alk. paper)
1. Women in motion pictures. 2. Motion picture actors
and actresses—United States—Biography. 3. Actresses—
United States—Biography. 4. Character actors and
actresses—United States—Biography. I. Title.
PN1995.9.W6R56   2002
791.43'028'0820973—dc21   2001004565

For Ann Dubé

Cil est fous à droit
Qui assez acroit
Et petit veut rendre.

Contents

Preface and Acknowledgments

I began this book for two reasons. The first was to flesh out how the narrative middle—the chaotic and confused point between opening and resolution—functioned as a way to permit the expression and influence of the other-than-heteronormative. A previous study, *Come As You Are: Sexuality and Narrative,* seemed to suggest that there was no way around the hegemony of the heteronormative, at least not within any logic that privileged ends or resolutions. However, it seemed to me that even within the structure that defines narrative as such, something else necessarily worked against the grain, not only to provide tension but also to afford a different view and sense of possibility. This study tries to discern what that something else is and how it works. This book is a view of narrative from the vantage point of the middle, the minor, and the perverse as it plays out in one of the most central sources of narrative in twentieth-century American culture: Hollywood cinema.

The second reason was an offhand remark I made at a Society for the Study of Narrative Literature conference in Albany, New York. A large group of women gathered around keynote speaker Tania Modleski were discussing a collection of essays they wanted to produce about their favorite actresses. When someone asked me which actress I would write about, I responded without even thinking, "Eve Arden." I wondered what fascinated me about her and realized much later that it was her middleness. As I thought about it, I realized that minor characters, such as those played by Arden, typify an odd mixture of perversity, middleness, and implied queerness. This study, then, also explores what is queer (both in the sense of eccentric and in terms of desire) in the middle and how that queerness functions both as a part of narrative and as an antidote to it. My examples of such middleness are the characters played by two female comic secondary characters: Eve Arden and Thelma Ritter.

Writing about the minor and the middle threatens to deform it by making it the center of focus, but I have tried to adhere to some consciousness of the narrative politics at work. To make an argument, I had to translate this middle to some other structural position; for this reason, making conclusions about the minor has the odd effect of feeling like déjà vu because in a way we had to be there to get there. I'm not sure that the middle affords any practical liberating site, but it does account for a much larger diversity of postures and pleasures than privileging ends and beginnings allows.

Ann C. Hall gave me the first opportunity to analyze these predilections in an essay for her collection *Delights, Desires, and Dilemmas: Essays on Women and the Media* (New York: Praeger, 1998), and I gratefully acknowledge permission to use rewritten portions of that essay in this book. The project was partially supported by a Research and University Graduate Studies grant from Indiana University, Bloomington. Individual chapters benefited from the generous comments offered by those who heard versions of them at the University of Louisville Twentieth-Century Literature Conference, the *Arizona Quarterly* Colloquium, the Indiana University Colloquium Series on Queer Studies, Antioch College, Bucknell University, The Free University of Berlin, and Michigan State University. I wish to thank Tom Byers, Harriette Seiler, Lynda Zwinger, Ed Dryden, Don Pease, Steve Sanders, Emily Crandall, Frank Smigiel, Tom Foster, Jean Gregorek, Ghislaine McDayter, Mike Payne, Jael Lehmann, Scott Michaelsen, Patrick O'Donnell, and Eyal Amiran for enabling these exchanges and providing insight. I also thank Joan Catapano for her kind and thoughtful guidance and support throughout the project. Finally, I am grateful to Ellen McCallum, Robin Silbergleid, and Dennis Allen for their careful readings of the draft manuscript.

All quotations of movie dialogue are from transcriptions I made from distributed versions of the films (usually video or DVD).

Introduction:
Some Minor Considerations

Our heroine walks into a police station accompanied by two nondescript plainclothesmen. As she enters the squad room, the camera leads her—the quietly desperate Mildred Pierce (Joan Crawford)—from the right side of the screen to the left, dollying slowly forward. The camera follows Mildred's sight line as she swings around, sees another woman, and quickly asks, "Ida, what are you . . . ?" before she is silenced by a policeman. The camera dollies in on the other woman, Ida Corwin (Eve Arden), as she starts to rise and says to the police officer restraining her, "Look, I bruise easy." The film cuts back to Mildred. The phone rings and another detective calls for Ida. Mildred turns again to watch Ida as she gets up and begins to walk out of the room. The camera tracks Ida from right to left as she stops to talk to another man—Wally (Jack Carson)—who enters the frame from the left. "Well, what is this? A class reunion?" she quips. "Looks like it," Wally responds grimly. The camera leaves Ida to track Wally going left to right, then returns to Mildred.

The midnight atmosphere of the high-ceilinged anteroom is a mixture of gangster and gothic, a noir milieu of cast shadows, winding cigarette smoke, fedoraed police, and sounds magnified in the empty predawn hours. This is the first time we have seen Ida Corwin, whose sardonic wisecracks toll brassily in the hollow grimness of the Criminal Division. At this point, thirteen minutes into the film, we know there is a dead body, and we suspect that Mildred is involved and that she has embroiled Wally. But in the police station Ida is a mystery woman whose fur coat

Ida Corwin (Eve Arden) and Mildred Pierce (Joan Crawford) in *Mildred Pierce*

and fashionable toque signal a refinement her witticisms belie and whose familiarity with both Mildred and Wally suggests their connection. Ida is neither a casual acquaintance nor a nemesis, however; the camera's imperative tug at Mildred as it pulls her around to see Ida, as well as the urgency and surprise expressed in Mildred's unfinished query, raise questions about who Ida is and what part she plays. But beyond the characters' stymied familiarity, Ida is a mystery at the scene's end and will stay that way for another twenty minutes until she is finally introduced in the long flashback history of Mildred's struggle for success.

Although Ida is intriguing, it is nearly impossible to follow her in *Mildred Pierce.* Despite her compelling, decoratively indecorous presence, the camera persistently moves away from her. Like Mildred, we too are restrained from further contact with her; we are tantalized, seduced, and kept away not only in this scene but throughout the film to various degrees. Secondary, a supporting player, one whose idiosyncratic difference marks her as minor and funny, wise and irreverent, Ida peoples the background fabric of the film, coming forward only occasionally to remind us of the different kind of sense that lurks throughout the story, a sense that might avoid Mildred's tragic decisions. Although films have many secondary characters (rejected love interests, hero's buddies, servants, children, functionaries, extras), wise comic female characters like

Ida, who perform modernized versions of the Shakespearean fool, occupy a crucial if eccentric position in film narrative, history, viewing, and operation. They not only figure audience knowledge in dramatic irony, they also mediate between characters and between the audience and the film. Main characters may triumph (or fail) at film's end, but female comic secondary characters play in the middle, producing and sorting confusions and anxieties, threatening short circuits of narrative, and helping the narrative along. They provide humor, wisdom, a point of identification, and the possibility of narrative alternatives until they disappear at the end. They are the site where minor, middle, and perverse overlap, undoing narrative as they do it and showing us another way to look.

Middle, Minor, Perverse

As David Bordwell points out, the "dominant" in classical Hollywood cinema (1917–60) is a "specific sort of narrative causality" (Bordwell, Staiger, and Thompson 12). This causality, he outlines further, consists of "causality, consequences, psychological motivations, the drive toward overcoming obstacles and achieving goals. Character centered . . . causality is the armature of the classical story" (13). This is another way of defining the parameters of a very traditional narrative structure as a series of cause-effect events organized in a trajectory from disturbing cause, through confusion and mishap, to achieved goal—or, more succinctly, beginning, middle, and end.[1] Most narrative analyses of classical Hollywood cinema focus on this dominant narrative, assuming that it defines filmic impetus and ideology.[2] Even though most of the energies and effects of cinematic production occur in relation to this dominant narrative, the whole structure must produce moments of uncertainty, chaos, and misdirection—a middle on which the narrative depends but by its very nature threatens to escape. This middle is the subject of this book, not in terms of plot but in the ways middleness becomes associated, via Hollywood's economy of characters, with a particular type of character: the female comic supporting (or secondary) character. The dominant may seem dominant, but it is not the only show in town.

Bordwell's narrative "dominant" is itself understood only as a whole. Peter Brooks tells us that "meaning in plot is the structure of action in closed and legible wholes" (280–81). Although Brooks is asserting the centrality of metaphor in narrative, he is also describing how narrative is typically perceived. "The beginning," Brooks declares, "presupposes the end" (283). "The fiction film is defined by its closure" (Heath 133). It seems that there is little in narrative that might escape the overwhelming urge toward holistic meaning. Wholeness conceived in certain terms—the ideologically proper beginning and end—endows meaning, and incompleteness or openness in narrative is not meaningful apart from this structure. The shape of narrative and this insistence on wholeness also expresses ideology, in particular that which emphasizes the joining of opposites in production or reproduction (e.g., heterosexuality, capitalism). Narrative therefore is a system of organizing and producing sense that constantly reproduces in its structure and operation dominant cultural ideology.[3]

But narrative doers have a middle that is more than simply the filling between the beginning's catalyzing irritation and the end. On one hand, Brooks's reading of narrative seems to suggest that the space and time between the beginning and end of narrative are a necessary postponement of the end—a postponement requisite to achieving the proper end at the proper time. But Brooks also suggests that the middle presents a real danger to narrative. Calling the middle a "détour," Brooks finds in it the potential danger of a mistake that will lead to an "improper end." "The improper end indeed lurks throughout narrative, frequently as the wrong choice: choice of the wrong casket, misapprehension of the magical agent, false erotic object-choice. The development of the subplot in the classical novel usually suggests . . . a different solution to the problems worked through by the main plot, and often illustrates the danger of the short-circuit" (292). But, Brooks points out, even the subplot "wards off the danger" of the short circuit by perpetuating narrative until it can end at the right place.

The middle is two things: a useful detour and a threatened short circuit. The useful detour is assigned to the "sub": the plot appended to and parasitic on the main plot. The short circuit is linked to wrong choices, misapprehensions, and false erotic object choices. These threatened mistakes veer toward the threat of too much sameness and hence stasis rather than toward the kind of radical difference that would exit the story altogether. Short circuits short narrative's circuit by prematurely discharging the energy of desire in a proximate spot, one too close and like, such as incest or homosexuality (where homosexuality is understood as like-to-like). In the context of meaning's grand narrative plan (or narrative's grand meaning plan), short circuits represent a stopping too soon and a settling for less, where sooner and lesser are choices that run counter to dominant ideologies of the proper, the right, and the valuable (e.g., heterosexual marriage, reproduction, death, knowledge, and victory). Short circuits suggest the possibility that desire will never get there but will circulate meaninglessly through the perversely short circuits of a middling homogeneity, forever dancing with itself.

In narratives we recognize as such, these short circuits do not occur, or if they do, their spark provides the tantalizing tension of threatened noncompletion that makes the ultimate ending more satisfying. But is the middle of narrative—even if overrun with goofs, flickering circuits, and lost directions—so completely foreclosed by the end that its peccadilloes can exist only if ultimately corrected by the end? Is the middle simply a structural designation that loses its middling menace when taken out of its narrative envelope, or are there middling elements that are ineffably and essentially middle? If the stuff of the middle could surmount the imperatives of current notions of proper narrative, how would we know? If unframed by the resolutely stiffening mainstays of a wholeness-endowing end, will the teeming mess of parts, fragments, wanderings, and filler provide a different kind of legibility? It will only if we understand narrative differently from the start or start at a different point in narrative. The problem is perspective, both as a sense-making device and as an assumption of ideologies. All the elements—sense and nonsense—of narrative are always there. We choose (sometimes consciously, mostly unconsciously) to privilege some over others based on the ways they comport with particular understandings of meaning, closure, and fulfillment. If we think the middle is interesting and we start there, the narrative may no longer make its proper sense, but the middle still works and it has its own sense. But its sense may not be the same either structurally or ideologically as the sense reaffirmed by the whole story. Perversely, however, its sense may not be completely different either. The middle is ambivalent and multivalent.

Let us then wallow in the middle; one model for so doing is the category of the minor. In Gilles Deleuze and Felix Guattari's terms, the minor is "rhizomatic";[4] minor characters hint at the possibility of multiple entrances to a text and a wandering away from organization, structure, and the "signifier" and "attempts to interpret a work." In their own dicta about the minor, Deleuze and Guattari note its self-contradictory qualities. On one hand, it rambles, multiplies, evades, and wanders, and on the other, like the psychoanalytical symptom, it is the site where unconscious meaning opens and becomes visible. The minor is thus quite a major point. Another model is the eccentric or marginal as defined by Jacques Derrida. Commenting on his own reading practice, Derrida remarks, "I do not 'concentrate' in my reading either exclusively or primarily on those points that appear to be the most 'important,' 'central,' 'crucial.' Rather, I de-concentrate, and it is the secondary, eccentric, lateral, marginal, parasitic, borderline cases which are 'important' to me and are a source of many things, such as pleasure, but also insight into the general functioning of a textual system" (*Limited, Inc.* 44). In the sophisticated readings of deconstruction, the minor often provides the elements that clash, undermine, or undo any sense of textual unity or consistency.

Although the middle derives its identity, at least initially, from the structural exigencies of narrative wholeness (a wholeness always understood already in terms of the narrative closure that makes it a "whole" story), the minor derives its character from the politics of hierarchies. The coincidence of middle and minor occurs as an effect of interpretation. As Derrida suggests, sometimes what we see and find meaningful depends on where and how we look. We tend not to look at the middle because we most often look to and for certain notions of meaning and wholeness, especially as those concepts translate into such categories as life and death or such ideologies as heterosexuality, reproduction, production, knowledge, victory, or other "fitting" ends. Or we may be so subjected to the operation of structure and ideology that we can look only where they point. The minor may persist ubiquitously, like white noise, but we don't notice it unless we look or listen for it. It may be that the middle is as ubiquitous as the minor. The "wrong" stuff seen as occupying the middle is always there, even at beginning and end, but like stars in the daytime, it is obscured by the scintillating radiance of cultural truths and the stark lines of narrative's familiar pattern.

If middle and minor coincide as they shift in and out of structural categories, what might focusing on them tell us about other possibilities that already operate around and within the predominant structures that seem to shape consciousness? What other kinds of meaning and knowledge will the eccentricity, obliquity, peregrination, irresolution, kaleidoscopism, and astigmatism of the middle and minor provide?

Repeating the Previous through Another Theoretical Lens, Briefly

Freud has made this case about the middle and the minor using the more concrete example of sexualities. Brooks's argument about narrative is premised on a reading of Freud's *Beyond the Pleasure Principle,* but Freud makes a case for the importance of the middle as the category of the perverse in "Three Essays on the Theory of Sexuality." In Freud's characterizations of the perverse, its role is quintessentially narrative, and it operates in the middle. In his account of the role of the perverse in

"Three Essays on the Theory of Sexuality," what we think of as the perverse—the elements of a story that lead to the wrong end or the wrong object and thus threaten premature satisfaction—are necessary to any normative or dominant narrative and yet deviate irrecuperably from it. As Freud puts it,

> We were thus led to regard any established aberration from normal sexuality as an instance of developmental inhibition and infantilism. Though it was necessary to place in the foreground the importance of the variations in the original disposition, a co-operative and not an opposing relation was to be assumed as existing between them and the influences of actual life. It appeared, on the other hand, that since the original disposition is necessarily a complex one, the sexual instinct itself must be something put together from various factors, and that in the perversions it falls apart, as it were, into its components. The perversions were thus seen to be on the one hand inhibitions, and on the other hand dissociations, of normal development. Both these aspects were brought together in the supposition that the sexual instinct of adults arises from a combination of a number of impulses of childhood into a unity, an impulsion with a single aim. (97–98)

The story of sexual development goes from a state where there are a number of possibilities to a conclusion where aim and object come together. The perversions exist as some of the possibilities, but they are significant as alternate possibilities only in relation to an end we already understand to be "normal" heterosexual intercourse. The perverse elements among the multiple possibilities help us to get to the proper end, but they also work against getting there by providing alternative paths to pleasure. They might consist of multiple potential mates, different career choices, the possibility of incest, death, homosexuality, or celibacy, for example, all of which lead in directions different from the impetus of the primary plot. Even if the story has a happy heterosexual ending, the perverse possibilities still persist as alternatives and threats to the singularity of the system.

Freud's theory plays out Brooks's story of the middle in the terms of sexual ideology. Its oblique relationship between normative and perverse offers another lens through which to understand both the middle and the minor, however. The middle of Freud's story, the perverse, functions like Brooks's notion of the middle. The middle of narrative is perverse because it consists of the same kinds of mistaken choices ("false erotic object-choices") as the perverse. The minor is structurally perverse—out of the center, out of focus, out of the mainstream. Minor things are perverse precisely because they are not the center of focus. It would be the case that not everything minor is perverse in terms of ideological alignments (the heterosexual marriages of servants, for example), but much of the minor is perverse in its structural relation to the end and to meaning. The three terms—middle, minor, and perverse—come together in their shared structural relation to the dominant, the normative, and the important.

But where can we see this all playing out? We could look at the middles of stories, or as Deleuze and Guattari do in *Kafka*, look at minor elements of the writings of a practitioner of a minor literature. Or we could go to the mainest mainstream (or at least one mainstream)—Hollywood cinema—and investigate one specimen of minor character whose main role exists predominantly in the middles of narratives. Through this figure, our perverse Virgil (Beatrice?), we might see how the concatenation of middle, minor, and perverse terms plays out as a moment in narrative, where the possibility of a different perspective produces a threat to narrative and meaning. We might also see how this medial representative embodies and operates perversity, otherness, multiplicity, and different registers of meaning and meaninglessness.

This book, following Bordwell's insight that classical Hollywood narrative plays out through an economy of character, focuses on the kind of middle linked to, synecdochized through, and enacted by a specific kind of minor character: the female comic secondary character represented by such actresses as Eve Arden, Thelma Ritter, Rosalind Russell, Mary Wickes, Whoopi Goldberg, and Kathy Najimy. The book assays several questions simultaneously: How do female comic seconds function in film narratives? What do they tell us about the nature of the middle and the minor in narrative? What does looking at the middle and minor tell us about narrative and filmic practice?

In Medias Res

The film industry has been long aware of the dynamics of major and minor, end and middle in more literal terms than Deleuze and Guattari, Derrida, or Freud. The relation of major and minor is reflected in the typing and casting of actors and actresses, the division of film production into expensive A features and cheaper B movies, and the conventional ways minor characters are presented, ranging from positions in the title credits (an arena where many battles of major and minor are fought) to the camera distances and angles by which various characters are filmed to movie narratives that themselves trace, sometimes obsessively, the relation between major and minor in show business and elsewhere. For example, one formula often exploited by Hollywood is the narrative of the underdog—the overlooked, the understudy, the outnumbered, the ugly duckling—who prevails over a major force in everything from backstage musicals to westerns, spy films, teen Sturm und Drang, and *Lawrence of Arabia*. In this formula, the minor is really major, and the middle is really the beginning that the end will correct. Films focus on these underdogs from the start and in the process deploy minor characters whose minor status is not the subject of the film. In fact, the direction of this formula is to make the major the desirable goal of the minor, the end the goal of the middle.[5]

Minor elements pervade cinema in the guise of comic gags that do not further the plot, incidental details, subplots that end up going nowhere, and a variety of types of minor characters. In terms of film narrative, these minor elements appear and work primarily at the beginning and in the middle of the film; they tend to disappear at the end, or they serve as structural echoes of the fates of the protagonists. Details and gags take up space and time, sometimes forming motifs that complement other patterns and themes in the film, sometimes working as seemingly idiosyncratic moments remarkable for their seeming irrelevance in otherwise very economical systems.

Films deploy many different kinds of minor characters, each of which works somewhat differently. The character types that enable an economical character-focused narrative are types, like the wise fool, that come from traditional theater and are more visible and operative in the literal middle of films.[6] According to Jay Leyda, Sergei Eisenstein saw film typage as "a modern development of the *commedia dell'arte*—with its seven stock figures multiplied into infinity. The relationship lies not in numbers, but in audience conditioning" (Eisenstein 9). Likewise, Bordwell suggests that classical Hollywood characters develop from earlier conventions that followed the practice of typing via occupation (Bordwell, Staiger, and Thompson 14). The importance of audience conditioning, or typage, as Eisenstein puts it, "included a specific approach to the events embraced by the content of the film" (8). Minor types such as servants provided certain perspectives on the action. My argument is that the perspectives and approaches attached to supporting characters are more important than we might think, precisely because film narrative works through character type.

As we shall see in chapter 4, minor characters themselves form structured, interdependent, interlocking communities in which each defines the others as well as the main characters. There are many kinds or degrees of minor characters. Extras are nameless, appear fleetingly, and merely suggest the presence of a person or a crowd. Functionaries perform specific stereotyped tasks (cab driver, waiter, cop). Stock players have names, lines, and a role in the plot, but they express little individuality. Character actors and actresses exhibit more personality than their function requires, and some—the comic seconds—specialize in playing sidekicks. These characters are comic both in comedies, where they tend to provide much of the comedy derived from character, and in serious drama, where their presence provides both relief and intensification (Thelma Ritter's character, Moe, in *Pickup on South Street* and Eve Arden's Maida Rutledge in *Anatomy of a Murder* are two examples).

That the role of wise fool is occupied almost entirely by female rather than male comic seconds has to do with the differing disposition of the masculine and feminine in narrative, the asymmetries of males' and females' relations to secondary status, and differing understandings of male and female stars. As Teresa de Lauretis points out, our conceptions of narrative are themselves gendered insofar as "the hero . . . is constructed as human being and male," whereas "female is what is not susceptible to transformation . . . she is an element of plot-space, a topos, a resistance, matrix and matter" (*Alice Doesn't* 119). Within this metaphorically gendered relation, only certain roles are possible for female characters: mother, girlfriend, or servant. Unlike most female protagonists, female comic secondary characters are degendered, masculinized, or queered; they are removed from salient action in any role except as facilitator or wise fool, even though their presence still hints at perverse alternatives of nonmarriage, independence, and business success. Female comic seconds are thus somewhat parasitic; male comic seconds can exist as independent entities.

Because of the differences in their relative positions in narrative, where independent but secondary females are more out of their expected narrative disposition than servant males (who merely look weak), female comic secondary characters tend to be more empowered, more knowledgeable, more threatening, and more liminal than their male counterparts. Unmarried or secondary male characters are not a problem to patriarchal systems, although just as female comic seconds tend to be desexualized or masculinized in relation to female protagonists, male comic seconds often are feminized in relation to male protagonists. However, this feminization—or queering—does not enable male comic seconds to have the same kind of disturbing effect as female comic seconds.[7] On one hand, feminization produces a palimpsest of the heterosexual (and the male homosexual or lesbian) couple; on the other, it seems to enable the feminized male to exhibit stereotypically feminine qualities such as sensitivity, nurturance, and female intuition.

Male comic seconds have a slightly different relation to the protagonist than female comic seconds, mostly because gender partly defines roles in narrative (and narrative defines possible gender roles, such as the stereotypical association between masculinity and activity). Although some male comic seconds such as Donald O'Connor and Phil Silvers are, like female comic seconds, fool figures, the quality and function of the fools they play are different from the roles played by such actresses as Eve Arden and Thelma Ritter, especially insofar as female comic seconds seem to have a magical insight their male counterparts often lack or exercise sparingly. The gender politics of the middle is complex and intriguing, mostly because of the possibilities for multiplicity and misalignment offered by the middle. In this book I focus primarily on the female secondary characters who occupy the role of the wise fool, exploring through them the middle's gender foibles, but this does not begin to exhaust the middle's gender permutations or the dynamics of their interplay.

This is certainly not the first book to focus on secondary or supporting characters and the significance of their position. From the angle of character type or stereotype, both Karen Stoddard (in *Saints and Shrews: Women and Aging in American Popular Film*) and Kathleen Rowe (in *The Unruly Woman: Gender and the Genres of Laughter*) have looked at the ways female characters defy gender expectations to become comic versions of excess, threat, or buffoonery. Stoddard focuses on the ways older women can break out of feminine typologies, and Rowe looks at female comedians. For the last fifteen years, critics have considered the representation (or representability) of gay men and lesbians in cinema, a category that has traditionally occupied the narrative middle. Richard Dyer, reiterating Eisenstein's claims about typage, suggests that gay men and lesbians often are presented either as stereotypes or within a set of types that enable their recognition as gay, carrying "within their very representation an implicit narrative" (*Matter* 15). In Judith Mayne's extended meditations on women and lesbians in film and media, "lesbian spectatorship is concerned with the space between visibility and invisibility" (*Framed* xviii). The lesbian's ambivalent status parallels and suggests the association of the middle with queerness as a category that opens up multiple possibilities while functioning as a necessary part of narrative. This is not to say that all middle characters necessarily have a lesbian or queer identity (either overt or covert) but that their middle position itself is the site of queerness—and that queerness almost always works in a way analogous to the contradictions and ambivalences of the middle. The question in this book is how characters both are and aren't stereotypes that work as necessary parts of narrative while they exceed or defy it.[8]

Patricia White's superb study of supporting actresses, *The UnInvited: Classical Hollywood Cinema and Lesbian Representability,* thoroughly and brilliantly analyzes the ways in which the marginal position and casting of supporting female roles in Production Code–era films enact, encode, and enable a decoding of lesbian presence in cinema. White examines the lesbian connotations of the outsider site provided in film and how in particular certain figures—Agnes Moorehead, Ethel Waters—signify lesbian presence in complex ways: the employment of actresses rumored to be lesbian, the imaging of inappropriate gender behavior, the suggestiveness of women's relationships with other women, and the sense of included marginality that clings to supporting roles. In his study of homosexuals and cinema, Michael Bronski notes the lesbian import of sidekicks: "The sidekick's role was generally to act as a confidante and to give the audience a pungent analysis of the plot. Sidekicks were sarcastic, unromantic, and sensible. They were cleverly self-deprecating . . . but could also turn the wit on men. Too smart ever to get the man, sidekicks had to settle for being funnier than everybody else" (102).

Instead of focusing on a particular identity or sexual economy, this book studies what a specific kind of secondary character can tell us about the metaphorically queer dynamics of the narrative middle in mainstream American cinema. Rarely overtly queer (though often encoding or retrospectively decoded as lesbian, as White, Mayne, and Weiss have shown), this middle site contributes a part of narrative that is not completely aligned with the heteronormative drives of mainstream cinematic narrative as outlined by David Bordwell, Teresa de Lauretis, and Stephen Heath.[9] The obliqueness or eccentricity of the female comic second is not quite outside but intrinsic and yet unconsidered. White analyzes the lesbian ramifications of the figurative outsider who is enfolded as a supporting character (both comic and not), whereas this study treats the comic insider who is too much inside—too middle—as a way of understanding how narrative in concert with cinematic practice provides multiple sites for consumption and identification within and yet beyond the automatic lessons of dominant ideology.

What follows focuses primarily on films featuring Eve Arden and Thelma Ritter such as *Stage Door* (1937), *Cover Girl* (1944), *Mildred Pierce* (1945), *All about Eve* (1950), *Rear Window* (1954), *Anatomy of a Murder* (1959), *The Misfits* (1961), *Move Over Darling* (1963), and *Boeing Boeing* (1965). Both actresses, whose work exemplifies the powerful essence of the female comic second, consistently and over a long period of time play the same type of secondary character in popular and critically reputable films. Although I am (perhaps ironically given my interest in the minor) focusing on two of the most prominent character actresses who appeared in Hollywood film, a part of the study is devoted to even more minor secondary, perhaps tertiary players who all define, refine, delight, and enlighten in their vital minor roles. As pretext and context for examining singular secondary characters, I consider films— *The Women* (1939), *The Trouble with Angels* (1966), *Soapdish* (1991), *Sister Act* (1992), and *Boys on the Side* (1995)—in which conventionally secondary communities of female characters are made prominent, showing not only how Hollywood represents the minor as a conscious construction but also how this minor enables perverse possibility, sustains the status quo, and defines the character of the eccentric secondary character. I also consider films that illustrate the intricate relation between secondary characters and tertiary characters played by blacks and children—*Holiday Inn* (1942) and *White Christmas* (1954)—and those that make central a character whose attributes mark her as minor—*Auntie Mame* (1958) and *The Associate* (1996). In addition to Arden and Ritter, I examine the work of such actresses as Rosalind Russell, Joan Crawford, Butterfly McQueen, Mary Wickes, Louise Beavers, Virginia Weidler, Peggy Cass, Kathy Najimy, and Whoopi Goldberg.

Vectors of Illegibility

Eve Arden's and Thelma Ritter's idiosyncratic sidekick personae translated into screen longevity. Arden's career lasted from the 1929 *The Song of Love* to 1982's *Grease 2* and included the successful radio and television series *Our Miss Brooks* (1952–57). Coming to the movies from a stage career, Ritter spent the twenty years from 1947 to 1968 making films; she was nominated six times for an Academy Award for playing secondary characters. Typecast almost from their entrance into film, Arden and Ritter never played a lead in the movies, although Arden often played leads on stage. Arden's fifty-three years on celluloid is matched only by Mary Wickes, who began acting in films in 1941 and was still cavorting as a gawky nun in *Sister Act II* (1993), and is closely followed by Joan Crawford, who performed in film from 1925 until 1970, and Rosalind Russell, who appeared from 1934 until 1971. Although Arden and Wickes might owe their staying power to the fact that secondary roles require personality rather than looks, Russell and Crawford show the value of versatility. McQueen's and Beavers's careers were limited by the parts available to black actresses in Hollywood, although Beavers performed such roles from 1923 until 1962, the year she died. McQueen, who quickly tired of her stereotyped roles, retired from film in 1947 after only eight years.

On the surface Arden's and Ritter's characters represent several different kinds of eccentricity: They are fool figures in the traditional Shakespearean sense, they embody class and gender differences in the middle's bubbling confusions, they represent safety, security, and reliability as an alternative to the imperatives of mainstream ideologies, and they embody the knowledge gained from occupying an ambivalent, inside-outside position. These functions are visible both because these characters operate in the middle, where multifarious differences are tolerated, and because the characters are not the "real" subjects of interest. This auxiliariness enables their narrative contributions but also enables their near invisibility or even our disavowal of them (they may be present, we see them, but we pay no attention). Their ability to be present and yet not be noticed permits them to support the primary story and simultaneously deviate from it without apparent conflict.

Although this quality of unnoticeableness seems to exist by definition (the minor are minor because they are minor), it is actually part of a hierarchy that is necessary to maintain the centrality of the primary characters. When we watch, we do not notice all that must come together to make a film. Much of it is there in front of our eyes, but the cinematic apparatus—the organized assemblage of imaging, editing, and narrative practices, cultural ideals, psychological mechanisms, and enunciative strategies—tends to focus our attention on the acts and emotions of the main characters in the primary plot. Because the apparatus elides most of its operations, we tend not to pay attention, for example, to the editing in a film that keeps us focused on one character or another, or consciously think of the star system as one reason we are interested in the major characters stars play or recognize how main characters inevitably dramatize the various moral dilemmas of a given era (unless for some reason they don't). When one tries to watch minor elements in a film, not only is the attempt nearly impossible, but the work of the apparatus becomes quite visible. Major characters wouldn't be major characters unless they enjoyed the results of the flattering style and adulative duration of camera attention, were the subjects of a narrative that focuses events and their outcome around the stars' actions and feelings, and could take for granted the maestro performances of supporting characters whose ostensible role is to do just that: support main characters, embellish their elegance, and make them look good and central and important while providing variety and contrast.

Arden, Ritter, and other female secondary characters are types with a long cultural history that have been transposed into the modern argot of Hollywood. In *The Comic Mind*, Gerald Mast notes that "comic types . . . line up our responses in the intended direction. Because of the pervasiveness of these types, critics have consistently identified comic character with 'the base,' 'the lowly,' 'the mechanical,' or 'the ridiculous'" (10). As Mast shows, classical Hollywood has evolved these types into more hybrid and less class-attached profiles. The types themselves seem to derive, as both Eisenstein and John Rudlin suggest, from the tradition of the *commedia dell'arte* developed through theater and vaudeville (Rudlin 7). Female comic secondary characters are hybrids of the Brighelle, a form of the Zanni, and the servant figure, the Fantesca. The Brighella is the boss of the Zanni (generally male wanderers with a strong survival instinct, persistence, hunger, and extreme loyalty). Both Arden and Ritter often play peripatetic manager types, bosses of the servant world, and like Zanni, they can directly address the audience because they are often the most sympathetic characters. Like that of the Brighelle, their address tends to be cynical, and often female comic seconds go further, more like the Fantesca, the female version of the Zanni, who is "collusive" with the audience because "she is a spectator herself" (130). Like the Fantesca, female comic seconds have a "very strong relationship with the audience, almost confidential in the sense that she too can see what fools the rest of them are" (Rudlin 130). Female comic seconds combine the cynical independence of the Brighella with the collusive character of the Fantesca.

The Hollywood manifestation of the fool as female (or hermaphroditic), unattached, and lower class perpetuates the wise servant figure but tailors it to reflect generalized cultural anxieties about the role of women, the larger problem of gender confusion, the potentials of class, and the alternatives of democracy. Shrewd, loyal, utilitarian, pragmatic, self-denying, perceptive, outspoken, witty, wise, and likable, these characters are able to cross the bounds of social groupings, gender expectations, and often propriety. They are privy to the main character's introspection, perform a metacommentary on the film's action, double the female protagonist and the audience, and mediate between film and viewer in various ways, continuing the ambivalence of the wise fool—the Jacques, Marias, and Touchstones of modern cinema. Like the predecessors, the characters are interpreters and intercessors, both inside and outside the film's narrative and time, ahead of the story and within it, existing as two personae at once. This inside-outside position accounts in part for the difference in tone displayed by Ida Corwin in the sequence from *Mildred*

Pierce described earlier. Like the others, Ida has been brought in for questioning, but unlike Mildred and Wally, Ida seems to take a view from outside, the perspective necessary for ironic observation (as in the "class reunion" comment). Ida's presence in the sense of her noticeable bearing or conspicuous essence is produced both by the conflicting signals of her dress and manner and by her being simultaneously within and distanced from the action.

As the figurative (or literal) servants, female comic secondary characters often play out differences in class, education, and expectation that account superficially for their different perspectives. On one hand, their class difference (which is often undefinable) gives female comic secondary characters a freedom of action more restricted upper class characters don't have. On the other hand, their class difference (constructed always in relation to the main character) is expressed through a gender difference where female comic secondary characters are less traditionally feminine than main characters because they are older, are children, or are simply taller and brasher (both Arden and Wickes). At the same time, reciprocally, their comparative lack of femininity is also an indication of a lower-class status. These differences free female comic secondary characters to be more daring because they have less to lose. They also have a verbal or vaguely voyeuristic rather than immediately physical relation to sexuality (if they have one at all). In communities of women, such characters tend to perform more masculine roles; they wear the pants, sit akilter, talk back. They can do "unfeminine" things in unfeminine ways because they aren't presented as sufficiently womanly. At the same time, their freedom actually presents a broader vision of what women can do and how they can do it. Among men, they are reluctantly maternal or aunt-like, crosses between buddies and moms who are definitely out of the mating game.

That female comic seconds are a version of the traditional fool figure results partly from their position as women who are unattached or unworried about mating. The fool is one way in which Hollywood cinema resolves the dilemma of the "loose" woman. Insofar as the prototypical narratives of many film genres are linked to a heterosexualized disposition of female characters—women are married, tragically not, fallen, recovered, all in relation to men—females who present only a distant or secondary relation to such hetero fates seem to fall out of narrative consideration. The good pretty woman gets married and the bad pretty woman gets what she deserves, but the really smart but gawky woman gets nothing, creating a loose end for the romance plot that is visible not so much at the film's end, where these characters usually disappear, but throughout the film in their example of a chronically reluctant liberation. This raises the question of why such characters are present at all if they pose such a problem. They are comic, they provide contrast, and they provide the very necessary middle material: the wrong choice, the bogus alternative, the threat to end that paradoxically perpetuates the story's tensions. They are perfect embodiments of the middle—the "détour," mistake, wrong choice—Brooks describes (to go full circle). Their transformation into fool or quasifool characters may be one way to deal with the excess they represent. At the same time, the fool character may appear in the guise of the loose woman as the most logical way to include the fool and its complex negotiations of knowledge and borders within the conventions of Hollywood verisimilitude. Or both.

Their differences in class and gender function as an entrée or privilege that enables these secondary characters to be compelling, if marginal, insiders, confidantes, and advisors. On one hand, as White suggests, this could be attributed to the characters' covert lesbianism; on the other, the fact that they are not explicitly lesbian enables a ranging queerness that may be lesbian and may be many other things. There is no doubt that the lesbian tone is often present. My question is how that tone functions within narrative. Unfettered by the niceties of class or gender, female comic seconds can acknowledge, ridicule, and negotiate—often through humor—the difficulties more major characters face. Their class-crossing hermaphroditism locates and distances threats to both heterosexuality and sexual difference, enabling the untroubled flow of the primary heteronarrative while permitting on the margins the excess that grounds irony. They often threaten to exceed the piece (e.g., to be too strong, to end better), exuding the power linked to borders and potential transgressions. The alternative they often represent—independence—does not cease to be desirable at the film's end, nor is the sense of another coexisting narrative cut off. As William Willeford observes, fools "represent destructive realities to be dealt with by culture, warded off or in some way made acceptable" (84).

At the same time, their class difference and associations with the everyday also align such characters with safe intermediate or liminal spaces in the film: offices, kitchens, rooms off to the side, more private, often domestic spaces that would, in relation to the dominant narrative, be off-screen spaces. As secretaries, managers, nurses, bus drivers, and housekeepers, they provide security that minor things won't fall apart, that there is a reliable base. We trust these characters to be in control behind the scenes; wisecracking characters gain the privilege to speak the otherwise unspeakable only because they don't make too many mistakes elsewhere. Associated with the space behind the scenes, these second-ary characters not only render such spaces a point of respite and more distanced perception but carry with them an aura of safety when they emerge in more public contexts. Ida exists mainly in restaurants, for example, moving, as the film progresses, from the dining room to the cash register and office. Mildred's office is where Mildred confides in Ida, but as the seat of power it is also the space where Mildred must take chances and make decisions. As the office grows more dangerous for Mildred, Ida moves out of it; she appears less and less in the office space with Mildred and is imaged instead in Mildred's home, where she tries to protect Mildred against the ravages of her plotting husband and social-climbing daughter.

Ancillary to the narrative's main drive like many fool figures, female comic secondary characters function as audiences within the world in which they are depicted, observing and commenting. Supplying and embodying perverse knowledge, they play a special role in relation to knowledge both within film and as an extension and embodiment of dra-matic irony. The snide observations of Ida Corwin or the folksy wisdom of Stella (Thelma Ritter) in *Rear Window* point to a knowledge of the shape of events that is obvious to those not immersed in the action. In their position as wise fools, female comic secondary characters provide alternative perspectives. By coming close to breaking filmic diegesis, they remind the audience of what the audience knows, particularly of their knowledge beyond the film itself, becoming the embodiment of the knowledge film viewers already have and reinforcing whatever dramat-ic irony the film allows. This knowledge provides a particular position for audience identification. Because female comic seconds know what we know, they provide a node of identification in a way analogous to the camera that sees what we see. They voice the directions of narrative and serve as a narrative consciousness in the film.

The quintessence of middleness, female comic secondary characters perform the alternatives and deviations of the narrative middle within what otherwise appear to be the fairly unified narratives of mainstream cinema. Although their eccentricities seem to be contained by the nar-rative's outcome (whether that ending is happy marriage, certain knowl-edge, death, or all three) and their deviations seemingly treated as such by a world that subscribes to normative narrative as the truth of existence, they also inevitably escape or evade that narrative by disappearing, by refusing closure, and by existing on the sporadic fringes where multiple possibilities coexist: in the middle, where fates are as yet uncertain. They enable a sort of mobile middle, a middle that travels by synecdochal connection to figures beyond the structural confines of the literal middle of narrative. Tracking characters such as Ida reveals the perverse multiplicity that resonates throughout Hollywood film, both as a supporting ground and as the suspicion of alternative narrative possibility that is never quite extinguished by the weight, glamour, or luminosity of the normative. It also implies a slightly different understanding of narrative as that which is never as certain as it seems to be, where the middling alternatives have as much weight as the end, and where what seem to be the certain alignments of accepted ideology (patriarchy, capitalism, heterosexuality) are revealed as dependent on and even constituted by a range of eccentric, perverse, and queer alternatives over which the dominant narrative doesn't triumph but with which it agrees to a peaceful coexistence.

Medial Bliss

In films, the presence of female comic seconds is unpredictable. Because film narrative and convention tend to sideline these characters and because they tend to occupy the middle instead of the surface or edges, their reemergence is always a vague surprise. Unlike protagonists whose roles augur their presence, these characters, though functional in the plot, have no defined expectations. The set scenes where they advise, witness, or calm occur less regularly and at points that are not so neatly trackable in the narrative. In addition, because of film's focus on the central plot and protagonists, we tend not to pay as much constant attention to auxiliary elements. Thus, we neither discount nor anticipate their appearances, which return like the repressed, not quite uncanny, but very much a site of "bliss" in Roland Barthes's terms. For Barthes, textual bliss is repetition, unpredictability, "the text that imposes a state of loss, the text that discomforts (perhaps to the point of a certain boredom), unsettles the reader's historical, cultural, psychological assumptions" (*Pleasure* 14). Although female comic secondary characters seem to be a part of a viewer's cultural assumptions, their sporadic return and representation of excess in many forms also enable them to work as the cultural performance of a certain countercultural pressure, as White demonstrates in her analysis of their lesbian import. They enable the enunciation of scandalous material in the form of wisecracks and sarcastic remarks that delight us not only with their wit but through our gratification at their pronouncements about what we already suspect to be narratively true. In a Hollywood that had since the 1930s learned to negotiate the restrictions of the Production Code, secondary characters served as one way to insert the more complex material sophisticated audiences enjoyed without necessarily endangering the values of those whose tastes ran to reinforcements of morality.[10] Characters without apparent fate, explicit narratives, or prominent star value could deliver pronouncements and commentary that could not come from protagonists or more serious characters. How these secondary characters function as one way of providing a more multivalenced and even sometimes counterideological film is part of the concern of chapter 2.

Such characters return like an old friend not only within the film but from film to film. They are usually cast from the same group of character actors and actresses, partially as a result of studio contract practices but also because of the way the whole notion of type works both as a stereotype and as a complex intercinematic code around permissible deviation (in appearance, manner, or role) that is normalized by the regular casting of the very same "outlaws" for all such parts. That the same group of actresses plays the same kind of comic second fool character through thirty to fifty years of filmmaking not only produces the sense of these characters as types but also contributes to an intercinematic consistency and a code of pleasure sustained through expectations attached to these particular actresses. Eve Arden, described as the "tart-tongued comic relief," plays the same kind of character from the 1937 *Stage Door* to the 1982 *Grease 2* (Siegel 13). Thelma Ritter, "the excellent character actress . . . typically in cynical, wisecracking, disarmingly outspoken roles," played more pathetic characters whose common-sense wisdom provides a sane lens for the action (Katz 976). Their continuity both within films and from film to film makes them seem unchanging and unchanged, subject to no continuous narrative or social movement. In this sense, these female comic seconds seem at the same time to be only superficial and functional placeholders whose claim to consideration exists only in the ways they enable plot movement and character reflection and a central privileged part of the narrative formula. At the same time, this constancy produces a familiarity with such actresses that signals their function and grounds their privilege to speak.

In tracking Ida and characters like her, this book begins, as *Mildred Pierce* does, by delaying Ida's second entrance in favor of the context and background that more thoroughly flesh out the character of the minor and the possibilities of the narrative middle in classic Hollywood cinema of the 1930s, 1940s, and 1950s. The first chapter, "The Minor Made Major; or, A Moment of Gooch," wallows in the effects produced by a film constituted entirely by secondary character types (even if some of them are primary players). Using *Auntie Mame* (1958) as a specimen text, chapter 1 elaborates the characteristics and politics of the minor and the middle and, through their reversal, the relations between minor and major. Reversing the relative values of minor and major exposes the mainstream investments of typical mainstream narrative as such and, in deploying the narrative middle as the constitutive frame of the film, makes visible a range of eccentrics whose presence makes apparent the pleasures afforded by the minor and secondary. Chapter 1 contains an overview of the narrative and characterological economy of major and minor as these categories work in mainstream Hollywood film.

The second chapter, "Spatial Attractions," studies films staged on the side of the secondary in all-female communities. *Auntie Mame* shows what happens when the typically secondary predominates, whereas female community films provide a view from the more minor and extended middle of normative heterosexual narratives. In these films, what would typically be secondary, though still understood as minor in cultural terms, becomes prominent. Featuring spaces that would normally be off screen enables these films to play out more visibly the dynamics of the middle part of narratives and permits the primacy of relationships that, in a more heterosexual frame, would be rendered unimportant. Although these films clearly share in a larger sense of normative direction, they also demonstrate a range of alternative narratives in making visible and central the secondary side of events that do not disappear. In other words, they present the possibilities of narrative's middle while still being attached to a larger, more normative narrative world. They also showcase the many variants of the female secondary character and their interrelations as the subject of interest, presenting what is for all practical purposes a study of them.

The third chapter, "Tracking Ida," returns to a full investigation of the characters played by Eve Arden and Thelma Ritter as they function as secondary in mainstream narratives. This chapter continues the study of the narrative middle as an economy of multiple possibilities embodied by these wise fool figures, showing how even what appear to be stable, definitive normative narratives still permit the expansive and eccentric potential embodied by the female comic second. It also investigates the identificatory possibilities these figures provide and supplies a sense of how the female comic second works in classical Hollywood cinema.

Chapter 4, "Reliant Constructions," studies the secondary of the secondary, or the even more minor characters who make up interdependent communities in relation to one another and to the film's protagonists. Often black, ethnic minority, or child characters, these figures repeat among themselves the dynamic of primary versus secondary, reiterating on another level the dynamic of minority and perversity enacted by starring secondary characters. At the same time, they reveal a *différance*, Derrida's term for a delaying play of variety and differences that puts off categorization and organization. If, as we see in chapter 3, primary characters are constructed in a dynamic with secondary characters, chapter 4 shows how secondary characters themselves are produced in relation to a wide range of even more minor characters against a backdrop of disorganized variety. It also demonstrates the racial and ageist base necessary to sustain what appear to be strong independent white women as well as other kinds of alterity that play in the middle.

Chapter 5, "From Sidekick to Associate," traces the fate of the female comic second through the 1950s' dissolution of the Hollywood studio system through the influence of television and ensemble comedy to her reemergence in the roles played by such actresses as Whoopi Goldberg and Kathy Najimy. This species of neosecondary character pulls together the structures of secondary and tertiary to produce a new configuration of the secondary that has far more cultural power and is no longer necessarily minor but instead occupies a central spot among a variety of characters and types that explodes the middle with the illusion of universal enfranchisement and commodity pleasure. This study tracks the female comic second from the discretely stylized economy of classical Hollywood to the expanded variety of 1990s commodity culture, showing changes in the form and function of the minor and the middle and demonstrating how a version of the middle becomes the context for masquerades of liberation.

1 The Minor Made Major;
or, A Moment of Gooch

Ito: What happen, Missy Gooch?
Agnes: I lived. I've got to find out what to do now.
—*Auntie Mame*

In the middle of *Auntie Mame* (1958), a film that luxuriates in the eccentric peccadilloes of the title character, Mame (Rosalind Russell), who is visiting the Georgia plantation of her wealthy boyfriend, Beau (Forrest Tucker), goes on a fox hunt to show how sophisticated and genteel she really is. Having never been on a horse, despite her claims that she rides only sidesaddle, Mame mounts the dangerous Lightning and triumphs over the field by first getting her ill-fitting riding boot caught in the saddle, then riding backward to corner the fox. Of course, she also captures Beau. Her methods illustrate how mishap and indirection can still produce a proper end; the entire film repeats the structure of this episode, focusing on the chaotic eccentricity typical of the middle as the celebrated center of Mame's liberated entourage.

A Hollywood version of the successful Broadway play, *Auntie Mame*'s story about a wealthy "character" and her entourage of eccentrics appears in the wake of the House Un-American Activities Committee hearings as a kind of antidote to narrow, rigid, sanitized notions of normativity and acceptable behavior.[1] Its success suggests that such an intervention was quite welcome; its aberrant variety provides a view of another side of 1950s American culture in which various perversities and countercultural practices thrive. The film emerges as a species of eccentric or queer pleasure that resonates with such strains in successive films such as Billy Wilder's *Some Like It Hot* (1959) or the Doris Day vehicles *Pillow Talk* (1959) and *That Touch of Mink* (1962). *Auntie Mame* was the highest-grossing film of the year, at $9 million, and was nominated for six Academy Awards. Russell lost out to Susan Hayward as best actress. "Comedies seldom win," Russell philosophized after the awards (Jordan 125). Ingrid Bergman is reported as having announced "that if Russell couldn't have won for her tour-de-force performance, the Motion Picture Academy should have given her a special Oscar" (Jordan 125).

When a film such as *Auntie Mame* focuses on a world that is clearly and deliberately eccentric—a world in which traditional mores and habits of thought are overturned—the customary envaluations of normativity stand out in stark contrast to a much more inviting world of deviance and difference. The apparent reversal of typical-eccentric, major-minor, normal-deviant draws attention to the righteous pomposity of convention. Fixing on material that normally occupies the middle situates polymorphous pleasure as convention's antidote and appears to make multiplicity and deviance triumph over traditional narrative ends. This apparent reversal plays out as an allegorical struggle between minor and major, illuminating from the vantage point of the minor what is indeed valuable in the minor and showing the value of people and ideas that do not seem to serve a normative imperative. Such narratives provide an opportunity to examine how narrative position, cultural values, and perverse pleasures are intertwined, which is useful as a first step toward appreciating what the female comic second might impart (and import). In *Auntie Mame*, however, the apparent ascendancy of the minor and perverse becomes itself the subject of a narrative that compulsively returns to normative ends.

When the middle is enlarged, as it is in *Auntie Mame*, it comes to occupy an ambivalent position, centric and eccentric at once, enacting a division between structure and quality where the quality of the middle is not necessarily only a function of its place in narrative. *Auntie Mame* produces a kaleidoscopic spectacle of middleness. The centrality of this middle enables a different perspective on such dominant ideologies as capitalism, racism, patriarchy, and narrative itself, and the film's framing comedy of marital felicity safely contains this riot of perversity within a very normative narrative structure. Featuring eccentricity, as *Auntie Mame* does, becomes one way the middle might appear to extend beyond its structural captivation. Such expansion shows simultaneously and paradoxically that the middle is as much a quality as a structural position and that it will always end up in the middle, even if its values seem to triumph at the end. It can be detached from narrative to exist as counterheteronormative, multivalent, and multidirectional, persisting in the continued (and somewhat perverse) operation of elements associated with middleness—a proliferation of indirections, the prominence of minor character types, and an economy of variety not yet reduced to oppositional sense.

The film's center, Mame, has the hallmark traits of someone who would typically be a female comic secondary character: She is loud, brash, irreverent, insightful, and wise, the quintessential aunt, eccentric to the parent, licensed to license.[2] Marked as minor in terms of her personality traits and manner, Mame takes the minor to campy heights, playing up her centrality in the bohemian cultural margins of her wealthy world from her initial prohibition-defiant announcement that more gin is on the way to her celebritylike weaving through bevies of bizarre party guests (everything from the Russian conductor "Klinkoff" to lesbians, intellectuals, an Eastern Orthodox priest, and a man who plays the piano upside-down and backward) to her enthusiastic proclamation to Patrick (Jan Handzlik): "I'm your Auntie Mame!" Her exploits and peccadilloes illustrate how conventional narrative ends—marriage, happiness, death—can be achieved through unconventional (Beau's dive off the Matterhorn), misleading (Patrick's school arrangements), and even deviant (riding the wrong way on the hunt) behavior.

Mame, already presented as "that crazy sister," befriends a teeming array of intriguing minor characters in a vision of equality and image of universal tolerance that makes the minor or middle a site of democratic acceptance. The film attributes characteristics of open-mindedness, generosity, and kindness to characters occupying the cultural margins and paints representatives of mainstream culture—bankers and businessmen—as narrow-minded, bigoted, and selfish. Mame's wealth enables her to fight for a less repressive environment with all the power money and a good decorator can bestow. Instead of sending Patrick to the conservative boys' school that his trustee, Dwight Babcock (Fred Clarke), recommends, she sends him to an alternative school in the village, run by her friend Acacias Page (Henry Brandon), where the children play "fish family" naked in the classroom. When Babcock discovers Patrick playing gentleman fish, he moves the boy to a private boarding school in New England. The status quo here, represented by Babcock and his straitlaced ideals, is not only repressive, it is cruel and antifamilial. When Mame finds out that Patrick's fiancée's parents intend to buy the lot next to their Connecticut place for Patrick (Roger Smith) and Gloria (Joanna Barnes) to keep the "wrong sort" of people from moving into their restricted neighborhood, Mame buys it and donates it as a home for refugee Jewish children. Mame is thus the heroine of a classic narrative of the underdog who triumphs over the evil and oppressive forces of cultural propriety with a different, more charitable ethic. She embodies a fantasy of social and aesthetic retribution against narrow-minded upper-class privilege, a fantasy that has haunted the American imagination since the nineteenth century in everything from rags-to-riches tales to melodrama and the novels of Sinclair Lewis. With Mame as its eccentric center, *Auntie Mame* enacts how even the most minor of us may battle a set of majority values and behaviors that keep the minor to the side but only because Mame's minority is safely conveyed through mannerism rather than class.

We read *Auntie Mame*'s plethora of minor characters as minor because of the way they are presented within the film's cinematic operations or apparatus, which are very much a part of mainstream convention—even perhaps more conservative than usual in the late 1950s because of the film's theatrical qualities. Like most mainstream Hollywood films, *Auntie Mame* is organized within a conventional narrative structure that, because it is made very conscious in the film's graphically theatrical marking of scenes, seems to be more an organizing frame or showcase for the eccentric. Although Mame is not conventional, her narrative ultimately is, focusing on her successful maintenance of her position as rich bohemian as she raises her nephew, Patrick, to be as open and tolerant as she is. While the film's mise-en-scène, cinematography, editing, and sound push our attention toward Mame herself and the elements of her story, they prevent us from following any divergent narratives. The film's massed eccentricity, while seeming to escape the fates ideology visits on the marginal, actually contributes in some way to Mame's narrative. Rendered episodically, the narrative is organized around conventional events in the trajectory of a woman's life: Patrick's schooling, the stock market crash, Mame's failure as an actress, Mame's marriage to a rich oil baron, the oil baron's death, Patrick's engagement, Mame's sabotage of the engagement, and her final marriage to Lindsey Woolsey and role as great-aunt. Nonetheless, the scenes built around these events also focus the many minor interactions with secondary characters, on aimless or misleading badinage, and on the sense of chaos and disorganization that Mame somehow manages to enlist to her purposes. Each episode also repeats the lesson that even if events do not immediately turn out well, they eventually will, as Mame finds a rich husband during the Depression and Patrick terminates his engagement to the empty-headed Gloria. The point is that *Auntie Mame* is ambivalent—a conventional narrative that celebrates the unconventional.

Through the use of the larger-than-life campy star, *Auntie Mame* constructs both an illusion of transgression and its containment. The character Mame is a lure that draws attention away from the narrative and cinematic structures that insistently recontain what appears to be excess. By using character, the film can seem to have it both ways. Deflecting our attention from the operations that reiterate the normative, Mame herself obscures the concatenation of shot distances and angles, camera movement, editing, sound, set decoration, and acting that work to make her central by playing overtly on our psychological investments in image and narrative (identifications), our participation in larger systems through which elements of the film become important (i.e., the star system, the film's history as novel and Broadway play, the codes such as wipes, cross-cutting, or close-ups on objects by which narrative events and relations are rendered elliptically), and our ideological associations with positions rendered within the film. All of these apparatuses and systems depend on practices of consistency, centralization (of both visual elements and the viewer's perspective), and a tautological economy of the dominant (that what is offered are cardinal points and that cardinal points are what the film offers). In other words, we have been conditioned to assume that almost everything presented in a film is important and that narrative cinema's tactics of representation are geared toward the optimal presentation of important material. The consistency of a film's focus on certain characters who perform certain roles in the narrative (such as protagonist or antagonist), the consistency of that narrative with prototypical cultural narratives (and ideology), and the consistency of character, narrative role, and actor or actress type all help maintain an attention to major events and also make it difficult to question the automatic and naturalized correlations between a film's plot, characters, and the ways these are represented. Thus, for example, even though *Auntie Mame* may present a sympathetic portrait of the culturally eccentric, it consistently focuses on Mame, whose acerbic wit makes her a particularly idiosyncratic type of leading lady, in a story about victory over misfortune (even if this is cast in the slightly aberrant terms of the really wealthy who becomes wealthy again). Its alignment of protagonist, plot, and the focus of its imaging and editing makes this film a spectacularly consistent vehicle (both in itself and in line with narrative and filmic expectations), which is why it can get away with its apparent valorization of the eccentric.

At the same time (to continue this ambivalence), *Auntie Mame*'s narrative seems stereotypically major: A rich woman manipulates everyone to very traditional marital reproductive ends. What makes the film a commentary on the minor or middle is the way it first hyperbolizes the central, then illustrates repeatedly that traditional ends are best gained through very perverse means and through the agency of an array of very eccentric characters. What the film makes interesting is not the satisfactions of narrative closure but rather the aberrant quality of characters and events, including Mame herself, as quintessentially perverse. The pleasure in *Auntie Mame* is not only a pleasure in Mame herself but also a pleasure in deviant process, in minor cultural transgression enabled by the net of narrative that surrounds it. Mame's presentation as major brings the whole category of major and normative into question. Her machinations consistently illustrate that deviance has its rewards. Mame is hyperbolically centralized, not only narratively but also visually. Throughout the film, the camera focuses on Mame, tracking her through rooms and through conversations, ending each scene with a key light focused on her. This makes sense in a film titled *Auntie Mame*, but the centralization of this single character simultaneously constructs and augments the dominance of her personality, even though what the character seems to offer is something different or capricious. The collaboration of narrative and centralized image makes Mame so central that she both commandeers the film and opens the plot into a series of lush possibilities, represented by the gangs of minor characters who surround her. In other words, her overcentrality simultaneously exalts and dissolves her centrality.

The beginning of the film provides a fairly clear example of how this works. The film opens after the credits (which list no fewer than seventeen supporting players), with a shot of Edwin Dennis reading and signing his last will and testament in which he characterizes Mame as "that crazy sister," making a specific provision that she will not oversee his son's education. The second shot is an iris shot of a newspaper headline that announces the death of Edwin Dennis. The third shot shows the boy, Patrick, and faithful servant Norah (Connie Gilchrist), carrying the newspaper with the headline in a cab in New York, going to Mame's house. The ensuing fifteen shots show Patrick and Norah arriving at Mame's apartment building, entering, getting in and out of the elevator, and ringing the bell of Mame's apartment. Although this section of the film literally focuses on Norah and Patrick, its ulterior focus is the mysterious Mame, about whom we have already been warned. Mame becomes an increasingly fascinating mystery as the apartment door turns out to be a smoke-belching dragon, and the servant who answers is an Asian man who announces, "Madame having affair now." The reverse shot sequence showing Norah and Patrick entering the apartment shows a series of scenes crowded with a wide variety of cosmopolitan partiers, including Arabian sheiks, monocled gentlemen, stodgy matrons, dogs, monkeys, women in jodhpurs, "mannish" women, and performers. Although Mame has not yet appeared, anticipation about her has become central even as the world has suddenly opened into a vast array of odd personages.

When Mame does finally enter in shot twenty-four, she is on a balcony above the crowd, wearing a flowing bright yellow lounge coat and shouting that more gin is on the way. From that point on, the film follows Mame religiously, but it also expands from the narrow bourgeois perspective of Patrick's father (and to some extent Norah) to the broad panorama of worldly characters who people Mame's bohemian universe. If we stick to the more narrow perspective and read and interpret the film from the frame of the dominant (a frame wherein we look only at the elements featured prominently), *Auntie Mame* becomes a fun portrait of a kooky but kind-hearted character who manages, despite her interest in the unusual, to keep the patriarchal line going in a healthier direction than the one in which it was headed. Weird women can heal a patriarchy that is veering from a course of humane values and the tolerant attitude that provides real wealth.

But if we shift our perspective, as the film also invites us to do through its provision of variety and perverse indirection, Mame becomes the manipulator of an assortment of secondary characters who people her duplex on Beekman Place and who stand as the critical mass of minority and cultural perversity from whom Mame gains her strength and over whom Mame asserts her "alternative" philosophies. In this heterogeneous ambiance, most of the characters are secondary in the sense that the film does not maintain a primary or sustained focus on their actions or emotions, nor does it contemplate more than in passing the ways they are countercultural, odd, or eccentric. Although no secondary character in the film is a female comic second like Mame, the group provides a useful laboratory for examining just how secondary characters function both singly and as ensembles to produce entrancing parts of the cinematic apparatus while providing faint hints of something around and beyond the imaged parameters of the film. Each secondary character reveals a different side of Mame and at the same time implies a world or trajectory different from the immediate world of Beekman Place in which we are immersed. These suggestions of something other broaden Mame's aegis, as do her own references to hobbies and causes taken up and discarded (sculpture, weaving, health food). At the same time, the infusion of variety seems to expand Beekman Place, just as the apartment itself shows remarkable versatility in its constant shift in style and decoration. The minor in *Auntie Mame* is expansive rather than restrictive, multiple instead of monolithic, and generous and open instead of selfish and self-centered.

The middle dynamic the film presents contains both males and females, rich and poor, idiosyncratic and ordinary who illustrate the many possible relations between major and minor, especially their social incarnation in mistress and servant, employer and employee, hostess and guest relations and the narrative conventions of the heroine-sidekick and heroine-suitor figurations. But they also show how those conventions don't always rule the character of the association or the value of the person. Vera Charles (Coral Browne), Mame's oldest friend, "the first lady of the American theatre," drinks to excess, spends half of the film unconscious or hung over, has a snide tongue when awake, and has a fairly good sense of what Mame is up to. Patrick is a wide-eyed boy who (at least while young) is both open to the world Mame shows him and sensitive to Mame's plights. Although as a young man he tends toward Dwight Babcock's conservative worldview, this is because of the influence of snobbish private schools and Babcock himself and is easily corrected when Mame contrives to demonstrate his fiancée's shallow bigotry. Babcock, Patrick's trustee, is the most extreme version of bourgeois conservatism, acting as Mame's nemesis and the representative of all that is pretentious, small-minded, and intolerant. Lindsey Woolsey (Patric Knowles), the publisher and Mame's erstwhile suitor, is the portrait of astonished yet accepting respectability. A species of normative performative, Lindsey responds to events in the manner of a representative "normal" being, showing both Mame's eccentricities and their ultimate acceptability.[3] Also normative is the maid, Norah, whose early comments on Mame's entourage as a "den of criminals" signal how someone from a more mundane world perceives Mame's style of living but whose later approval of Mame suggests the triumph of values beyond superficial niceties. Ito (Yuki Shimoda), Mame's manservant, is in many ways the sad stereotype of the Asian servant with broken English, a will to please, and a slightly obsequious manner. But Ito is also Mame's coconspirator, delighting in Mame's subterfuges and parties, putting the drunken Vera to bed in the "Marie Antoinette room," discomfiting stodgy visitors such as Babcock by asking him to hold a dress while he removes Babcock's coat, and laughing in a fierce giggle whenever the small-minded march out in a huff.

The members of Mame's menage are augmented by other recurring secondary characters including Acacias Page, the Greenwich village experimental educator who follows quite literally the adages of Greek thought; Jackson Beauregard Pickett Burnside (Forrest Tucker), a southern oil baron from Georgia with a penchant for photography who marries Mame and then falls off the Matterhorn; Brian O'Banion (Robin Hughes), the horny, opportunistic faux Irish ghostwriter and poet (author of "The Parched Garden") whom Patrick hires to help Mame write her autobiography; and Agnes Gooch (Peggy Cass), the secretary from Speedo who follows Mame around the apartment, capturing her every word. Each of these secondary characters has a role not only in the spectrum of bourgeois normativity and relative idiosyncrasy the film focuses on but also as a different kind of foil or recipient of Mame's badinage. They also present in themselves alternative stories that intersect with Mame, even though Mame's centrality motivates their presence in the film. The film's emphasis on movements in and out of spaces emphasizes the wandering divergence of characters each going a different direction and only loosely but joyfully amalgamated by Mame, whose liberality permits such differences to coexist.

Though central, Mame also enacts a perversity characteristic of the middle, often taking indirect, deviant routes to get to fairly normative ends. Relying on others' erroneous assumption that she is a demure lady, Mame quietly does the opposite of what they expect. Defying the limiting stereotypes of class and gender and yet playing on those stereotypes at the same time, Mame embodies a froward independence that becomes the premise for the film's many episodes where the normative is turned on its head but so turned only to effect a more humane kind of family in the end where parents allow their children to miss school to go to India and everyone "lives, lives, lives." Mame manages this through manipulation of narrative. Her comic reinvention of Agnes Gooch, for example, plays off of her simultaneous management of Patrick's wrong-headed romance with the snobbish Gloria. Finagling Patrick's encounter with the independent Pegeen (Pippa Scott), Mame contrives a dinner in which the Upsons and Babcock are revealed to be the small-minded bigots they are. Mame's arrangement for Agnes exhibits Mame's mastery of the perverse as a way to get to the "proper" end—in this case the merger of Agnes with the pesky O'Banion. As Mame's secretary and "sponge," as Agnes puts it, Agnes is an admiring disciple who literally follows Mame through the apartment, taking down every word she says. In this she seems to be the model for simple, and in Agnes's case uncritical, Mame adoration as well as a kind of same-sex anaclitic identification. "Everything Mrs. Burnside dictates," she says, "is so wonderful. When I think of the things she's done and think of the things I haven't done, I could just die." Agnes models a comic, somewhat self-conscious version of the film's ideal viewer. Agnes often gets so caught up in the action that she forgets herself and crashes into the conversation; "How bleak was my puberty!" Agnes exclaims after hearing Mame and O'Banion repeating the same line. She takes Mame's advice to "live, live, live" faithfully, allowing Mame to talk her into substituting for her in a night out with O'Banion against her better judgment: "I think I know what you want me to do," she complains, "I'm not sure I want to do it." But Agnes's role as perfect viewer is emphasized by Mame's persuasion: "Oh, Agnes, where is your spine? You've been taking my dictation for weeks and you don't get the message?"

Agnes literally reproduces in the film, becoming pregnant on her night out with O'Banion but forgetting the circumstances in a drunken haze. She then becomes even more evidence of Mame's kindness, telling Mame, "You're so wonderful. No one else would have taken me in, an outcast of society." As it turns out, Agnes isn't an unwed mother, having married the opportunistic O'Banion (who thought she was a banking heiress) sometime during their single date. At the end of the film, when publisher Lindsey brings the proofs for the autobiography Mame has been writing, Agnes exclaims, "I'm so proud. The whole last chapter is about me, fighting the stigma of the unwed mother." With such supervision, Mame gets Agnes out of the perverse realm of the spinster and into the marriage bed, a proper conclusion for her eccentric story.

The economy of *Auntie Mame* is such that secondary characters and their narratives proliferate, splitting their functions in a kaleidoscope of possibilities (much like the kaleidoscopic graphics of the film's title sequence). Setting the film in the 1920s, during a prohibition Mame gaudily ignores in the movie's first scene, enables its critique of the restrained values of the midcentury when it was produced. Its flouting of mores is politically loaded as a response to the repressive ambiance of early 1950s McCarthyism and a postwar drive toward (and anxieties about) normative suburban values. The stylistic exaggerations of *Auntie Mame*'s minor characters have a liberating effect that looks simultaneously like camp playfulness and serious daring in that drinking, sexual libertinism, and liberal attitudes are imaged (or mentioned) at all. But although the film seems liberating in that regard, its ultimate lesson is fairly safe: Marriage is happy, financial woes will be solved, and liberality leads to the same safe nuclear productivity but through an alternate route. The eccentric can ultimately become a tradition, as Patrick's son chants Mame's "Live, live, live" motto.

Despite her eccentricities, Mame is ultimately tame, performing as the good perverse should and getting us to a good nonperverse end. But what about the perverse side of the perverse—the "inhibitions" and "dissociations" that threaten not to rejoin the normative narrative stream? *Auntie Mame* has disposed of all of these characters, tying up the loose ends in a Shakespearean comedic manner. The lesson we might take from the film is Freud's understanding of the perverse but with a vengeance. Eccentricities certainly do lead back to the normal, especially if shepherded by someone who seems to understand and operate the perverse as a narrative tool. *Auntie Mame* takes more care of its secondary characters than less perverse films, giving them fates, tying up loose ends, and ultimately permitting little deviation at all. It is as if because the world of the film seems so permissive, its narrative frame must be more restrictive, must seal in the riotous elements that, like Mame, always threaten to escape. The world of the film is also a middle poised on the brink of liberation, however, which extends the dynamic of the middle and illustrates the spirit the female comic secondary character imports in her much more minor roles in other, more traditional films. This spirit, as *Auntie Mame* demonstrates, can exceed its frame. In fact, in *Auntie Mame* the middle seems ultimately to define and produce the entire narrative. Narrative is produced from the inside out in this case.

The qualities endemic to *Auntie Mame* are reiterated in the character of Mame herself. The similarities between Mame and other female comic seconds suggest that insofar as Mame emblemizes the middle, so female comic secondary characters do as well, both in other films situated overtly on the edges and in those that wallow in the mainstream. Like Mame, such characters have a license to speak and can operate narrative (or at least function as the site of narrative consciousness). Despite the cloying frame of conventional success, *Auntie Mame*'s jubilations exemplify how the middle can slop over, exist both within and beyond the structure that would seem to generate it, raising a question of which comes first, the middle or the structure, openness or closure, variety or organized binaries, perversity or normativity.

2 *Spatial Attractions*

Eve Arden: Peaceful little haven we have here.
—*Stage Door*

Insofar as narrative structures cultural representations (and perhaps even culture itself) by producing justifying divisions, categories, and hierarchies and by helping envalue the valuable, both events and spaces are marked by their narrative roles. Certain events—birth, coming of age, marriage, death—are major. Other events—brushing teeth, gossip, cooking—are minor. The spaces associated with these events are also organized narratively within this hierarchy. Ritual spaces (churches, football fields) are reserved; public spaces are central sites of important commercial and political events; domestic spaces are the behind-the-scenes locus of preparation, trivia, and safety. Although these latter spaces are minor compared with the first two, they have no obvious or necessary relation to a narrative middle. They are often treated in mainstream cinema as women's space, the domestic, private space where minutiae circulate. They are certainly spaces imagined as the sites of support: the utilitarian locus of preliminaries, the anteroom of machinery, the places where arrangements for other events are planned and negotiated. In this sense, they are middling by analogy to the way the middle relates to other parts of narrative. Embodying a relative disorganization, illustrative of the gears and parts that produce the main spectacle, these off-center spaces and those who tend to occupy them often are very middle stuff.

Culturally linked to the domestic, these generally feminized spaces can function as more than merely ground for male action. In the absence of males they become the site of their own parenthetical drama that takes place as if tacitly on the side (eccentrically) and typically in relation to some other, more primary action somewhere else.[1] In dramas featuring such spaces, patriarchal hierarchies often suffer a certain loss of influence, and the rules that define class differences among women relax sufficiently to allow interchange and even challenge. Just as *Auntie Mame* provides a specimen example of a film that openly examines the dynamics of the middle and the minor, films situated in primarily female spaces showcase a swarming array of minor characters among whom female comic secondary characters represent a centralized eccentric strength and even charisma. Those who are simply female comic secondary characters in the typical mainstream filmic world betoken strength, independence, loyalty, and leadership in an all-female environment. They survive more successfully in this off-center world than others do or than they do in more heterogeneous spaces. They also anchor the queer modes of desire that circulate in single-sexed spaces, enabled by the single-sex character of the space. *Queer* in this context means both implied lesbian desire and other-than-heterosexual modes of attachment. It is worthwhile to examine some of the few Hollywood films set in all-female spaces to understand further what happens in this space, which is defined as eccentric, to explore the female comic secondary character's operation both as and in this figurative middle and to see what of those middle operations is suggestively carried by secondary characters into more heterogeneous mainstream spheres.

The figuratively mediated space most often depicted in Hollywood cinema is a domestic space occupied by women. All-female films (or those primarily so in that the major characters are all women and the action takes place predominantly in single-sexed spaces) constitute only a minor genre in Hollywood cinema, aimed at female audiences but perhaps representing the extreme version of Hollywood's rendition of a space that would normally be off-screen or appear only as the site of domestic interchange. All-female films are a subgenre of the women's film, "romantic melodramas designed to appeal to female audiences and constructed around a popular female star."[2] They take the woman's film concept one step further from the mainstream by locating the action in women's boardinghouses or convents and focusing more on the women than on the romance. Films such as *Stage Door* (1937), *The Women* (1939), *The Trouble with Angels* (1966), and *Sister Act* (1992) make the typically secondary, off-screen spaces of female existence primary in a way that illustrates not only the dynamics of women's communities but also how gender politics coalesce with notions of minority, enabling less traditionally glamorous figures to emerge as important and interesting. Produced as cinematic renditions of Broadway curiosities, films such as *Stage Door* and *The Women* promise the mud-wrestling thrill of female competition and bitchy backbiting. They also provide thorough renditions of how Hollywood imagines the single-sex space that spawns such characters as Ida Corwin. Contrasting with these "henhouse" dramas are the all-female films set in convents and girls' schools, whose dynamic is simultaneously pedagogical and sensual. Girls' schools generally serve as a pretext for depicting awakening sexualities, and convent films essay the transposition of sensuality into dedication. This latter dynamic—sexuality restrained by a more compelling duty—also characterizes the libidinal dynamic of many female comic secondary characters whose desires are, for one reason or another, repressed or sublimated. Both the subcultures and the dynamics presented in these films are analyses and etiologies of the alternative narratives embodied by female comic seconds as they circulate through other kinds of films.

All-female films also effectively illustrate the complexity of the middle's multiple conflicting lines of action and its multifarious polymorphous gender-desire politics, where sex or gender binaries are more fluid and flexible. In this environment, female comic seconds may be subtly masculinized, not only according to some heterosexual narrative logic but also as an effect of the middle's misalignment of sex and gender. This subtle masculinization clings to female comic seconds in other contexts, providing a useful ambiguity that renders them ineligible for male desire as they alibi and mask the potential eroticism of women's relations to one another.[3]

Ladies Ensemble

Stage Door, Gregory La Cava's 1937 adaptation of Edna Ferber and George Kaufman's Broadway play, provides a scampish view of off-screen and off-stage space occupied by a crew of character actresses. Focused around stars and featured players who portray aspiring actresses, *Stage Door* plays on the real-life reputations of its impressive cast in a backstage drama that presents a fantasy of communal existence as the backdrop for the heroic struggle to succeed in show business. Although some of *Stage Door*'s players, such as Katharine Hepburn and Ginger Rogers, were already established and others, such as Lucille Ball and Ann Miller, were in the process of becoming stars, most of the cast consisted of character actresses.[4] The roles of Hepburn and Rogers matched their Hollywood reputations, Hepburn's as an Eastern blueblood intellectual and Rogers's as a clever showgirl. The fact that Ball and Miller were not quite yet stars enabled their deployment as ensemble players with such noted or rising character players as Constance Collier, Gail Patrick, and

Eve Arden.[5] The film also includes at least twelve uncredited actresses as residents of the boardinghouse and six men, including the predatory producer Tony Powell (Adolphe Menjou), who manipulates Broadway roles behind the scenes; his butler; and a group of lumbermen (including Jack Carson) whose main function is to squire the women to dinner. The ensemble cast of more than a dozen actresses and actors often worked improvisationally, producing hugely successful group scenes that bettered the Broadway version.[6]

Stage Door follows the careers and relationships of the house's denizens, showing how the fortune of one results in the suicide of another but also how an ensemble composed of a mixture of lead and secondary character types enfolds, critiques, and heals. The film's action occurs in two intertwined but somewhat competing forms: a conventional melodramatic plot featuring starring players and a group ensemble full of minor characters that functions as more than ground or context for the plot. The various directions of these conflicting or inapposite plots produce something akin to the narrative middle's confusion and threat. In fact, the energy of the film comes from the disparate tensions evident among the residents. The witty manner in which these tensions play out tints this middle chaos as urbane, comic, and a little cynical as the "proper" end of the success narrative seems permanently delayed. The female comic secondary character is entirely the norm, her ironic wisdom conscious of the match between environment and fate. The film's several examples of female comic secondary character types—Lucille Ball, Ginger Rogers, and Eve Arden—all exhibit a consciousness of the actresses' dilemma.

Stage Door's middling quality is underlined initially by its beginning *in medias res*, opening in the middle of the boardinghouse's preprandial chaos as the residents gather in the living room. The soprano yowling of the maid, Hattie, drowns out the jibes and laughter of a group of boarders, led by Eve Arden, who are making fun of a sweetly naive girl from Louisiana. The ensemble sorts itself out into separable personalities (and separate locations) as Jean Maitland (Ginger Rogers) attacks roommate Linda (Gail Patrick) on the staircase, accusing her of stealing her stockings and establishing the existence of a long-running disagreement about Linda's status as theatrical producer and womanizer Powell's "squeeze." Jean provokes Linda with the announcement (in fake upper-class accent): "Oh, need I remind you that Mr. Powell's car awaits without?"

> Linda: Maybe if you spoke a little louder next time everyone in the house could hear you.

Jean: Oh, I'm sorry, I forget that you're old and deaf.
Linda: If you were a little more considerate of your elders, maybe Mr.
    Powell would send his car for you some day. Of course, he would
    probably take one look at you and send you right back again. But
    then you have to expect that.
Jean: Is that so?
Linda: I think I could set you up with Mr. Powell's chauffeur. The
    chauffeur has a very nice car, too.
Jean: Yes, but I understand Mr. Powell's chauffeur doesn't go as far in
    his car as Mr. Powell does.
Linda: Even a chauffeur has to have an incentive.
Jean: You should know.

Making drolly evident the tensions of class privilege in the house, Jean
and Linda's conversation also illustrates the residents' propensity (a propensity exactly like that of the female comic second) to attack and de-
bunk all pretension—in this situation the flimsy pretense of Powell's
scurrilous attention Linda claims as basis for precedence. From the beginning Jean is not fooled by Linda's air of superiority, commencing the
film's project of exposing privilege's often false premise, undercutting
those who would dominate with the perspicacity of those who have fewer
advantages but much greater insight.

The multiple directions of the various streams of action continue
after Jean's skirmish with Linda, when Judy (Lucille Ball), an aspiring
actress from Seattle, asks Jean whether she would like a double date with
some lumbermen for dinner, warning Jean not to make fun of them as
she usually does, exposing Jean also as a snob (though a more comic version). During these various desperate bids for fine dining, the wealthy
Terry Randall (Katharine Hepburn) tries to get into the boardinghouse
through the wrong door, an act that metaphorically characterizes her
approach throughout the film. When she finally finds the right door and
asks for lodging, her three steamer trunks and the $50 bill flashed as pay-
ment confirm her wealth. Her imperious manner and hyperbolic self-
confidence establish her as a major force who demands to be reckoned
with. Her air of command seems to promise both more conflict and a
direct route to success. She settles in the room with Jean, who has kicked
Linda out and who has neither awe nor charity for the self-assured rich
girl. Terry refuses to accept the status quo, opening windows, asking why
the actresses don't have work, implying the others' lack of gumption, and
preaching industry and intellectual activity.

The daughter of a wheat baron, Terry has decided to make a career
as an actress, proclaiming the power of "common sense." Her self-righ-
teous up-by-my-bootstraps morality and discussions of Shakespeare with

the house's aged, pathetically pompous tragedienne, Miss Luther (Constance Collier), do not please the group of struggling actresses who have skipped lunch to buy stockings and scrabbled for bit parts while hoping for better luck. Gathered in the living room after Terry's first lamb stew dinner at the club, the other residents deflate what they see as her bookish bombast (which is a displacement of Terry's obvious privilege). Eve (Eve Arden) begins with the observation that "The new gal has an awful crush on Shakespeare." Another girl replies, "I wouldn't be surprised if they got married."

> Girl from Louisiana: Oh, you're foolin'. Shakespeare's dead.
> Another girl: No!
> Louisiana girl: Well, if he's the same one who wrote *Hamlet* he is.
> Eve: Never heard of it.
> Louisiana girl: Well, certainly, you must have heard of *Hamlet*.
> Eve: Well, I meet so many people.
> (*Terry Randall enters*)
> Another girl: Hang onto your chairs, girls, we're going to get another load of Shakespeare.
> Randall: Is it against the rules of the house to discuss the classics?
> Eve: No, go right ahead. I won't take my sleeping pill tonight.

If Terry enjoys privilege in the world outside the house's domain of the minor, she enjoys no privilege here, as the ensemble challenges her assumptions and values. The leader of her deflation is Eve, who, though a strong voice among the group, seems the most marginally situated of all. She often has the last word, which reflects a combination of apparent cynicism, resignation, and feistiness.

Only one actress in the group, the impoverished Kay (Andrea Leeds), has enjoyed any critical success in a lead part, and she is desperate to win the starring role in Tony Powell's upcoming play. Modest, humble, and serious (in contrast to Terry's brash perkiness), Kay is the once-major character who has become all too minor through the unfair vagaries of a slightly off-color Broadway, haunting the house wraithlike in her poverty, self-denial, and modesty while she is protected by the others. Early in the film, when she returns from a day of hunting work, the others gather around her when she announces that she has seen a manager.

> Kay: I've got great news. I actually saw a manager.
> Eve: Hey, the whole town is under water. Kay saw a manager.
> Another girl: Was it much of an interview?
> Kay: It wasn't an interview. I just saw him as he rushed out of his office.
> (*various noises of appreciation*)

Judy: Well, at least you know there is such an animal. What's he look
    like?
Kay: Like any other animal. He had on pants, tie and collar.
Another girl: Did he have hooves?
Eve: Smoke come out of his nose?
A second girl: That's what gets in your eyes, silly.
Judy: Did he say, "Maa, maa," when you squeezed him?
Kay: I didn't get that close to him.
Eve: You didn't see a manager, dearie, you saw a mirage.

Their protective spirit continues throughout the film as Judy and Jean often check on Kay, who is the subject of and often the participant in many of the film's two-character scenes. Terry also becomes her champion, chewing out Powell after Kay faints in his office when he has broken an appointment with her.

Powell meanwhile has "discovered" Jean and Ann Miller and has gotten them a gig dancing at a nightclub. His motive is an unsavory interest in Jean, who takes Linda's place as Powell's "love" interest, although her assumption of the role is a comic version of Linda's worldly affectation. Jean gets too drunk on Powell's champagne and, despite her earlier remarks to Linda, doesn't seem to know what the producer wants from her. However, Terry's career seems to take off as she is offered the lead part in Powell's new play. A representative of Terry's father approaches Powell with an offer of financial backing from an anonymous investor if Powell casts Terry as the lead in the play. Terry's father's idea is to show Terry once and for all that she has no talent as an actress so she will return home. Despite her resolution to make it on her own talent, Terry has been undermined by her father, who disapproves of her stage career. Indeed, Terry shows no acting ability whatsoever, arguing with the playwright and director and stepping woodenly through her part as she performs with her "brain." Terry also fleetingly replaces Jean as Powell's current squeeze, although for the self-confident Terry a visit to Powell's apartment is business only.

On opening night, the desperate Kay jumps out a window and kills herself, and Jean tells off Terry in her dressing room before Terry goes on. Seeing that she has callously destroyed the talented Kay in her own ambitious experiment, a tearful Terry finally acts with her heart, gives the performance of her life, and becomes a hit. Instead of returning to the trappings of privilege and wealth to which she is accustomed, the humbled Terry remains at the Footlights Club, where all continues as usual. Linda returns to Powell (or vice versa), Judy decides to marry a lumberman and makes a tearful exit, Hattie continues her screeching, and a new ingenue arrives.

This plot summary demonstrates some of the quality of *Stage Door*'s multiple lines of action, the differing and clashing aims of the characters, and the indeterminacy that colors all. The plot itself is a bit unusual and difficult to align. Elizabeth Kendall sees the plot as a romantic comedy with the parts of the traditional lovers played by the class-differentiated Hepburn and Rogers (168). But although Hepburn's and Rogers's tussles provide one pole of action, it is only one of a number of conflicts in the film. Though tracing the events that seem to define the film's narrative movement toward death, success, and knowledge, plot summary doesn't even begin to define the business or the central importance of the film's populated group scenes, the character of which is represented more accurately by the samples of group banter. Hitting the major events in terms of the traditional parameters of plot omits this matrix of women, their comedy, insight, and ethic, which constitutes a competing major force in the film and certainly provides a sustained example of the economy that characterizes the female comic secondary character both in this film and in films more focused on the mainstream. Despite its all-star cast, *Stage Door* isn't about individual success or failure but rather is about how women can succeed in a struggle with the larger world when they help each other. It is also about the mixture of bravado, common sense, and heart that enables their survival, showing the source of such strength to be a group of supportive women. To explain the film's ultimate indeterminacy, Kendall suggests that the romantic comedy transmutes into friendship (175). But the problem with structure comes from thinking only in terms of the dominant and closure and ignoring the film's very active ground.[7]

Most films' group scenes simply provide context within which individual characters act: *Auntie Mame*'s parties, *Mildred Pierce*'s restaurant scenes, *Cover Girl*'s backstage cast scenes, or *Anatomy of a Murder*'s courtroom scenes. However, *Stage Door*'s group ensemble scenes are not only a central setting but also a central agent. Returning regularly in the film as the site of pleasurable ribbing and philosophical humor, the group constitutes the dominant culture of the world of the film as it supplies choral comment on action to come or reverberation, response, and description of action past that has not been presented directly in the film. The bravura group, like the female comic second, is a highly sympathetic eccentric center, off the main track of the conventional plot, located in a homogeneous all-female space that returns regularly and reassuringly. The group is wise, safe, and perverse in a way that enables the conventional plot to continue but also hinders and expands it through commentary, doublings, and diverting excess. But if the group is the film's eccentric center, it does not serve as a protagonist; instead the film downplays the importance of singular roles in favor of an ensemble effect where plot lines, perverse lines, and general badinage produce an atmosphere of multiple possibilities.

The central, eccentric, and rhizomatic nature of the group is rein-forced by the regular return of group scenes and by the way the film rep-resents action within the group space. Scenes shot in the living room of the boardinghouse, for example, deploy both shallow and deep space and involve the constant movement of women in and out of the frame. This chaotic motion in diverse tacks defines the ensemble shot as a shifting group that generally occupies the frame's shallow space. The groups of five to seven characters (joined or abandoned by yet other characters) are imaged in long-duration shots broken down occasionally with medium close-ups of various individuals, although these breakdown shots provide only momentary focus on individuals (and not only on the film's named characters) rather than any shot–reverse shot editing pattern that would emphasize individuals over the group. The group's busy stability makes it a comforting, supportive, exciting milieu for individuals and a site for good-natured ragging, complaining, and a broadly comic airing of anxi-eties.

The group's joking commentary makes clear its ethic of unselfish survival, communal support, and low tolerance for prima donnas and poseurs—in other words, it makes clear that to be minor and generous are preferable to being major and selfish. Generosity is the ethic of the middle, whereas self-centeredness and individuality are the means to an (the) end. This ethical clash is played out through the film's meditations on class. Introduced early in the film, class is less a signifier of identity or value than a matter of pretense. Upper classness, as manifested by Terry, Miss Luther, and even Linda, is regularly exposed as a pretentious inability to comprehend that one is really no better than anyone else and that knowing this becomes a matter of survival. For example, when Ter-ry goes to her room just after she enters for the first time, a group of res-idents discuss her.

> Judy: Did you get a load of that hat? I expected a rabbit to jump out of it any minute.
> Another girl: I thought old Orcutt [the manager] would fall over in a faint when she handed her that $50.
> Louisiana girl: If she has a $50 bill, what's she doing here?
> Eve (entering): Ah, it must have been counterfeit. There's no such thing as a $50 bill.
> Judy: You know, I think she's as phony as that bill.

Another girl: Well, I must have missed some class.

The first unnamed girl: I'll say you did. When she asked if the meals came with the $13, I thought I'd bust a ligament.

Eve: Maybe she's a social worker doing a little slumming.

Judy: She picked the right place.

Eve: Say, speaking of slum, when do we eat?

Although the jokes are a way for the residents to exert some control over the conditions of their existence, their savaging the signs of prosperity makes it clear that in this enclave wealth is perceived as phony because to admit its existence would be not only to admit to one's poverty and lack of good fortune but also to acquiesce to a class system and a particular narrative of success that has no place for ambitious unmarried women. Their banter suggests an idealism, a willingness to stay with their dreams, that both subscribes to the conventional success narrative and denies (or defies) the ways and means attached to such plots (such as marriage). Commenting on Terry's uppitiness, for example, the group cools its envy and resentment by making jokes not only about Terry but also about their own circumstances. Their criticism of Terry and apparent anti-intellectualism have to do with an attempt to maintain a sense of possibility; if the intellectuals are deposed, then there is a chance for them. Joking itself becomes a means of control, an alternative means to an end that is itself quintessentially indirect. At the same time, joking's hard edge works as a defense against circumstances over which the residents feel they have no control, such as the whims of managers, the scarcity of work, and the whole system within which they struggle. The group's urbanity and toughness work as weapons against what is at best a serendipitous business but also cover over kindness and feign a jaded quality we don't really believe from any of them. These are the hallmark qualities of the female comic secondary character as she functions through the 1940s and 1950s; they suggest that this type of character emerges from battles against gender and class odds. Female comic secondary characters are those who have survived the system without having given into it—who have found another way and who represent this other way in films focused on more end-oriented, conventional narratives.

Like *Auntie Mame, Stage Door* enacts a drama of major and minor as that constitutes the stuff of the middle. The Terry-Kay plot of *Stage Door* represents a version of majorness in very conventional narrative terms (major stars seek major roles by besting their competition). This plot competes with the myriad plots of the group for importance and interweaves with the group's equalizing tendencies and pleasurable forays into social and personal critique. Although it is obvious that Terry, for example, will never be a minor character, Jean Maitland (Rogers), who has the comic attributes of a secondary character, is actually as major in the film as Hepburn even though the character is only a fledgling success story compared with Terry's spectacular stardom. Jean has the most nongroup scenes, the most two-person scenes, and stands physically outside the group in the group scenes; she becomes the major spokeswoman for the values of the group. Her nemesis is Terry; her counterpart is Eve, who accomplishes within the group what Jean accomplishes for the group. Instead of remaining the focus, the Terry-Kay plot dissolves into other plots that repeat, reverse, and transform the competition between the two headliners into the general chaos of the community.

As a variation of Jean, Eve is a major voice of the group and fervent champion of Kay. She is also the quintessential second, often coming into scenes from off-screen space or occupying the edges from which she makes her terse commentary. She is the only character who refuses to attend Terry's opening night, remaining in the safe space when the others have gone, mourning Kay in her own fashion. Throughout the play, Eve wears a cat named Henry over her shoulders like a mink stole. The two are as one; Henry is the only male Eve can trust. At the end of the film it turns out that "Henry" has had a litter of kittens. The regendering of the cat retrospectively recharacterizes Eve's relationship with it and with gender in general, her heterosexual association becoming an interspecies lesbian one.[8] Although this specious lesbianism both exposes and explodes any covert suspicions about the investments these women have with one another, at the same time it suggests that there is a queer gloss on their energies. Most of the women are dubious about the mostly pathetic males who inhabit the boardinghouse entrance hall. They are more interested in their own struggles to succeed and those of their friends, investing their energies in a different kind of success and perpetually suspicious of male power and desire.

This deviation of attention typifies the film's larger dynamic as the group's standouts such as Judy and Eve offer a different version of interest than the plot's major players, and the major points of plot interest compete against the intriguing interplay in the group environment. Plot and group clearly work together, but *Stage Door* makes the group so visibly prominent that its challenge to the mainstream is not only part of the group impetus to succeed against all odds but also a challenge to the coalition of star and main narrative as the site of desire and identification in this film and in cinema in general. By boosting the complexity and energy of the group scenes, *Stage Door* enables a different kind of viewership. Contrasting the singular with the plural and making the plural lively, perceptive, down-to-earth, and sometimes in the same spectator position as the film's audience, the film invites a joining in, a positioning of the viewer in alignment with the group who watches and comments on the characters involved in the film's melodramatic plot of success. As female comic seconds will accomplish in more mainstream films, this group provides a site that parallels the situation and knowledge of the viewer and aligns this position with comfort and fun. This has the effect of producing both critique based on their knowledge and a sense of belonging that clings to the female comic second as she embodies this group in films focused on more public scenes.

What's to a Door?

Terry: How many doors are there to this place?
Jean: Well, there's the trap door, the humidor, and the cuspidor. How many doors would you like?

—*Stage Door*

The various sites depicted in the boardinghouse in *Stage Door* are liminal and mediate, like doors, into which women enter on their way to something else. The film's feeling of movement and multiple direction comes from depicting the women's space as a site of constant unbridled transition as women come and go through and around scenes, in and out of the frame. The single-sex living room space of the boardinghouse is neither public nor private but exists as an intermediate world of safety and homogeneity that characters leave only at their own risk. The film's subtext about doors—Terry trying to enter by the wrong door, Jean's joking suggestion that there are many doors, the film's title—suggests that the film's world is somehow posed not only in the door's liminal space but also on the threshold of a number of possible choices and in a fairly literal middle of the story. Although Terry doesn't appreciate Jean's joking rejoinder, Jean's list of possibilities is actually quite accurate. Once inside the safe liminal space of the Footlights Club, the only ways out are via the stage door (success), or other, less appealing alternatives whose symbolism could be read in any number of ways (e.g., marriage as a trap, suicide as the cuspidor). Just as the door is liminal, it is also ambivalent, connoting alterity and danger on either side. But in the Footlights Club, all is safe—or at least the dangers of being stripped of pretense and ribbed unmercifully are already familiar. By deploying a mediate site of action—the common space of the boardinghouse—that hosts a spectacle of competing interest to Terry's success, *Stage Door* makes visible and central what is otherwise understood to be eccentric, unimportant, utilitarian space, situating in that space multiple and competing lines that also work as a matrix for the story of Terry's success plot. In so doing, *Stage Door* makes an implicit connection between the unfairness of the gendered predation of show business and the underestimation of the importance of seemingly unimportant female spaces. The clash of patriarchal and women's values is resolved as Terry learns the lesson of pride from the women in the house and enjoys a success emblematic of the struggle of them all.

Although all-female spaces usually are either sites where nothing perceived as major ever happens (such as a kitchen) or where nothing important can happen because the spaces are occupied by women, *Stage Door* challenges this not by attempting to make the matrix into an element of the success plot but by rendering it an alternate site of pleasure while making it appear that despite the living room's continuous movement, nothing ever changes there. This combination of apparent stasis with perpetual transition and heightened pleasure of a sort different from that gleaned in following the success plot renders the minor all-female space a perverse site of enjoyment, a way station, a middling plethora of possibilities and constant circulation—of bodies, jokes, anxieties, ideas. Typically, the stasis of the middle is resolved either by producing the impression of sexual difference among female characters (as in women's prison films or lesbian romance) or by grounding such a world in a heterosexual imaginary that is often referenced in the film but only sporadically appears.[9] *Stage Door* does both, contrasting more aggressive, bepanted characters with meeker, more feminine ones while also playing out the subplot of Tony Powell's affairs and Judy's dates with lumbermen. But none of these overshadows the economy of the community.

But just as *Stage Door* is made safe for heterocracy, as in most all-female films, it also lingers on something eccentric or queer that thrives in the middle, as if the lack of visual heterosexuality renders the characters (or at least some of them) vaguely suspect. The liminality of the space is itself queer in the sense that it is neither public nor private, neither here nor there.[10] Given the characters' gender homogeneity and the potential stasis threatened by it, all-female spaces must work hard not to be queer. Narratives set in all-female spaces are attentive to evoking the heterosexual ambitions of their occupants, even while intimations of lesbian desire filter through indirectly in everything from dress and body language to relations with one's cat. All-female spaces straddle a strange line between innocence and suggestion; part of the subtle titillation of these films is the way single-sex spaces revise or double the coding of female relationships. The physical amity and easy familiarity among women in these spaces codes as ingenuous, whereas the same degree of intimacy in a heterogeneous space would be unusual and suspicious. In all-female spaces, this communal recoding defers suspicion even though its suspension of disbelief never really erases the hinted eroticism of homosocial interactions. This female homogeneity, like homosexuality, is the typical threat of the middle. The narrative is unresolvable without the intrusion of some agent of heterogeneity such as a male, the considerations of a different realm (the worldly into the convent), or a shift in space itself.

Terry Randall seems to represent such an agent in *Stage Door*, her differences in wealth and will providing the apparent heterogeneity to shake up what seems to have been the residents' inertia. Randall's aggressiveness and refusal to accept a sit-and-wait status quo mark her initially as different. On the surface, her gumption certainly seems to produce change: Jean and Ann get jobs, Linda is deposed, and Terry herself challenges the pecking order in Powell's office. But Terry's insistent spunk, though genuine, is not what moves the world or breaks the residents out of their slump. The changes that occur after Terry's arrival occur because of the whims of the men outside. Jean and Ann are discovered by Powell because of Powell's interest in Jean, which also dethrones Linda; Terry's part is arranged by her father's agent. Terry's apparent ability to move the world is overrated; it is an effect of focusing on a very traditional plot and assuming that the rest is background. Rather, like the house's other residents, she becomes an unwilling (but in her case unknowing) victim of the machinations of men in the larger world. After Kay's death, the Footlights Club becomes a safe haven for Terry as well. In this sense the film's canny insight into the relations between major and minor, heterogeneity and homogeneity, and change and inertia seems almost cynical. It is as if no real action can ever take place in an all-female space, even in a film set in such a space.

When all-female spaces function as the primary setting of a film, as in *Stage Door*, the clear distinctions between a major public, heterogeneous space that is the site of plot development and a minor space that typically operates as a site of narrative inaction break down. Because everything in an all-female space is already minor, the basis for any preeminence or majorness becomes a matter of negotiation; even the automatic centeredness of stars is brought into question. *Stage Door* maintains and plays on a very ambivalent relation to the notion of stardom. On one hand, it works on the actual reputations of its lead actresses. On the other hand, its plot is about the making and unmaking of stars. It performs a critique of stardom and questions its pretension.

Elizabeth Kendall exhaustively documents the relation between *Stage Door* and the star personae of Rogers and Hepburn. About the production of stardom, the film certainly played on a fairly certain public perception of the film's stars, their problems, and their personalities. On the level of the "star" it is fairly obvious that the film industry and the actors and actresses themselves constructed, nurtured, and produced a commodity image that attracted viewers to films. The star was a primary mode of defining and advertising a property.[11] Jackie Stacey suggests that female stars are "a key source of idealised images of femininity" (9) and that female spectators responded to stars as stars outside their location and function in specific film texts. Furthermore, spectators' responses to stars produced an independent, sometimes parallel process of consumption. In the case of secondary characters and the people who played them, the politics of stardom worked differently. Secondary character types such as Rogers and Rosalind Russell could become full-fledged stars, but most secondary actresses were minor stars who occupied the odd (or liminal or ambivalent) position of being recognized while still being anonymous—"Oh, there goes what's-her-name." Though also carefully cultivated media images, secondary characters resonated more with what Richard Dyer calls "personhood" than the "idealised images of femininity" represented by first-tier stars (*Heavenly Bodies* 10). This personhood was a continued reaffirmation of both the idea of the individual and of individuality itself, manifested through the performer's idiosyncrasies of speech and manner. If *Stage Door* worked as an image corrective for Hepburn by having her play her own image, it began the establishment of the images of its supporting cast—Ball, Arden, and Miller—who pretty much followed through their careers in the same persona they manifested in *Stage Door*, though elaborated and magnified.

The Lass Menagerie

> Jean: Which keeper is on duty today, Hattie?
> —*Stage Door*

The figure of the female comic second derives both from the narrative middle and from the politics of an all-female space—both from the dynamics within the space and the ideological and structural forces that can conceive those dynamics only as contained and secondary. Although most female comic secondary characters are not overtly linked to such spaces in films set more in the mainstream, they still carry with them an aura of this somewhat eccentric community, which, as *Stage Door* demonstrates, is of interest in itself. It is useful to see the complexity of the phantasmatic site from which such characters are imagined to emerge, even if such an origin is conveyed only by the behavior of the character herself. Female comic seconds telegraph this complexity, but without understanding the nature of the social location to which they refer, it is difficult to account for their richly evasive qualities and modes of interaction with other characters. Whereas *Stage Door* locates a large part of its action in a centered ensemble that contrasts the stuff of the middle with all sorts of potential ends, the 1939 all-female film *The Women* demonstrates how dangerous the middle really is. As in *Stage Door*, *The Women*'s secondary characters deflate the pretense and pride of more central characters, but unlike *Stage Door*'s pleasurably chaotic mix, *The Women*'s characters are distributed around a much more traditionally allegorical array of good and bad, primary and secondary types and functions. *The Women* organizes the middle because it is a threat; it also organizes the middle into a threat devised of challenges to traditional heterosexual commitment. Whereas *Stage Door* fills foreground and background with a field of minor characters who seem to be pretty much on par with featured personalities, *The Women* presents a clear class division between the wealthy women who play key roles in the film's complex plots of marital disarray and the mainly lower-class servants and service personnel (such as the personal trainer, the manicurist, the cook, the maid, and even the divorce ranch proprietor, Lucy [Marjorie Main]), who function as witnesses, informants, and foils. Rather than being supportive, all of *The Women*'s women, regardless of class and function, are purveyors of information; gossip and pride drive the women's choices in a complicated plot of marital lost-and-found that portrays women as animals snarling over male meat. The film interweaves these plots of mating competition with portraits of various relations between women that seem to serve as context, but as in *Stage Door*, these "secondary" relationships are of competing importance and interest.

   In contrast to *Stage Door*, *The Women* enacts a much tenser version of a middle-like homogeneous chaotic space. Its secondary character types, here represented most obviously by Rosalind Russell's gossipy Sylvia, are correspondingly more threatening. The terms of this threat have everything to do with maintaining a fragile and contingent heterosexuality in the face of more complex, riveting, and intense relations between women. Contrived to present only the women's part of the action, *The Women* shows the dangers of homogeneity—the perils of a (gender) sameness that occupies the liminal ground of the domestic—when what is at stake is a husband and lover instead of theatrical success. *Stage*

Door presents a hint of this threat in the altercation between Jean and Linda over Powell, but *The Women* makes competition over men its central focus. In other words, *The Women* allegorizes what happens when events and choices get too caught in the middle, where that middle is quite obviously not what is desired at all. Rather, in *The Women* the middle is a continuous point of tension enacted around the film's palpable absence of men.

Poised much more overtly in relation to a dominant patriarchal world, *The Women*'s secondary characters all imperil normative marital relations, not by forming competing relations with other women but by jeopardizing the heterosexual relations that already exist through indiscretion (generating the flow of too much information) or competition. They are quintessential elements of a narrative middle's chaos, provoking disruption and misalignment. Unlike the supportive secondary types in *Stage Door*, they are much less insightful, but they still work on the margins to manage knowledge and to provide a perspective into the blind foibles of more major figures. At the same time, what might be discounted (paradoxically) because the film includes only women is the centrality of their relationships with one another. *Stage Door* offers a world in which the ensemble and group values dominate, but *The Women* presents a compendium of clashing types—the virtuous wife, the wise mother, the meddling friend, the "other" woman—linked predictably and self-consciously to their roles in conventional narrative but also presenting a complex portrait of exchanges between women that exacerbate potential failures of heterosexuality.

The exchanges within the film echo the complex star relations involved in making the film. Functioning as a showcase for MGM's set of highly cultivated stars, *The Women* emerged in a year of heavy competition with Selznick's *Gone with the Wind*. Known for its careful development and deployment of such screen queens as Norma Shearer, Joan Crawford, and Greta Garbo, MGM featured both Shearer and Crawford along with the emerging star Rosalind Russell heading a cast of 135 women (and no men except for a shadow at film's end) that included columnist Hedda Hopper, Marjorie Main, and an uncredited Butterfly McQueen. Although the film originally was to have been directed by Ernst Lubitsch, when George Cukor was removed as director of *Gone with the Wind* (ostensibly because of his conflicts with Selznick but also because an antisemitic and homophobic Clark Gable reportedly complained that he wouldn't "be directed by a fairy"), MGM moved Lubitsch to *Ninotchka* and brought in Cukor, whose reputation for understanding women made him the perfect choice.[12]

And Cukor delivered, turning Anita Loos and Jane Murfin's screenplay (which had been stripped of even the most innocent jokes about sex) into a fast-paced, witty whirlwind moving around the sedate central character, played by Norma Shearer. He had both Loos and Donald Ogden Stewart sitting on the set, ready to offer "clean" one-liners where necessary. He urged Rosalind Russell, for whom this was a first comic part, to play her role in an exaggerated fashion. He paid acute attention to details. He cleared the set of all but the necessary personnel to avoid clashes. He managed to control tensions on the set between Shearer and Crawford, who, as the studio's top stars, did not much like one another (and, according to one report, did not speak to one another after the scene in which Mary confronts Crystal). But those who would be regal on the set often were bested by supporting actresses. In one scene, Sylvia (Russell) is supposed to be whispering to Mary in a dressing room. Afraid that Sylvia's active buzzing would draw attention from her, Shearer donned a leftover costume from *Marie Antoinette* with a hoop skirt that would not allow Sylvia to get within three feet of her. Cukor, seeing the comic possibilities of such a scene, moved several mirrors into the dressing room, which multiplied Sylvia's image many times.

The headliners (no matter how hard they fought over billing—and they did fight, Rosalind Russell calling in sick for four days when Shearer wanted her name put beneath the title) are not what is interesting about *The Women.* Crawford comments,

> Now, *The Women*—quite a different kettle of fish. It was brilliantly written and directed, better than the Broadway Play it was adapted from because the screen gave it mobility. And that cast. Norma Shearer, as usual, played the perpetual virgin, the wronged wife. Roz Russell played one of the bitchiest, funniest women ever put on film. Paulette Goddard was beautiful and a real Minx, and all the supporting players, including Mary Boland, or especially Mary Boland, were perfectly cast. My part— I knew it was dangerous for me to play Crystal, but I couldn't resist. She was the epitome of the hard-headed, hard-hearted gold digger on the big make, a really nasty woman who made the audience want to hiss. I knew that Norma would walk off with the audience sympathy and that Roz Russell would walk off with the picture, and that I'd be hated. (Newquist, *Conversations with Joan Crawford* 84–85)

John Baxter agrees except that he thinks Crawford is the film's center: "Norma Shearer's bland niceness smooths her scenes and those with her daughter, but the more astringent Rosalind Russell, arch-gossip, with her bizarre clothes, gawky walk and shrill insistent dialogue, and Joan Crawford's Crystal, greedy, ambitious and cynical, soon divert attention from her. . . . Joan Crawford is the film's true star, but in such a production it is bound to be the supporting cast that attracts most attention" (*Hollywood* 124).

Critics also point out the performance of child star Virginia Weidler; she is singled out for mention in *Variety*'s review of the film and in a May 1940 essay, "The Youthful Stars That Mostly Wane." *New York Times* reviewer Douglas Churchill notes that "Virginia Weidler, acknowledged by critics to be the most competent child actress on the screen, is another who is protecting herself against a rainy day. Of all the performers on the Metro lot where she is under contact, she is the most in demand. Producers try to write parts in script [sic] for her and established artists watch her to see that she does not steal the picture. In order to protect Mickey Rooney, one of Metro's most valuable properties, the studio re-shot a substantial part of 'Andy Hardy Out West' because Virginia completely blanketed their star." *The Women* was highly successful, making the *Film Daily* and *New York Times* Top Ten lists and launching Rosalind Russell's career as a comedienne. But it also stoked her career as a leading lady, spurring a move to Warner Brothers in 1944.

The central character of *The Women*'s marriage and divorce plot is Mary Hanes (Norma Shearer), who is married to the film's most desirable male, the reputedly wealthy, handsome, and fun-loving engineer, Stephen Hanes. Mary has a very wise mother, Mrs. Morehead (Lucille Watson), and an equally wise daughter, little Mary (Virginia Weidler), as well as a collection of friends ranging from the impish scandal monger Mrs. Howard Fowler (Sylvia, Rosalind Russell) to the naive and docile Mrs. John Day (Peggy, Joan Fontaine) to the more traditional fool figure, author Nancy (Florence Nash). Trouble starts when a manicurist at the sumptuous salon all of the women frequent tells Sylvia that Stephen Hanes is seeing a salesgirl on the sly. With mother of eight Mrs. Phelps Potter (Edith), played by Phyllis Povah, Sylvia engineers it so that Mary visits the same manicurist and learns the same thing. Counseled by her sage mother to let Stephen have his fling, Mary lets the situation slide until she meets the salesgirl, Crystal Allen (Joan Crawford), at a fashion show. The confrontation between Crystal and Mary produces society headlines; the publicity provokes a heated off-screen discussion between husband and wife (reported by the maid), and Mary decides to get a divorce.

She takes the train to Reno, accompanied by Peggy, who has also had a fight with her husband, and on the train they meet the Countess deLave (Mary Boland), who is divorcing her fourth husband, and Miriam Aarons (Paulette Goddard), who is also going to the Reno ranch. Mary, who really doesn't want a divorce, keeps waiting for Stephen to call, but when he does, his respect and consideration prompt him to say the wrong thing. Meanwhile, the countess finds a cowboy, Buck, whom she marries after her divorce and puts on the radio as a cowboy crooner. On Mary's last day at the ranch, Sylvia arrives, her husband having produced evidence against her so he could marry a showgirl, who turns out to be Miriam. Peggy discovers she is pregnant and makes up with her husband, and Mary finds out that Stephen, gentleman that he is, has married Crystal. Back in New York eighteen months later, Sylvia, who has now befriended Crystal, discovers that Crystal is seeing cowboy Buck behind Stephen's back. Mary, hearing from little Mary that Stephen is unhappy, sets out to reclaim him by getting Sylvia to divulge Crystal's affair. When challenged in the women's restroom at a popular nightspot, Crystal admits her relationship with Buck and tells them all to go to hell because she thinks Buck is rich, only to find that Buck's wealth comes from the Countess. The film ends with Mary joyfully exiting the women's room to rejoin her ex-husband.

The Women's allegorical quality comes not only from its enactment of middle stuff as distinctly wrongheaded but also from the film's crowd of culturally and narratively minor characters, which the film controls by characterizing them as types and locating them within several classificatory schemes. The film tries to present the minor as a series of stereotypes in a parable. All the characters are obsessively classified, located within at least three conscious taxonomies—a bestiary, woman versus female, and categories of love—and typed implicitly by their stereotypical roles in the various versions of marital narratives the film presents. This obsessive categorization suggests that without such framing devices, this homogeneous mass of interrelating women might be threatening to the patriarchal status quo. The film's layers of character classification fail to contain such personae as Sylvia and little Mary, who consistently exceed their roles, the former to lengthen the middle's complications, the latter trying to resolve them but in the meantime providing both insight and pleasure. Within the film's restrictive taxonomies, the women serve as contented helpmate, naive spouse, fecund mate, complaining wife, snarling interloper, mother, and spinster. In these diverse versions of the patriarchal family, what imperils are the agents who threaten to tear the family apart, and what comforts are the characters who try to preserve it. At the same time, the women's various responses to their husbands' infidelity suggest the possibility of rebellion incited by noncompliant wives who demand an equal part in the marriage contract.

Emphasizing the film's inclinations toward marital parable, the characters are openly compared to animals at the beginning. In a curious departure from typical Hollywood practice, *The Women* opens with an extended list of credits and characterizations unusual in that the film actually renders the credits twice, once in a traditional list of hierarchized names (Shearer, Crawford, and Russell on the first frame, with Shearer and Crawford above, Russell below), followed by six of the featured players, and the production credits. The names then appear again in a series of comparisons between the actress, an animal such as a doe or a leopard, and the character. Each shot in this second list consists of an iris frame of a live animal labeled with the actress's name at the top, then a dissolve of the iris image to an image of the character with the addition of the character's name (married name, then given name in parentheses) at the bottom. There are ten such comparisons made with a doe (Mary), a leopard (Crystal), a cat (Sylvia), a monkey (The Countess), a fox (Miriam), a lamb (Peggy), an owl (Mrs. Morehead), a cow (Edith), a fawn (little Mary), and a mule (Lucy).[13] This sequence is followed by another roster of ten names of secondary actresses not listed in the opening credits. This top-heavy opening seems to underscore the film's preoccupations with organizing quantity by means of character types and displays. It emphasizes the large number of characters (many of whom are minor) and invites us to read the film in terms of the simple allegory of predator versus prey suggested by the animal counterparts. In comparing the characters to animals from the start, the film not only makes a wryly humorous commentary on stock female personalities but also signals the basic outlines of the film's narrative, which we are quite able to construct before we even see the film. This bestiary, sometimes verging on the melodramatic, also belongs to the tradition of fabliaux (medieval satirical tales featuring animal protagonists that substitute animal characters for people in stories where the trickster is tricked) and moralistic fables. The film shifts between these forms, inviting and referring to multiple perspectives through the very bestiary that seems to pin the characters down. Its multiple narratives of domestic strife import melodrama (the Haneses), irony (Sylvia), fertile productivity (Mrs. Potter), comedy (The Countess), and felicity (Peggy) so that there is no firm sense of any single register that dominates the film. Ironically, while urging a simple reading, the bestial apparatus suggests that all is not quite so easy; the hyperbolic listing seems tongue-in-cheek, a knowing wink to the misogynist possibilities such beastly comparisons invite.

Although the creatures seem to function as a gesture of control, animals nonetheless haunt the film somewhat uncontrollably, paralleling, undermining, and reinforcing the various gender and romantic taxonomies that participate in its assorted versions of familial romance. The film's first scene opens with two lapdogs fighting in front of the beauty parlor. The scenes introducing mother and daughter Hanes open with the two on horseback, and the Haneses have two dogs, who figure prominently in domestic scenes with Mary and little Mary. Throughout the film, the women wear minks, and the Reno divorce ranch returns to the motif of the horse when Sylvia battles Miriam. Occasionally, characters link other characters to animals, as when little Mary says she saw Mrs. Potter visiting the snakes when her father took her to the zoo in her mother's absence. Such a connection is implied in the association between stylish women and caged monkeys in the technicolor fashion show that forms an interlude before the film's climactic meeting of Mary and Crystal. Even the posh environment of New York nightlife is compared to a jungle; the color of fingernail polish sported first by Sylvia and at the end by Mary is "Jungle Red." The use of animals in both *Stage Door* and *The Women* as the recipients of displaced affection and aggression suggests that animals take the place of men, who are largely absent in these films. Animals fill in for sexual difference and at the same time trivialize (in a very speciesist manner) women's relationships with one another and their pretensions to any real importance.

But this bestiary and the simple narratives it suggests are not enough to organize this on-screen off-screen world. Other taxonomies are devised by perspicacious secondary characters who work to describe and define the terms of combat. For instance, the film's spinster writer character, Nancy, organizes characters as either "women" or "females." When troublemaker Sylvia first gleans the tidbit about Stephen Hanes's affair, the writer comments on her scheming and observes that there are "women" like the contented and happy Mary Hanes and "females" like Sylvia who are ready to ruin others' good fortune through their envy and meddling. When asked how she would classify herself, the writer replies, "I'm what nature abhors, an old maid, a frozen asset." The woman versus female scheme aligns with the marital plots in which "women" are the characters who make the marriage narrative work for them, such as Mary Hanes and Mrs. John Day, and in which "females" don't seem to understand their place, such as the predatory Crystal, Sylvia, and even the fecund Mrs. Potter (who aids Sylvia in her machinations). Nancy's association between female type, marital status, and economics also signals both the film's insistent connection between marriage and wealth (marriage as a means to financial security for women who otherwise have none, wealth as an incentive to marriage) and the connection between marital status and narrative utility. A spinster may have wealth, but she can't be used for much narrative profit.

Mary Hanes's mother and daughter, both on the margins of Mary's own tale of marital woe, are also interested in establishing categories. When her daughter discloses her marital troubles, Mary Hanes's mother elaborates the writer's observations, urging her not to confide in her friends. "I'm an old woman," she says; "I know my sex." Like the spinster writer, Mary's mother understands that marriage is intrinsically a story about gender in which women work for the happy ending and females become the antagonists who try to produce tragedy. Mrs. Morehead believes in happy endings and tells Mary, "It's being together at the end that counts." Mother also produces a taxonomy of love, counseling Mary that there are two kinds: the unshakable love of a husband for a steadfast wife and the fleeting sexual interest that typifies adulterous affairs. Women enjoy the former, females the latter. Throughout the film, Mary's mother reminds her of the way the story should go, as Mary deviates further and further from the part of the woman to the part of the female, first mentioning the affair to her husband, then demanding that he choose, then retreating to Reno even though she still loves him. To her mother, all of these are wrong choices, and with the mother we must watch proud Mary stumble into the realm of tragedy, a woman lost among the females.

Caught between women and females, the child, like the writer (but an unmatured investment instead of a frozen asset), presents the sober, common-sense perspective of one caught between forces she cannot control. From the child's point of view, the parents' marital complications are a confusing set of mixed messages. Daughter Mary evinces a wisdom similar to but more instinctive and less calculated than the advice of her grandmother. From the beginning a competitive "oedipal" daughter who wants her mother to inform her father that she beat her mother in a horse race, little Mary directly questions the premises of her mother's choices. She asks Mary whether she loves her husband more than she loves her daughter, and when Mary goes away to Bermuda with her own mother when she first finds out about Stephen's affair, little Mary asks her whether she returned because she missed her daughter or missed her husband. Little Mary's juvenile jealousy often leads back to yet another taxonomy of love. Adjusting her own mother's relational taxonomy of romantic love and sex, Mary Hanes explains to her daughter that there are two kinds of love: the kind one has for one's child (parental love) and the kind one has for one's husband (romantic love). But little Mary's questions also faintly echo the complications of the other triangle Mary and Stephen Hanes are entangled in, daughter doubling the "other woman," competing with her mother for her father's attentions. When Mary tells little

Mary of the impending divorce, little Mary questions her mother's love typography, asserting just as her grandmother did that familial love should be more compelling; and just like her grandmother, little Mary brings Mary Hanes's narrative choices into question. At the same time, she also questions the father's adulterous privilege, suggesting that women, females, and men all act silly.

Although decoding the film in terms of these three taxonomies is both tantalizingly simple and difficult to sustain, the film's comparison between the women and animals both renders the familial narrative predictable, in that we expect characters to perform the roles suggested by their animal counterparts, and shakes it up when it becomes clear that even animals are multivalent. Although a predator-prey opposition seems to inform the link between the animal metaphors and the film's narrative of husband hunting, the bestiary's typology does not line up with the film's taxonomies of gender and romance, nor is it so clearly binary. Although characters connected to various sweet furry creatures play the sympathetic parts in the film's various romance narratives, sweet furry creatures are not necessarily all "women," nor are the small predators— fox and cat—all "females." The various animals of the bestiary, especially the monkey, the mule, the owl, and the cow, don't align with any of the other categories (they are neither "women" nor "females" in the film's terms), which indicates that instead of working closely together, these different taxonomies diverge, echoing one another, perhaps, but also presenting multiple perspectives on diverse versions of a familial formation that ultimately doesn't appear to be stable.

It also suggests that despite the film's multiple efforts, some characters cannot ever be classified. The clash and bad fit of taxonomies typifies the female comic secondary character, who in more mainstream films is neither one thing or another but who represents a conflicting amalgamation of the categories so finely parsed by *The Women*. The threat of the unclassifiable woman is reflected in the film's ultimate undecidability. Even if the film ends with Mary Hanes's victorious reconquest of her ex-husband, such an ending does not necessarily only reaffirm dominant patriarchal values. It also implies that the patriarchy itself has undergone an adjustment, at least on the Hanes front, and the other familial narratives provide alternative possible endings, from divorce to pregnancy to happy marriage to doomed marriage to being single. Within all this marital emplotment, the advice of various secondary characters rings through as the insight we all have in relation to such predictable narratives.

The difficulty in aligning the film's taxonomies parallels the difficulty in locating characters within the typologies, despite their overt comparison in the opening bestiary. The disruptive agent Sylvia, who in the opening sequence is compared to a hissing cat, is not entirely unlikable or completely evil. In fact, Sylvia is perhaps the most overtly comic character in the film; her lines are crisp and witty (anticipating the future delights of *Auntie Mame*), and her physical comedy in the exercise room and the fight scenes at the Reno ranch break free from the otherwise restrained demeanor of ultrafashionable New York matrons. Although Sylvia's manipulations seem to revel in the destruction of others' domestic arrangements, Sylvia at least alibis her behavior with the fiction of her helpfulness and good will toward her friends. Even if she is fooling herself about her charitable motives, Sylvia expends her energy among the women (or the females) rather than in preoccupied relation to men, whom she treats rather carelessly. Although she is a troublemaker, Sylvia is an interesting and entertaining knave whose respite from Mary Hanes's goodness occasionally reverses the valences of the film. Mary's virtue seems to get her nowhere, whereas Sylvia's mischief is at least interesting.

The leopard—the grasping, dangerous, truly immoral one in the film—is Crystal Allen (Joan Crawford), who shamelessly manipulates Stephen and doesn't care about what damage she inflicts. At the same time, Crystal's type is completely predictable within the economic terms of marriage in this film; she represents the "female" for whom marriage is both an economic matter and a matter of proving her own power. She is clearly presented as a working girl, without the social class of the others, and her conquest of Stephen is as much a matter of gaining social or economic currency. Her calculated play for Stephen shows up Mary Hanes's naivete but also hints at the hidden mercenary qualities of some of the other marriages. Although she intends to take advantage of all the patriarchal goodies marriage can offer, Crystal is also another means by which that patriarchy is shown to be an economic system, built around male insecurity, vanity, and boredom. All the women take seriously marriage's economic benefits. One of Mary's mother's arguments to Mary is that she should not relinquish her economic stability; all the women are overtly conscious of marriage as a way to continue living well. As soon as Crystal thinks she has hooked Stephen, she shows up at the fashion show and begins ordering thousands of dollars of clothes charged to his account.

If Crystal is evil because she steals Mary's husband, her sin is not only in her adulteries but in her treatment of other women, particularly the black maid, played by Butterfly McQueen.[14] Grabbing her in the back room of the store, Crystal orders her to go to Crystal's apartment and fix dinner so that Crystal could claim she had cooked for Stephen. Although McQueen complains that she has a date and that there is probably no food in the refrigerator, Crystal brushes all of that aside in her self-centered desperation. Unlike the other women who present a veneer of politeness, Crystal is openly abusive and insulting, not only to the maid but also to Mary Hanes and her friends at the department store. Obscured by the marriage plots, this kind of meditation on female (womanly?) relationships seems secondary, a field of interaction whose main function is to disseminate information. *The Women* presents a world where competition for men and envy seems to make female friendship a minefield. "Females" seem most likely to betray their friends, in contrast to "women," who appear to be supportive and generous. But the opposite is also true: Patriarchal power incites "women" to betray "females." The problem among women is men, and although the film's vision of a women's world seems sometimes treacherous and unkind, it is so because of the male infidelities and lack of economic independence that pit women against one another.

The film's narrative of familial salvation might constitute melodrama if it developed unself-consciously and if it were the only marital narrative in the film. But the actual narrative of Mary Hanes's successful reintegration of her family is only one of several marital stories the film weaves together. Though in many ways more central to this film than the Terry Randall plot was in *Stage Door*, the Mary Hanes plot is still one plot among many in *The Women*. If we do not focus entirely on it and instead see the proliferations and variety of exchanges that actually constitute *The Women*'s economy of information, communication, and miscommunication, the film becomes less about marriage per se than about the relationships between women of different generation and class as they are inflected by the looming presence of romance narratives. The film's diversity demonstrates simultaneously different interpretations of the same story of marital woe. The flow of information through such characters as Sylvia and little Mary is not a flow that defines the direction of the story but is rather a catalyst that forces the action to fan out into several different coexisting stories. For example, the knowledge that Stephen is seeing Crystal engenders the following varied responses: Sylvia reconfirms her own husband's fidelity, although she is unknowingly also in Mary's predicament; Mrs. Morehead counsels Mary to be the forgiving wife; Mary counters with a narrative of marital equality and wants to confront Stephen to force him to return to his vows; Crystal sees a future as Stephen's wealthy mistress; little Mary sees only family happiness; Peggy wishes she could afford to get pregnant; and Nancy suggests that envy prompts people like Sylvia to meddle with the happiness of a true woman such as Mary. Each of these responses actually depends on a different narrative—the narratives of the demure and obedient wife, the happy family, the irresistible other woman, and marital equality—and each comes true in the film. Sylvia ends up in Reno, Mrs. Morehead is right, Mary gets her way, Crystal enjoys Stephen's favors, the family comes back together, Peggy gets pregnant, and the envious and vicious destroy themselves.

The Women thus presents multiple, covalent marital alternatives that result in a mixed and ambivalent sense of marriage, an iffy take on the virtues of friendship, an exploration of the problems of patriarchal privilege, and yet another view of the chaotic hotbed that typifies the middle's dynamic. The presence of myriad interweaving versions not only is comic proliferation typical of the narrative middle but also demonstrates both how predictable the plots are and how powerless the women are unless they take matters into their own hands—unless the "matrix" rises and acts. Though often frivolous, the women are both complicitous and irreverent, believing in and eschewing the romantic alibis that enable the continuation of patriarchal privilege. Although *The Women* is organized around a primary narrative of marital difficulty, the importance of its secondary figures makes visible the ways this film and the women must actually labor to make the marriage narratives central. In *The Women*, the narrative of the nuclear family is not necessarily natural but is instead the product of a great deal of work both on the part of the characters within the film's diegesis and on the part of the film itself, which elaborates, doubles, repeats, and interweaves multiple variations of types and possibilities around the themes of gender propriety and fidelity.

Instead of being about one central narrative with enough subplots to enhance it, *The Women* is in some ways about narrative itself. All imperiling, preserving, and rebelling in this film coexist with a tacit acknowledgment of how the story should go, what roles people play, what can go wrong, and why. The film self-consciously emphasizes the process of plotting around both the literal author, Nancy, who draws attention to whatever plotting goes on in her presence and often likens it to her writing endeavors, and the more figurative author, Sylvia, whose intricate plotting to deliver information requires that she both actively spy (as she and Mrs. Potter do when they visit the notorious Crystal at her perfume counter) and manipulate various characters and situations to produce scenes of revelation (such as the manicurist telling Mary about Stephen). In a case of poetic justice, Mary uses Sylvia's modus operandi against her at the end to get her to spill Crystal's secret. Throughout the film, Sylvia is responsible for comic plotting as well as a sustained consciousness of the plotlike nature of her orchestrations. This metanarrative consciousness and the film's subtextual insistence on types make the film both the anatomy and critique of the marital tale and an excellent example of one. The conscious wielding of information and story defines female comic secondary characters such as Sylvia, who carry such talents beyond this film and are licensed to use them in others. The presence of such information-wielding manipulators—agents of the middle—opens up the possibility of multiple perspectives on the narratives that are present, demonstrating that narratives are never simply true but are instead contingent products of desire and position.

The presence of multiple possibilities brings any single choice into question. For example, if the central plot is driven by Mary's "female" rather than "womanly" choice to let her pride get in the way, her choice is tragic only if we perceive her trajectory from the side of patriarchal privilege espoused by her well-meaning mother—from the "woman"'s perspective. Rather than being tragic, Mary's own determinations may also enact an alternative view of patriarchy's privilege. If her mother counsels patient endurance, Mary sees Stephen's defection as his failure, his breaking the bonds of fidelity and intimacy. Instead of allowing Stephen his duplicitous pleasure, Mary forces him to acknowledge his trespass. Although she relinquishes some of her material well-being in divorcing Stephen and although she still loves him, Mary's decision not to play the complacent wife—the woman—brings patriarchal privilege into question. In divorcing him, Mary teaches Stephen a lesson about the value of the faithful wife; even though she suffers from what her mother calls "pride," she wins him back on her own terms. Although one side of the story seems to comply with patriarchy, from Mary's angle patriarchy looks rather cruelly self-indulgent and misled. Although Mary seems to have slipped from womanliness to femalehood, in preserving the family Mary actually redefines the woman as a less passive and more active agent in the familial scenario.

If we look at the film from its "female" side, patriarchal privilege (the right to exchange women freely) is hampered often by the noncompliance of the women themselves and has a cost. Marriage in *The Women* is not the exchange of women between men but the exchange of men between women as well as the exchange of one's independence and pride for material wealth. And yet the film is not a strident indictment of male privilege. It seems finally to track a series of interlocked variations that are situated as minor in relation to the film's primary focus on the Haneses' marital narrative while locating the Haneses as simply one example among many. But looming within and behind the marriage plots is the field of women whose relationships might just as well constitute the film's main entrance, a field as intriguing as marital variety and mishap, a field that exists somewhere in the neighborhood of the spinster, the widow, and the child, who are, finally, the wisest characters in the film.

Focusing on the nature of the women's interactions—focusing on the secondary of this already secondary space—reveals a film that is not about competition over men but about competition around Mary herself, as Sylvia, Nancy, Peggy, Mrs. Morehead, and little Mary all contend for her attention and favors. Sylvia's motivation might well be envy, as Nancy suggests, but Nancy and Peggy seem motivated by admiration, Mary's mother by knowledge of her daughter's potential folly, and little Mary by an oedipal and almost romantic interest. The crazy physicality of Sylvia's encounters with Crystal (when she falls into a merchandise cart), her workouts in the spa, her fight with Miriam, and her being locked in the women's room closet when she threatens to warn Crystal contrast with the oddly sexualized presentation of Mary and little Mary's relationship. Beginning with the horse race little Mary wins, the two compete for absent Stephen's attention but play out between themselves the absent spousal relation. Little Mary films her bent-over mother from the rear (a rear view Mary herself offers); the two cuddle, kiss, discuss love, and get in bed together in ways that are read as completely innocent parental affection but that also seem to be the displaced site of both Marys' frustrated sexualities. If this is the case in a familial context where such affection is understandable, that suggests that much of the other physical comedy is displaced sexuality as well. And although we are loath to consider intergenerational incest as a form of sexuality, there is nothing to prevent us from seeing the physicality between the other women, particularly Sylvia, not as displacements of a frustrated desire for the absent men but rather the absent men as a pretext for playing out frustrated desire among the women. This is again particularly true of Sylvia, whose nosiness can be read as a kind of intimacy, as a desire to become indispensable to other women.

As in *Stage Door*, the single-sex nature of the environment alibis all female relations, but if we look at the minor—at the narratives that seem secondary to the looming but absent Stephen Hanes—they may well tell a different story, a story that finally can be told only indirectly because to center it would be to transform it into romance or to suggest an overt lesbian eroticism. The story of the women's relations is like Eve Arden's cat in *Stage Door*; it is there all the time, but we rarely pay much attention to it, and its true character is revealed only retrospectively. Although we see the women's affection and interdependence, the nature of the relationship evades us because we are paying attention to other matters. In this sense, the heterosexual romance narratives function as lures, presenting a version of desire that stands in for but is not the same as the other desire that can continue to exist because we are focused on the lure. Not only is indirection the only way anything but the orthodox heterosexual is permitted by the Production Code, but it is the quintessential position of the queer and eccentric anyway, whose pleasures are conveyed across and through the rigidly taxonomic marriage fable.

Conventional Stories

> Mary Clancy: Welcome to Happy Acres!
> —*The Trouble with Angels*

Stage Door and *The Women* both demonstrate the complex single-sex dynamics that play out in sites coded as metaphorically in the narrative middle—that is, events that occur in a space and time before more conclusory action (weddings, jobs) take over and finish the narrative. The narrative middle undergirds the female comic second, who rules this liminal domain by controlling the flow of information (which in both films is the catalyst for further action) or by her constant reflection and meta-commentary on the action. The female comic second's knowledge is not the kind of grand insight to which might one come as the fitting end of a narrative; rather, it is a common-sense knowledge that produces a tension in relation to the conventional story's proper course. It is what the audience generally already knows about the ways stories go. It is thus ironic rather than noble and practical rather than conventional, producing a second tone in the narrative that plays off and makes more evident what is at stake in the "proper" course.

This tension between tones becomes palpable in films seemingly cut from the single-sexed middle because minor elements become far more prominent there, both in themselves and because the film focuses on what appears to be a slice of narrative (although of course these films are themselves complete narratives). This slice substitutes the middle for the whole, substituting what are within a larger "ideal" narrative frame the middle's chaotic or irrelevant and aimless foibles of an excessive sameness for the more important differences introduced by such mainstream agents as men or major events such as marriage, reproduction, and death. This excessive sameness is rendered as heterogeneous if not heterosexual, which forestalls any overt queer erotic among the characters but paradoxically produces a more covert and thus alluring scenario. In both *Stage Door* and *The Women* the plot's framing devices—the ultimate marriage or success of characters—gloss the women's interactions as temporary, whereas convent films have only religion (and chastity) to alibi the innocence of the women's relations to one another. Although matters of morality and character might seem to take precedence, the convent's rarefied atmosphere draws attention to interpersonal relationships that emerge with intensity. Off the beaten track and out of the way of heterosexual romance, both *The Trouble with Angels* (1966) and *Sister Act* (1992) disclose the eccentric—even queer—investments of women with women, providing another imaginary etiology for the dynamic incarnated by the female comic secondary character.

Girls' school, women's prison, and even some convent films make up a subset of B-film erotica, which is often sadomasochistic, but only the convent provides a respectable setting for more contemporary mainstream Hollywood all-female stories.[15] Even more sheltered than the boardinghouse of *Stage Door*, cloistered spaces usually are considered to be the epitome of sanctuary. Many films use convents as sites of safety and innocence; *The Sound of Music* (1965), for example, uses the convent as a site of retreat and renewal where the kinds of narrative problems plaguing the outside world don't exist.[16] Unlike the boardinghouse denizens' libidinal investments in producers and lumbermen, the quiet, static, private, celibate, and undifferentiable nuns seem in themselves to provide no narrative impetus, representing a field even more inert than any female matrix because nuns are disqualified from even imaginary romance.

Both *The Trouble with Angels*'s St. Francis and *Sister Act*'s St. Catherine's are mother houses and schools set away from secular culture, St. Francis on a large estate in a little town called St. Francisville and St. Catherine's fenced and walled away from the San Francisco cityscape. Both convents are simultaneously imposing and crumbling, their physical plants conveying the strange ambivalence of their status in the world as both abiding symbols of a contemplative, self-sacrificial life and the outdated inutility of such an existence. In both films, the normally minor (out-of-the-mainstream, eccentric) locus of the convent is the primary setting for a drama of transformation. As in *Stage Door*, the convent provides a liminal middle site where transition can occur. In *The Trouble with Angels*, the convent converts an impious outsider into a pious insider; in *Sister Act*, an outsider transforms the convent from the otherworldly to the worldly and actively charitable. The contrast between the two films reflects a mid- to late-1960s shift in ideas about where socially relevant action might take place. The 1966 film represents the waning moments of an interest in internal transformation manifested subtly and indirectly in outward actions. Notably, *The Trouble with Angels*'s sequel, *Where Angels Go, Trouble Follows* (1968), reflects a late-1960s interest in activism. *Sister Act*'s communal turn toward the outside world reveals nuns (most of whom display an eagerness and talent that are merely wasted in a convent) who are hip to contemporary possibilities; its sequel, *Sister Act II* (1993), takes worldly involvement even further.[17]

The *Trouble with Angels* and *Sister Act* both present the changes that occur when a radically different agent is introduced into the convent setting. In *The Trouble with Angels* troublemaker Mary Clancy (Hayley Mills) and her friend Rachel (June Harding) arrive at St. Francis Academy, a convent and girls' school headed by Reverend Mother (Rosalind Russell) and populated by a group of mainly elderly nuns including Sister Liguori (Marge Redmond), Mother Superior's assistant and best friend, and the indefatigable physical education instructor and bus driver, Sister Clarissa (Mary Wickes), who functions as the group's honorary masculine member. Mary, who is an orphan, and Rachel, who has been unsuccessful at other schools, cannot follow the school's rules, giving false names when they arrive, smoking in the bathroom, charging admission for tours of the sisters' forbidden living quarters, smoking cigars, replacing the sisters' sugar with bubble powder, encasing Mary's cousin in plaster of Paris—all "scathingly brilliant ideas" that signal Mary's apparent disrespect for the institution. Given their merely annoying rather than destructive quality, the pranks also hint at an aggressive desire to occupy the inner recesses of the sisters' existence as Mary penetrates to Mother Superior's bedroom, alters the nuns' after-dinner coffee, and whiles away her time smoking in the basement. Mary's seeming disdain for institutional order and the sisters' privacy sets her in opposition to the Mother Superior, who is always uncannily on the spot just when Mary and Rachel think they've gotten away with something. Mother Superior's ability to anticipate some of Mary's pranks is certainly the result of insight and experience, but it also hints at some incipient affinity with Mary or the superpower humorously attributed to imposing nuns.

The Trouble with Angels is also single-mindedly single sex, the portrait of the kind of middling sameness Brooks draws our attention to as part of the middle's infelicity and threat. With the exception of characters called "the outsiders" in the credits, no men appear in the film, and even the male outsiders consist only of Mary's uncle, Rachel's father, and the male head of Rachel's previous school. Mary's troublemaking does not extend to seeing boys on the sly, there are no convent dances, and

none of the nuns leaves her vocation for romance. Except for one passing reference Mary makes to a boy in France with a scooter and Mother
Superior's observation of Mary's uncle's "secretary," the film is hetero-
sex (and even sex) free. Although the absence of heterosexual references
is justified by the film's setting, the film's focus on women's relations
enables it more clearly and overtly to portray their interrelations, especially as they are still safeguarded by the religious nature of the setting.
Although the sanitized homogeneous nature of the convent allows the
relations between women to take center stage, the power of these relations can still be conveyed only indirectly.

The film's structure seems to repeat a whole narrative several times
rather than represent some middling indeterminacy. However, the series
represents finally the same pattern (and a pattern of becoming same),
following Mary and Rachel through a series of mishaps that always end
up the same way: with Mother Superior catching them in the act, taking
them to her office, and disciplining them. As the film moves through the
girls' education at St. Francis, the pattern of episodes begins to change
when Mary and Rachel begin to cause trouble on behalf of, instead of in
defiance of, the school. Their change is matched by a change in Mother
Superior, who, always fascinated by Mary, begins to see the possibility
of her salvation. Mother Superior starts to help the two, staying up all
night to help Rachel resew a dress for the fashion show, confiding her past
and "real" name to Mary. With the death of Sister Liguori, it is as if
Mother Superior subtly invests Mary with Liguori's spot in her affections.
When Mary decides to join the convent, she seems literally to take Liguori's place, and Mother Superior must try to make Rachel, who behaves
like a jilted lover, understand. The aimless and ambivalent Mary's high-
spirited pranks (in spirit if not daring like the pranks showcased in summer camp or campus films) reveal a desire for attention specifically directed toward Mother Superior. Because there is so little motivation for
Mary's recidivist misbehaviors and because the arena of relevant action
is so small, Mary's shenanigans operate as part of a coded conversation
with or even seduction of Mother Superior as the repository of wisdom,
meaning, and love. And Mother Superior, seeing in Mary the same qualities of strength, will, and pride she herself battles, identifies with Mary
and sees her as a soul well worth turning to the good. This subtle and
seemingly minor interchange becomes significant in a film where nothing else happens, but the film's presentation of it, apart from the episodic pattern of transgression and punishment it establishes, is as subtle as
its gentle and captivating erotic.

The dance of magnetic indirection (or watered-down sadomasochism) between Mary and Mother Superior is effected through the thrust and posturing of Mary's mischief and Mother Superior's discipline as well as through the less obvious deployment of the look during more contemplative scenes of respite and inaction that seem to function simply as matrix or static background in the film. Constituting apparent interstices between episodes of frantic disobedience, these contemplative moments are focused on reflection as Mary gazes thoughtfully at Mother Superior from a window or across the convent's luscious gardens as Mother Superior herself is contemplating the gardens or a statue of the Virgin. In contrast to episodes of crime and punishment, these scenes of apparently minor pause, which occur with increasing frequency, exert a powerful captivation through the chain of looks that plays out in a very subtle and indirect exchange the complex lines of desire that structure those moments. On one hand, these scenes are a way of developing the narrative of identification and choice that organizes the film; on the other, these scenes impart a sublime, a desire that exceeds narrative necessity.

The series of looks exchanged between Mary and Mother Superior occur, as they did in *Stage Door* (though here more figuratively), through an architecture of liminality—the literal frames of windows or the space divisions of pillars. Mary's association with windows signals not only her marginality as a "bad" girl in a good girl culture or an adolescent in transition to adulthood but also her search for something beyond the teen pursuits of clothes and smoking that define her existence. The window is a safe and protected margin for Mary where she can give in to her fascination with Mother Superior unseen and undisturbed. Mother Superior, too, is attached to windows as not only the vantage point of her superior knowledge but as emblems of the knowing wisdom incarnated in her return looks at the challenging but wistful Mary. Generally, the looking sequences very simply but powerfully convey both desire and connection. Generally they consist of a shot of Mary looking, her point-of-view shot of Mother Superior who in two of the sequences looks back at her, a reverse shot of Mary looking out the window seen from Mother Superior's perspective, a closer point-of-view shot of Mother Superior, then a final shot of Mary looking. The series contains a system of exchanged glances that convey simple attention as well as an acknowledgment of the special nature of that attention, its potential significance in terms of Mary's connection to her nemesis, both characters' desire to be the object of the other's contemplation, and the enactment of that desire in the exchange of looks that actually completes a circuit. Usually wordless, these exchanges also incorporate or suture the spectator into their system of looks, inviting us to identify and desire through looking as well.[18]

The looking occurs twice from the window, twice in the chapel, once in a confrontation on the grounds, and once at a Christmas party. The window exchanges are wordless and mesmerizing. The other exchanges have the dual purpose of circulating desire and providing an education for Mary. The chapel scenes situate Mary as the willing but covert voyeur of the nuns' mysteries, the first time at a Christmas service where Mother Superior notices her curiosity and the second as Mother Superior mourns at the coffin of her best friend. The first of these seems to indicate Mary's interest in the contemplative life, the second an interest in Mother Superior herself as Mary witnesses the grief Mother Superior had masked earlier. One social encounter is also educational in that, upon interrupting Mother Superior in her contemplation of a statue of the Virgin, Mary makes fun of the German Sister Ursula, whereupon Mother Superior tells her the story of Ursula's bravery in hiding Jewish children from the Nazis and her subsequent imprisonment. Mary's reaction is stunned and rebellious, and she tells Rachel that she "hates" Mother Superior. The second encounter occurs at a retirement home where the convent girls are helping with a Christmas party. Mary watches Mother Superior comfort an old woman whose family has forgotten her. Moved by Mother Superior's kindness and affection, Mary hides her desire for the same with the comment, "I hope I die young and very wealthy." Both of these responses present a defensive Mary who struggles with having been touched and who proudly masks with overt hostility her own desire for Mother Superior's good opinion and affection.

Despite the spiritual nature of the convent and the difference in their ages, the quality of Mary and Mother Superior's attraction is akin to romantic love. Mary becomes increasingly riveted to the figure who is stronger than she. Mother Superior identifies with Mary's strength and will as well as with her need. But rather than being clearly like parent and child or teacher and student, Mother Superior and Mary are more like equals. The indirect and nonverbal manner through which the film represents their attachment conveys a feeling that is beyond classification but is nonetheless vaguely erotic, romantic, obsessive, and compelling. Their relationship motivates Mary's transformation from a troublemaker to a woman devoted to God while transforming Mother Superior from a rigid figurehead to a sympathetic woman. The charge between them is even portrayed in the film as animated lightning (supposedly emanating from an irritated deity) in the film's title sequences and at the end.

The film's minor characters do not play as prominent a role as plot devices or comic doubles as they do in *Stage Door*, *The Women*, and *Sister Act*. Instead, they almost function as a matrix against which the battle of Mary and Mother Superior stages itself. The other nuns and students manifest only the stereotyped characteristics that might vaguely distinguish them from one another, with the exceptions of Sister Clarissa, the convent's jack of all trades and comic subcommandant; Sister Constance (Camilla Sparv), the "flawless beauty" who leaves the convent to minister to lepers in the Philippines; and Marvell Ann (Barbara Hunter), Mary Clancy's suspicious and unfortunate cousin. Sister Clarissa, the honorary masculine figure, is the convent's utilitarian link to the world as she drives the school bus to and from the train station and the band competition, sees to its maintenance, and busily bosses Mr. Grissom, the station master, about the luggage, the timetable, and anything else. Embodying the kind of literal discipline for which convent schools are noted, Sister Clarissa teaches physical education and religion, urges the students to stand with their "heads up and chests out," and flourishes a whistle with which she directs the group jogging and swimming activities. Unlike Mother Superior's calm command, Sister Clarissa struggles for efficient control, overdoing the details and being taken in by Mary's name-changing prank (Mary calls herself Kim Novak and Rachel is Fleur de Lis) and by the two girls' string of illnesses during three years of swimming instruction (which forces Sister Clarissa to jump into the pool to rescue them in the end).

Sister Clarissa is the closest thing St. Francis has to a man; her garrulous efficiency and ultimate incompetence reflect the film's general attitude about men. The three men who actually visit the convent Mother Superior bests easily, shaming Rachel's father and Mary's uncle and constantly outtalking the head of a competing school when he comes to complain, first in response to a letter Rachel wrote to him and second to the convent's skimpy uniform ploy by which they won the band contest and the much-needed prize money to fix the boiler. In fact, the change in Mother Superior's attitude toward Mary is catalyzed partly by her noticing Mary's uncle's "secretary" waiting by his swank convertible in the parking lot. Although the sisters are at the mercy of cultural generosity, they are well able to take care of themselves in their circumscribed world, dramatizing again in comic terms the safety of the homogeneous eccentric space. Furthermore, they dramatize forcefully but subtly the magnetism of emotional (and even erotic) bonds between women as they become visible when other kinds of more "central" or "major" possibilities are absent. This is not to say that women resort to bonding with women only if men are absent but that such bonds become important and visible only when we (or a film) focus on the minor.

Because of the intense relationship at its core, *The Trouble with*

Angels, like *Stage Door* and *The Women,* is dressed as a comedy. More in the tradition of the prank-plagued teen films in which Mills had already starred (such as the *Parent Trap* [1962]), *The Trouble with Angels* opens with a Depatie-Freleng animated title series and hops with a quirky score by Jerry Goldsmith. As in the other films, comedy defrays the anxiety produced by imaging fervent relations between women. And unlike those in *Stage Door* and *The Women,* the nuns' relations aren't alibied by absent men. Hedging the center with proliferated types and droll characters insulates the viewer from the potentially serious single-sex relationships that actually occupy most of the film's activity. At the core of these relationships is an undefinable quasiparental, quasiromantic relationship that in mainstream Hollywood films typifies the relations between female comic seconds and their protagonist friends. The masked imputation of incest (as in the relationship in *The Women* between Mary and little Mary) or impropriety both translates and sustains the eroticism of the relations. They are erotic because they are forbidden, and they are not erotic because such relationships are not countenanced. They are thus highly ambivalent moments where desire circulates in the short circuit, and these moments show exactly how such desire can circulate. The economy of this desire typifies a middle dynamic as opposed to (or as an alternative to) the closure economies of narrative.

There Were Never Such Devoted Sisters

The Trouble with Angels dramatizes how the liminal and all-too-same space of the convent transforms the troublesome outsider and produces its own brand of intensity. In contrast, *Sister Act* portrays how the outsider converts the convent, changing it from an inward-looking community desperately grasping for the last shreds of safety to an intrepid gang of aggressive activists who try to improve the neighborhood and stymie mobsters. Although it has the least homogeneous space of all the films discussed in this chapter, *Sister Act* is most overtly conscious of the functions of single-sex safe spaces, as lounge singer and crime boss girlfriend Dolores van Cartier (Whoopi Goldberg) is hidden in St. Catherine's convent after she has witnessed her gangland boyfriend order a hit. The most secure hideout the police lieutenant can find, the convent generously absorbs the wildly out-of-place Dolores even though the stern and conservative Mother Superior (Maggie Smith) initially opposes her sanctuary.

From her entrance into the order, Dolores imports differences in energy, attitude, race, and sexual enthusiasm barely hidden by her disguise as Sister Mary Clarence, a nun from a more "progressive" order. Aided by bubbly Sister Mary Patrick (Kathy Najimy) and novice Mary Robert (Wendy Makkena), Dolores grudgingly (but good-naturedly) adjusts to the convent's discipline. Like Mary Clancy, Dolores cannot resist breaking the rules, but her trespasses are the clear effect of sudden restrictions on an adult accustomed to a certain license. Dolores's infractions provide the occasion for conflict with Mother Superior, who reminds Dolores of her peril and must try to protect her. Mother Superior finally hits on the idea of restricting Dolores's activities to the nun's choir, a pathetically off-key and lethargic group led by Sister Mary Lazarus (Mary Wickes—Sister Clarissa returned). Dolores cleverly enlists the crusty and suspicious Sister Mary Lazarus as her confederate and proceeds to turn the lackluster chorale into a white Catholic gospel group belting out Motown hits whose secular lyrics have been sacrilized ("I Will Follow Him," "My God" sung to the tune of "My Guy"). Dolores's show-biz approach catalyzes the parish, filling the church and giving Dolores the opportunity to propose a more active ministry in the name of Mother Superior. The sisters enthusiastically adopt Dolores's suggestion, take down the fences that surround the convent, and begin cleaning up the neighborhood. At this point in the film, Dolores has become a central figure among the nuns, accompanied devotedly by Sisters Mary Patrick, Mary Lazarus, and novice Mary Robert.

Right after the newly inspirational choir is scheduled to perform for the visiting pope, Dolores's hideout is discovered by her ex-boyfriend's crime network, and his henchmen kidnap her and take her to Reno. The newly activist nuns commandeer a helicopter, go to the Reno casino, and rescue Dolores, first by acting as nun decoys to the pursuing hitmen and then literally surrounding her with a wall of black-and-white-clothed bodies. Delivered from danger, Dolores returns briefly to the convent to perform for the pope, her victorious salvation and choir leader accomplishments celebrated by the press.

The convent's prototypically middle community transforms Dolores as much as she transforms it; Dolores goes from a selfish, cynical, second-rate performer to a generous, optimistic, inspirational leader, most directly as an effect of the convent's enactment of joy and openness as ends in themselves and their commitment to the group over the interest of the individual. Although the group provides a competing plot to the dilemma of Dolores's escape, it offers a different answer to the question of survival. Although the film focuses primarily on Dolores, the agents of her change—the secondary characters who surround her—are crucial elements in the film who not only provide Dolores with examples but also mediate her integration into the community and provide pleasure in their sheer joy, approval, and excess. This relationship is figured by the choir itself, with its leader, Dolores, orchestrating a cooperating group with prominent soloists (Mary Robert and Sister Mary Patrick) and noteworthy contributor (Sister Mary Lazarus). These three function almost harmonically to set off Dolores's solo but in very different specific ways related to the difficulties Dolores poses. They also enable Dolores's supplanting of Mother Superior, who feels useless in the new regime until she engineers Dolores's salvation.

The most conspicuous of the secondary characters is Sister Mary Patrick, a carnivalesque corpus of bursting mirth and soaring soprano glee. She is the first to officially welcome Dolores; she follows Dolores to the biker bar, is instrumental in getting Dolores to direct the choir, and generally acts as spokesnun for the group despite her youth and unholy exuberance (or maybe because of it). In these roles, Sister Mary Patrick negotiates and detoxifies the protagonist's threatening racial and sexual differences. Because the differences imported by Dolores are differences in race and sexuality (she has some, the nuns pretend they don't), Najimy might be seen as mediating the dangers represented by both sides: the excessive sexuality of Dolores and the frightening celibacy of the nuns. Incarnating the bodily excess Dolores's references to sex and rhythm represent, Sister Mary Patrick transmutes raw sexuality into the joyous carnal surplus of her dancing and singing. Sister Mary Patrick is the unsexed sexual figure, an Eros unlimited who makes the convent safe for Dolores and Dolores safe for the convent and the whole film, with its prospect of single-sex celibacy safe for consumption by a general audience.

One brief episode in the film illustrates graphically how Sister Mary Patrick buffers differences. One night when Dolores sneaks across the street to a biker bar, Sister Mary Patrick and Mary Robert follow her. In the bar Sister Mary Patrick begs a quarter, plays a song on the jukebox, and begins to dance enthusiastically with Mary Robert, who, horrified, quickly pulls away. Taking as substitute partner the only black biker woman in the bar, Sister Mary Patrick leads a jitterbug until Dolores pulls her away, at which point she tries to dance with Dolores. Shifting from Mary Robert to an unknown black woman to Dolores dramatizes her literal mediation of bodies as she shifts from the white to the black, from the virginal and timid Mary Robert through a cooperative black stranger to Dolores, whom, we might suspect, is the person she wanted to dance with in the first place. Although we can pretend there is nothing sexual about this musical exuberance, the nuns' status is exactly why this scene can also impart sexuality. Because any homosexuality is veiled by a code of assumed innocence. However, Dolores is not so innocent—in fact, she is too sexy—so Sister Mary Patrick's actions have a way of taming Dolores through a chain of associations that leads back to Mary Robert, the most innocent of all.

Mary Robert, it turns out, has the voice of gospel singer, a hidden talent Dolores discovers and encourages. Mary Robert is curious about Dolores—about her vocation as a nun and her experiences ministering on the street. When Dolores is kidnaped, Mary Robert is taken as well, although Dolores saves her by pushing her out the door when the car briefly stops. Mary Robert then becomes the source of information about the kidnappers' plans, paying Dolores back for her care and reassurance.

The irascible Sister Mary Lazarus plays another mediating role, as her penchant for discipline (she preferred her former convent in Vancouver, where there was no running water) and subcommandant's role over the choir make her a substitute for Mother Superior and a means by which Dolores can turn the convent's philosophy around. By overtly appealing to Sister Mary Lazarus's dedication to hard work and discipline—in fact, appealing to Sister Mary Lazarus as she would to a male ego—Dolores seduces her into cooperation as she takes over the choir. With Sister Mary Lazarus on her side, Dolores's endeavors bear the stamp of old-guard approval. But in a way slightly different from Sister Mary Patrick, Sister Mary Lazarus's role as the convent's "male" member (evident in her gruff toughness and her love of work) also mediates Dolores's excessive sexuality by embodying a substitute partner, a masculinized assistant who carries out Dolores's ideas but who translates them from danger into virtue.

Sister Act is an allegory of the transformative processes of the middle. Dolores, like Terry Randall and Mary, enters as a self-centered prima donna who, through the intercession of a multifarious middle, becomes a more generous and single-minded character. Although Dolores transforms the middle almost as much as it changes her, the motley group proves its worth as a strategy and philosophy, overcoming such extreme patriarchal vestiges as the police, the mob, and the Catholic church. Like the other female community films, *Sister Act* is not simply the same old story of a triumphant underdog but the narrative of the value of the middle and an exegesis of its economy.

The Perverse's Perverse

Insofar as boardinghouses and convents are eccentric—out of the cultural center, homogeneously female, minor—these films center on elements that appear to deviate widely from more traditional stories and locales. The pretext of same-sexed safety provides license to wander in fields of what appears to be indirect or corollary action. Because of the supposed off-the-beaten-trackness of the films' settings, the action is posed as secondary, as behind the scenes. The imaging of what is typically off-screen space gives these films a sense of being both a voyeuristic vision of "women as they really are" and an exploration of behaviors and actions usually too insignificant to captivate an audience's attention. As the middle and the eccentric, these single-sexed spaces are a structural version of the perverse; they are perverse because they contain too much sameness. When the structurally perverse becomes the center, as it does in these films, then characters such as Eve, Sylvia, Sister Clarissa, and Sister Mary Patrick, who are secondary to a centered perverse, become the perverse's perverse. This may seem to produce two possible scenarios: Either secondary characters in perverse settings are so weird (as they often are in John Waters's films) that they surpass all bounds of verisimilitude and become simply caricature, or in a logic that two perverses make a normal, the secondary characters demonstrate a common-sense normalcy that lassoes the main characters into their ultimate compliance with a normative world.

In these all-female films, I suspect that a third mechanism also operates. Although some secondary characters fill both of the aforementioned roles, the most aggressively interesting—Eve in *Stage Door*, Nancy in *The Women*, Sister Liguori in *The Trouble with Angels*, and Sister Mary Patrick in *Sister Act*—are those who have some sense of the shape of the story and who act as mediators between the disturbing protagonist and the otherwise safe world of the middle's multifarious space. Their arbitrations are enabled by their common-sense insight, their ability to impart their wisdom in ways that still enable them to exist on the fringes, and their sense of their own relative place in the world as watchers rather than doers. Their role as knowledgeable onlookers makes these characters most like the film's audience; in a sense these characters embody the audience in the film and model at least one mode by which the film can be pleasurably consumed.

In addition, these characters' knowledge tends to keep straight the relation between the perverse middle of a single-sex world that has taken center stage and the larger world in which it is immersed. Because these films end up resolving some larger-world dilemma by recourse to this perverse path—stars are discovered, marriages are saved, vocations discovered, and criminals apprehended—the scope of these characters' insights keeps tabs on the multiple contexts of the film's action, enabling it to work within the limited context of the single-sex space yet also act as a productive deviation from a mainstream that will ultimately benefit from the actions of these corollary environments. All-female spaces thus turn out to be sites where more mainstream patriarchal problems can be explored and remedied. They illustrate both the pleasures and functionality of the middle and the perverse as it inevitably serves a more dominant patriarchal worldview while providing some limited respite from it.

The entire complex of overt relations between women, rendered "innocent" by their contexts, provides an elaborate source and anatomy for female comic secondary characters, such as those played by Eve Arden and Thelma Ritter, as they operate in more mainstream films. Although these characters often have no developed background, and when they do it is not the single-sex spaces examined here, they nonetheless carry with them the libidinal and epistemological economies explored in these films. They inevitably reference through their individual bravado this safer but more literally perverse world. That they are a synecdoche of this economy is important because it means that part of female comic secondary characters' fascination and power comes from their bearing more than just themselves; they are both individuals and the residue from an entire history and group dynamic that they telegraph. Their types carry the machinations of the middle in the way characters bear a narrative in themselves, as both Eisenstein and Bordwell suggest. This synecdochal function enables a layering of different economies within single films while permitting the films to appear fairly unified and coherent. There is pleasure in this, as the license from these other worlds provides an opportunity for a very different kind of economy.

3   Tracking Ida

Ida: Don't look now, but you're standing under a
   brick wall.
Monty: I don't get it.
Ida: You will when it falls on you.

—*Mildred Pierce*

"Alligators Have the Right Idea"

What kind of film is Michael Curtiz's *Mildred Pierce* (1945)
if we track the secondary character, Ida, instead of the protagonist,
Mildred? Rather than immersing ourselves in the film's central story, we
might engage in the pleasures and frustrations that come from watching
for the sporadic appearances of secondary characters with their knowledge, familiarity, and class and gender flexibility. We might engross ourselves in the confusions and indeterminations of the middle, aligning
ourselves with the fool figure as the middle's Virgil. Reading for the secondary and perverse agents who threaten a short circuit, lead away from
a proper end, or suggest alternative and not-quite-so proper stories is not
necessarily a resistant looking against a film's insistent star-studded grain
but, as we have seen, is already an intrinsic part of the scene. Even if we
adopt a deliberately perverse viewing practice, this perversity, like the
characters who interest us, inevitably leads back to the main story. The
all-female spaces of the films discussed in chapter 2 offer a generous site
for the middle and the minor; in a more conventional film such as *Mildred
Pierce* the ethos of the middle has become personified by the female comic second, the supporting fool figure who bears the mysterious history
of the middle in her actions, attitudes, and relationships. Watching for

such a character against the film's impetus provides uncanny but pleasurable glimpses into the atmosphere of the now-invisible off-screen
world and a taste of the familiar competing tone such characters represent. Instead of functioning primarily within a clearly defined all-female
site, this tonal difference between major and minor works throughout the
film both on the level of dramatic irony—producing tension between
characters' ignorance of the story and the fool figure's common-sense
commentary on it—and as a contrast between the seriousness of the
embroiled protagonist and the awry perspective of the observing friend.
With Ida as a possible vantage point, *Mildred Pierce* becomes a much
more varied, multiple, intricate text with a wide range of complicated
viewer-film relations.

Ida Corwin is the quintessential female comic secondary character
who, mooring a line of perverse narrative possibilities, embodies the virtues of the wise fool, sets a cosmopolitan and arch tone, mediates and
neutralizes threatening female behaviors, and affords a site of knowledge
that provides one lens through which the film may be consumed. Because
we have already begun tracking Eve Arden in her first substantial appearance as a minor character in *Stage Door*, this chapter follows Eve Arden
from her performance as the exemplary female comic secondary character, Ida, in *Mildred Pierce* back to *Cover Girl* (1944), where she plays
"Stonewall" Jackson, the talent arbiter for a fashion magazine, and to
Anatomy of a Murder (1959), where she plays Maida Rutledge, wisecracking secretary to defense attorney Paul Biegler (Jimmy Stewart). But because Eve Arden is by no means the only example of a female comic secondary character, this chapter contrasts Arden's roles with those of
Thelma Ritter, who also consistently played a fool character but who,
with her six Academy Award nominations for Best Supporting Actress,
was more recognized for her performances.[1] The chapter tracks Ritter
from *Rear Window* (1954), where she plays the prophetic insurance nurse,
Stella, back through her roles as friend and assistant Birdie in *All about
Eve* (1950), snitch Moe in *Pickup on South Street* (1953), dipsomaniac
maid Alma in *Pillow Talk* (1959), and divorcée Isabelle Steers in *The
Misfits* (1961).

Before we have even seen these films, however, we might already
anticipate delight from these actresses' intertextual survival, from Arden
and Ritter playing the same quirky characters from film to film: Arden
in *Stage Door* to *No No Nanette* (1940), *Ziegfeld Girl* (1941), *Comrade X*
(1940), *Cover Girl*, *The Kid from Brooklyn* (1946), *Night and Day* (1946),
One Touch of Venus (1948), *Tea for Two* (1950), *Anatomy of a Murder*,
The Dark at the Top of the Stairs (1960), *Sergeant Deadhead* (1965), and

Grease (1978), and Ritter in *Miracle on 34th Street* (1947) to *All about Eve, The Mating Season* (1951), *With a Song in My Heart* (1952), *Pickup on South Street, Rear Window, Pillow Talk, The Misfits, Birdman of Alcatraz* (1962), *Move Over Darling, Boeing Boeing,* and *What's So Bad about Feeling Good* (1968). If we see Eve Arden or Thelma Ritter's names in the opening credits, we already expect a particular kind of character playing a particular kind of part. There is not only pleasure in their roles and our knowledge of them, there also is great gratification in having our expectations about those roles fulfilled. This satisfaction is not quite the same as our expectations surrounding headliners such as Joan Crawford or Doris Day, even though they, too, may play the same character—or at least act the same way—from film to film. With secondary characters, our recognition tends to be subliminal; familiarity might be evoked by their name, but it is more likely to be elicited by their first appearance in the film because our experience of them as actresses or as types brings us the small glow that comes from recognizing someone whose reappearances seem more day-to-day. There is the sense that we know who they are, if only we only knew who they were. I can't emphasize this feeling of incipient recognition and mastery enough; it functions from film to film and within film culture in the same way female comic seconds function in individual films, providing us with a safe repetition, reliability, and a haven of comfortable familiarity.

This intertextual knowledge of a minor element suggests at the outset that not only are decentered and corollary elements of a film more important than we might think but also that they operate fairly consistently from narrative to narrative, at least in Hollywood film. This means that if the minor is perverse, it is not depraved, hugely unpredictable, or wildly deviant. Rather, it is also a "normal" part of the mechanism by which the "normal" is rendered and perceived as normal. The normal thus is produced through multiple and deviant lines and agents that work together toward certain ends, some, such as headliner stars, working at the center and retaining an aura of normalcy and others, such as more extraneous female characters, working at the edges and occasionally falling away, conveying a feeling of eccentricity and downright orneriness.

Although the middle is a "normal" part of narrative, its elements, particularly those that seem minor, work differently. Because they are not in the center, appear sporadically, and are partially rather than fully drawn characters, female comic secondary characters played by Eve Arden and Thelma Ritter operate as one of the instruments of the middle and its associated perversity and multivalence. They bring to film sites of pleasure that exist alongside, in cooperation with, but differently from the pull of the central narrative featuring a film's headliner stars. Even if Ida-like characters rule the narrative middle, that middle is itself never in the center of our attention but always poised toward the fulfillment (or failure) of something else. I would prefer—perversely, of course—always to keep Ida out of the center, to have you acknowledge her out of the corner of your eyes and attention, but then you would think I am writing about something else. Here, then, I focus on Ida Corwin as a fully developed example of the quintessential female comic secondary character type.

Mildred Pierce, a comeback vehicle for Joan Crawford and the film for which she won her only Academy Award, is a murder mystery that begins with the shooting death of Mildred's second husband, Monte (Zachary Scott). The film proceeds through the questioning of her partner, Wally; manager, Ida; Mildred; daughter, Veda; and ex-husband and Veda's father, Bert. The film oscillates between the film noir police station situated in the film's present and the brighter domestic drama of home and restaurant in a series of flashbacks through which we learn Mildred's history as she is interrogated by the police. She relates her separation from Bert, her struggle and rise as an entrepreneur, the death of her younger spunky and unspoiled daughter Kay, her relation to the lounging playboy Monte, her spoiling of Veda, and finally her marriage to Monte and his sale of the share of the restaurant she paid him as his "dowry," which brings her to the brink of fiscal ruin. The murder mystery is at last solved as we learn that Veda, thinking Monte was going to run away with her, shot him in a fit of childish pique when he refused. Mildred, who is willing to sacrifice herself for her daughter, does not succeed in saving her and leaves the Justice Building at dawn with her ex-husband.

Both Joyce Nelson and Pam Cook extensively analyze the workings of narrative in *Mildred Pierce*. Nelson argues that the film's refused reverse shot at the beginning allows the inspector to become the voice of truth in the film, making patriarchy the answer to the women's dilemmas. Pam Cook shows how the film's "problematic" is uncertainty and duplicity centered on Mildred's body as the "location of sexual ambiguity and the return of an infantile fantasy about the body of the mother" (78). "This fantasy," Cook demonstrates, "allows for a potentially more democratic structure of sexual relationships based on bisexuality, a structure repressed by the heterosexual division which the Oedipus complex attempts to enforce" (78–79). Critics see the film's problem as a split between the representation of a woman's difficulties on one side and the patriarchal—and inapposite—answers provided through narrative and cinematic practices (imaging in particular) on the other, figured through the film's own stylistic bifurcation between past and present. Pamela Robertson demonstrates how even "the female voiceover is undermined and superseded by the 'masculine' ideology of the implied filmmaker, not only in the final assertion of Truth, but also, more insidiously, in the flashback segments themselves" (43). While Robertson points to the "defeatism" of reading *Mildred Pierce* with an end orientation, the problem of making *Mildred Pierce*'s parts cohere in any way that doesn't ultimately punish the women is difficult to resolve. Even Ida, according to Robertson, "reinforces the equation in the film between female independence and loss of femininity" (49).

Cook points out that on one level this problematic is "signified . . . by the relationship between Veda and Mildred" (79), but I suggest that on another level it is expressed through Ida, not only as an attribute of her character but also as a part of her narrative function of mediation, alternative, and escape. If the film's figurative father, the inspector, always knows the truth, as Cook observes, Ida is the father's parody double who, knowing another truth, functions vainly from inside to try to avoid its consequences. If, as Nelson suggests, the film sets up an enigmatic structure by refusing the reverse or answering shot, Ida—and the Ida position— work to allay anxiety by both mediating and temporarily substituting as the reverse shot and provisional answer. This means that the kinds of multivalence and alterity represented by Ida are situated as provisional possibilities in the film, including female independence itself.[2]

Other readings of the film emphasize its postwar context in which the successful self-starter Mildred embodies threats to a masculine uselessness and superfluity. If the film works to showcase and contain (and even discipline) the dangers of too much female independence permitted by the war, then Ida is the character who is permitted to continue that independence but only as a version of dependence on others, particularly on women.[3] Whether *Mildred Pierce* is read as gender duplicity or social ambivalence about women's roles, because Ida is not central she can both mediate that duplicity and escape its punishment, evince alterity and evaporate from the scene, but at the same time hold the place and perpetuate its possibilities.

Woven into the narrative of Mildred's rise to restaurateur fortune, Ida performs such serviceable plot functions as giving Mildred her first job, teaching her how to be a waitress, collecting the earnings from Mildred's restaurant's first night, acting as friend and confidante, and signaling the whereabouts of Mildred's self-centered daughter and husband. Mildred first meets Ida when, exhausted from job-hunting, Mildred drops into a busy restaurant for a cup of tea. Restaurant hostess Ida seats Mildred and comments on the waitresses who are squabbling around them. Mildred asks Ida for a job, and Ida kindly gives the inexperienced Mildred a chance, becoming her restaurant mentor. When Mildred scrapes together enough money to open her own restaurant, Ida comes along as aide-de-camp, running the cash register, managing the importune Wally, and keeping a wary eye out for Veda. As Mildred's success multiplies and she loses control of Veda, Ida seems far more aware of impending tragedy than Mildred, trying to warn Mildred about Veda's excesses and protect her from the nastiness of the whole truth. Throughout, the low-key, loyal, and reliable Ida provides the sense that there is competence in the world, that when things seem to fall apart, Ida will be there to take care of the details.

But lest Ida now seem too much in the center, while watching the film we cannot sustain our attention to Ida. The film's visual practice will not let us make of her the kind of fetish or overvalued object Laura Mulvey defines in her famous essay "Visual Pleasure and Narrative Cinema." Ida's narrative perversity is instead matched by her perverse imaging. Because classical Hollywood edited films for continuity of action and narrative and lit scenes to focus on central aspects of this action (which mainly involve protagonists), it is difficult to pay any sustained attention to elements of the periphery such as secondary characters, transitional spaces, and other minor features that seem to be produced as a byproduct of such centralizing constructions.[4] The film's editing and framing focus on Mildred, following her from locus to locus and from time to time. When the film cuts on Mildred's action, it cuts for a continuity around Mildred, ending scenes at points of closure in her narrative and rejoining her at another place and time. This same editing prevents us from following Ida through space or time in any sustained fashion. Interrupted in mid-act and rarely rejoined except in the few sequences that focus on her, Ida's place in the logic of continuity is discontinuous and irrelevant. She is decentered and dismembered, occupying the sides of the images and running in and out of the frame. Mildred often is framed in medium close shots that focus on her face, whereas Ida is framed in medium long shots that disallow any facial detail. In contrast to Mildred, who is always lit with special key lighting so that her face is especially luminous, Ida, like many other secondary characters in the film, is lit in the same ways as the larger mise-en-scène. The effect of this, like the editing practice, is to emphasize Mildred while making the other characters fall into the background.

Unless we pay specific attention to our assumptions about the relative place and importance of such secondary characters, we tend to see female comic seconds such as Ida only in relation to the film's protagonist; our understanding of Ida Corwin, for example, is based primarily on the ways she advises and protects Mildred. But even though she appears sporadically and often opportunely, Ida is more than a functionary; she offers advice, provides knowing but cryptic commentary on characters and events, highlights irony, and generally furnishes a balancing, pragmatic voice against which to measure the obsessions, hubris, and cruelties of the other characters.[5] She is a head taller than Mildred, and when standing on a stool to adjust her stockings, she presents an image of clownish power that exceeds both the heights to which one woman can rise (in a covert complement to Mildred's success) and the inappropriate display of lingerie politics. On one hand, Ida is homely and practical; on the other, she is possessed of a higher power, a greater perceptiveness, threatening to exceed the piece and exuding the power linked to borders and potential transgressions.

In many ways Ida does ward off dangers. As an agent within the film, Ida protects Mildred from the truth about Veda's and Monte's behaviors, trying to warn her gently about the extent of their profligacies. She bristles at Wally from the beginning, a behavior accepted as the comic sideplay of the spinster and the tacky playboy, but Wally also turns out to have been a legitimate threat because he, like Monte, sells Mildred out.

Ida Corwin (Eve Arden) on stool in *Mildred Pierce*

Ida is the intercessor between Mildred and other characters at points when Mildred faces difficulties alone, most notably during her absence from Veda's birthday party, when she is fighting off fiscal doom. But Ida also wards off the dangers represented by Mildred herself as an aggressive, unsentimental, successful, driven woman. Because Ida is even more hard-bitten than Mildred and because Ida's hardness is sidelined in sarcasm and wit, her presence acts as a decoy to attract attention to her own more comic breach of gender propriety, thus deflecting possible anxieties about Mildred's inappropriate gender behavior. (This is also true in a slightly different way of Wally, a male comic secondary character whose unsubtle advances to Mildred distract from the more insidious and calculated romancing of the gigolo Monte.) Ida's brand of spinster hermaphroditism distracts us from Mildred's desperate masculine qualities, funneling the entire category of gender infringement off to the side through the realm of the minor as an attribute of the secondary that then seems to account for the character's secondary status.

And Ida does have a hint of hermaphroditism, if not literally in her height or carriage, then metaphorically in her appropriation of the privilege of speaking to the point. When Mildred asks Ida whether she was ever married, Ida, with the understated sarcasm that typifies her role in the film, explains, "When men get around me, they get allergic to wedding rings. You know, big sister type, good old Ida, you can talk it over with her man to man. I'm getting awfully tired of men talking to me man to man." In the limited world of the kitchen and restaurant, Ida also wards off the dangers presented by the male characters by being the "man" and helpmate for Mildred that none of the males in the film are. If Monte and Wally are untrustworthy, selfish, and grasping, Ida represents all of the qualities of strength, support, and know-how sometimes attributed to men while maintaining the comfort and familiarity of women together. Ida also negotiates the class problem instigated by Mildred's rise to fortune and represented most trenchantly by Veda. Veda wants no association with the "grease" that founded her mother's wealth; Ida often intercedes between mother and daughter, warning Mildred that Veda has been borrowing money from the waitresses, taking Veda's snide barbs about work in Mildred's place (Veda tells Ida that she's "provincial"), and becoming the displaced representative of Mildred's previous lower-class status.

Ida's hermaphroditism and class flexibility are also symptoms of her inside-outside narrative position, her almost queer positionality that seems, through its marked eccentricity, to provide Tiresian insight. Ida is an Auntie Mame before Mame was liberated from the margins, even

Ida and Mildred, *Mildred Pierce*

though such characters' marginal positions account for their perspective and its accompanying wisdom. Ida provides not only knowledge of plot events and psychological insight but also the kind of knowledge that comes from correct anticipation, from being let in on a secret and from having superior insight. She contributes a kind of scandalous knowledge because she enables the enunciation of unacceptable material in the form of wisecracks and sarcastic remarks, and she supplies recurring but irregular points of pleasure and contrast in our gratification at her pronouncements about what we already suspect to be true. For example, when Ida quips, "Basically Veda has convinced me that alligators have the right idea—they eat their young," we are gratified not only by the line's sarcasm and its apt commentary on what most viewers must have already realized about Veda but also by its slightly counterideological drift, its taunt at the sacrosanct nature of maternity.

In a Hollywood that had since the 1930s learned to negotiate the restrictions of the Production Code, comic seconds such as Ida served as one way to insert the more complex material sophisticated audiences enjoyed without necessarily insulting the values of those whose tastes ran to reinforcements of morality. Like fools, characters without apparent fate or explicit narratives could deliver pronouncements and commentary that could not come from protagonists or more serious characters. Ida thus can not only openly comment on the foolishness of Mildred's brand of maternity but also candidly fondle cash, as she does after the restaurant's first day, riffling a stack of bills and asking, "Isn't that a lovely noise?" and commenting to Mildred, who observes that she "must be dead," "Well, if I am just bury me with this." Ida's overt delight with money not only defuses the other characters' more problematic avarice but also plays up the crassness of a larger cultural lust for lucre. Her comments about men contribute comically to the film's gender war subplot and characterize the nature of most of the males in the film; "Oh men," she says, "I never met one of them who didn't have the instincts of a heel." They also reflect an embittered perspective that by all rights should be Mildred's but is expressed safely through Ida.

Despite the apparent unimportance of female comic secondary characters such as Ida, as Charles Higham and Joel Greenberg comment, "it was often the minor characters who set the tone of the period" (11). The lack of narrative and star commodity centrality relegate Ida to the realm of decoration—of tone—but as we have seen in the all-female films, this tone is an essential part of the tension that builds around the possibilities of narrative fulfillment and closure. As a tonal element in a film focused on the mainstream, Ida appears to work as part of the film's ground, coming forward only occasionally, like an instrument in the orchestra that accompanies a soloist, to add a highly empathetic and sometimes contrapuntal note or two. As a contributory strain, Ida produces tone by contrasting with Mildred, her blondness setting off Mildred's chic brunette, her frankness showing up Mildred's reticence, her quick repartee providing the performance of a sophisticated cosmopolitan atmosphere even as Ida herself stops just short of being cosmopolitan. Mostly, however, Ida accentuates, undergirds, and illustrates the film's tone of bravado, of women not accepting the fates necessarily handed to them and battling with their labor and wits the systems of marriage, wealth, and social consequence that otherwise would keep them behind the scenes.

But the tone Ida sets is even more complex than its competing ambiance and attitude in a film such as *Stage Door*. What seems like tone also includes the secondary character's suggestion of an alternative or perverse story in addition to the matrix or off-screen liminal middling world of the all-female space such characters embody. This alternative but mostly missing story is also structurally a part of the narrative middle because, like the perverse, it threatens a deviant course, but only for Ida herself rather than for the entire narrative. When a character such as Ida intimates an alternative story, her presence provides contrast, titillating threat, and deviant variety in addition to her introduction of visual difference and the lively wit of her verbal style. *Mildred Pierce* hints at this other narrative by joining Ida *in medias res* as she sits waiting in the police station, as she manages the restaurant where Mildred gets her first job, or as she confides her failures in her relationships with men. This sense of another narrative existing alongside but not entirely contained within the narrative of *Mildred Pierce* suggests both the expansive potential of the film's story (*Mildred Pierce* is linked to a large web of intertwined narratives that extend beyond the film itself) and the presence of alternate narratives within the film that vaguely threaten its unity and the inevitability of its final return to the familial.[6] If at the end of the film Mildred leaves the police station with Bert, Ida presents a potentially different trajectory that is aligned with the dominant narrative and takes its own way as we are left to assume that Ida will stay pretty much the same as when we first saw her: uncontained, single, feisty, unthreatened, competent, and wise.

Ida's narrative supports Mildred's, comments on it, and suggests that all narratives don't have to be like Mildred's. Mildred is dangerous because she can succeed on her own, whereas Ida is dangerous because she presents the possibility of living generally without any male interference, even though she complains about that. Within the heteronarrative frame of Hollywood narrative practice, the possibility of the independent existence Ida represents can exist only as minor and implied, as an alternative that makes Mildred look normal and even admirable in her success. Ida's danger is constantly held in check by Wally, who simply denies that she is a woman at all. Wally says, "I hate all women," to which Ida replies, "My, my," to which Wally responds, "Thank goodness you're not one."

The tone Ida represents also provides one entrée to the film's consumption. Female comic seconds such as Ida obscure and effect a very complex set of operations, like an enzyme, that enables us to digest the film. This enzymatic function includes not only warding off various threats of female excess but also performing a series of negotiations between the characters and between film and audience around issues of knowledge. Comic seconds such as Ida double the audience in the film, providing metanarrative commentary. For example, sensing Mildred's trouble at the end of the film, Ida says to Monte and Veda, "Something's going on. I'm worried. I think she's in some kind of business trouble." In saying this, Ida only reconfirms to the group of people celebrating at the house what the viewers already know. When Monte flippantly comments that "It happens in the best of families," Ida telegraphs the later discovery that Monte was behind the takeover, telling him, "Don't look now, but you've got canary feathers all over your face." Such verbalizations masked as sarcasm function as a shared secret, providing a place for the audience in the film through a kind of reciprocal irony, acknowledging the viewers' wisdom and complementing their sagacity. Ida is the character who lets us in; if she is the protagonist's best buddy, she is ours as well.

Consumption of cinema is conceived through two slightly different but related processes: identification and spectatorship.[7] Identification, a category of psychoanalysis, is a mode of engaging with a film based on some mechanism of internal and often unconscious connection (or cathexis) with a figure or position variously defined. Spectatorship, a category associated more with the sociocultural conditions of film viewing and the ideologies expressed by film texts, raises the question of how viewers consume films and how their consumption is affected by gender, class, race, and other cultural overdeterminants such as the star system and ideology. Identification and spectatorship are not distinct categories; rather, they slide from one to the other in various attempts to discern just how film texts work on viewers and how viewers engage with film texts.

Theories about identification in cinema have evolved from the simple to the complex. Spurred by the early (1970s and 1980s) work of feminist theorists who made a psychoanalytic understanding of sexual difference central, thinking about mechanisms of film engagement has gone from seeing identification as a set of passive processes closely defined by Freud's understandings of identification to a dynamic web of connections enabled by viewers' active fluidity between a range of alternatives. Freud's understanding of identification was binary: One either wanted to *be* or wanted to *have* someone else. Which one wanted depended on one's gender in a heterosexual matrix: Girls want to be other girls and want to have boys and vice versa. Following Freud, Laura Mulvey also initially assumed the automatic identification of women viewers with women characters in a tradition where films constantly reiterated patriarchal scenarios in which women were either fetishized objects or absent altogether ("Visual Pleasure"). This meant that female viewers either witnessed their constant location as object or absence or had to occupy a masculine viewing position against their interest and experience.

Of course, this rather rigid analysis raised the problem of how women could enjoy film at all if their identifications were so restricted to ideological orthodoxy. The resolution of this problem has occupied feminist film theorists ever since, producing a rich and provocative set of hypotheses about identification and spectatorship. As Miriam Hansen notes, "The difficulty of conceptualising a female spectator had led feminists to recast the problem of identification in terms of instability, mobility, multiplicity, and, I would add, temporality. Likewise, a number of feminist critics are trying to complicate the role of sexual difference in identification with the differences of race, class, with cultural and historical specificity" (591) and, I would add, sexuality. Briefly—and to locate the significance of what the female comic second might add to the conversation—film identification and spectatorship have been interrogated from almost all possible angles: from the assumptions of viewers' passivity in the face of the psychocinematic machine to shifting the operative paradigm away from gender and heterosexuality, to enlarging the mechanics of identification (the how), to enlarging the field of what can be identified with (the what).

Arguing for less subjected viewers, such theorists as Mulvey, Mary Ann Doane, and Rhona Berenstein engage masquerade and drag as models enabling viewers to wield gender (and hence also paradigms of activity and passivity). In a follow-up essay, Mulvey suggests that female viewers use masculine masquerade as a mode of viewing ("Afterthoughts"). Doane suggests a tactic of masquerade through which females take up their own feminine position elsewhere, allowing them to distance themselves from the image and view it as if they are in another, still feminine but distanced and hence more critical position ("Film and the Masquerade"). Berenstein understands spectatorship as an active process, "a mode of performance" or drag in which a viewer voluntarily and with great pleasure engages in a gender play that reflects not only the gender ambiguities of horror films' monsters but also the essentialized gender identity of viewers themselves. Hoping to evade the binaries that moor most theories of identification, Berenstein takes as her point of departure the lesbian viewer and drag as a process that enables the viewer to pleasurably identify "against oneself" (58). "Spectatorship-as-drag transposes horror's gender ambiguities from storylines and publicity campaigns to viewing," she suggests. "As a framework for spectatorship, drag suggests both that transgressive identifications and desires work beneath or on the surface of gender displays and that the lure of conventional roles does not counteract social expectations" (58). For Berenstein, gender itself is not a singular category but always already multiple and contradictory in its constitution.

Deemphasizing sexual difference itself as the central defining paradigm, Miriam Hansen, Tania Modleski, and Linda Williams adopt models of ambivalence. Hansen proposes an ambivalence located both in the figure of Valentino and in the viewer's ability to occupy both sadistic or voyeuristic and masochistic positions. Instead of adopting an either/or structure, Hansen suggests that viewing is more a both/and defined by the combination of position, identification, and desire (Valentino). Modleski explores what she sees as the essential bisexuality of both male and female viewers (*The Woman Who Knew Too Much*), whereas Williams emphasizes the dual nature of identification (be and have) as coexistent ("When the Woman Looks"). Operative ambivalence points toward the continued usefulness of the fetish model as it has been redefined as a site of productive ambivalence (see McCallum, *Object Lessons*). As Berenstein observes, however, ambivalence and bisexuality still adhere to covert binaries as the foundation for understanding viewing relations.

Adherents of spectatorship such as Jackie Stacey and reception such as Janet Staiger see the more empirical evidence of viewer experience as resolving the insistent binaries of theory. However, Stacey's painstaking elaboration of the different modes of cinematic delight are still versions of the desire to be or have in psychoanalysis (126–70). What Stacey adds to the discussion is a more finely tuned attention to the variations in the received forms this "wanting to be" might take. Stacey is certainly right when she suggests that spectatorship is mobile and empowered and not entirely defined or even described by theoretical endeavors. The variety of empirical impressions she collects do, as she suggests, have "cultural meanings" that are to some extent inscribed in the text (29). Tamsin Wilton follows Stacey in extolling the potentials of "social experience" for curing the rigid binaries of freudianism (143). Judith Mayne also suggests that specifically lesbian viewing "involves much more than a simple identification with (or rejection of) cinematic images" (xvii). Unfortunately, the split between spectatorship and identification reiterates the same old theory versus empiricism debate that continues to haunt feminist studies in general, but if studies of spectatorship show that those processes are neither rigid nor entirely predictable (empiricism), they also suggest that something (or many things) accounts for the variety and mobility of reception (theory).

The issues of how viewers identify and with what they identify are not distinct from the question of the paradigm (heterosexuality, sexual difference, psychoanalysis, empiricism) used to define identification as a mode of cinematic engagement. Privileging other paradigms such as apparatus theory or narrative produces slightly different possibilities. Theorists who study the constitution and effects of the cinematographic apparatus locate identification as the combination of psychic and cultural processes with the operations of imaging, editing, and narrative that bind a viewer into the world of the film. Jacques Aumont, Alain Bergala, Michel Marie, and Marc Vernet, following Roland Barthes, see identification as a "question of place, an effect of structural position" (223). This position is partly produced by the material practices of cinematography and editing that compose multiple and varied points of view throughout a film as well as through the labors of narration that create tension and empathy on behalf of certain characters. Mechanisms of identification are displaced from gender and ideology to the varied enunciatory operations of cinema. This doesn't solve (rather it ignores) the dilemma of the female spectator, especially if we understand crossgender identifications as inherently oppressive. But it does provide the basis for understanding identification in terms other than similarity and desire based only on gender.

For example, seeing identification in relation to a structural position suggests that fantasy (the ability to imagine oneself in multiple sex or gender roles) might account for how viewers pleasurably cross-identify. Identification is not so much a matter of the operations of a hegemonic patriarchal narrative within the circumscribed identificatory routes of identification in relation to gender but of the viewer's positional fluidity underwritten by fantasy and enabled by the apparatus itself. Although we seem to come full circle—this identification against interest is exactly what Mulvey was worried about in the first place—we come around to a sense of the greater complexity and inherent multiplicity of both cinema and identificatory mechanisms, a much broader sense of the "how."

We also have a much more varied sense of the "what." The apparatus and narrative might not be as insistently patriarchal as originally imagined. Teresa de Lauretis points out that cinema does address female spectators as female spectators; in other words, cinema is not as hegemonically masculine as first thought. De Lauretis quotes Chantal Akerman, the director of *Jeanne Dielman*, who suggests that a female viewing position is produced as much by content and style as by the politics of the apparatus. "I give space to things," Akerman comments, "which were never, almost never, shown in the hierarchy of film images. . . . But more than the content, it's because of the style. If you choose to show a woman's gesture so precisely, it's because you love them" ("Rethinking" 145). Developing de Lauretis's and Akerman's more women-centered modes of spectatorship, Andrea Weiss ("Queer") traces the various ways lesbian spectators find clues and codes in content and style in much the same ways Ackerman suggests women identify with content. For Weiss, lesbian spectatorship is a matter of decoding characters, language, and behaviors from the perspective of lesbian countercultural knowledge. Such identification, though not heterosexual, is identity based and assumes a tight relation between knowledge, identity, and identification. Patricia White combines the insights of de Lauretis and Weiss, showing how the apparatus, the star system, narrative, and processes of cultural encoding and decoding provide a site for the "outsider"—the lesbian viewer—within Production Code–era films.

Just as de Lauretis, Weiss, and White see female content as already inscribed, it is possible to see other kinds of positions produced by narrative itself. Narrative, understood as much more complicated and multivalent than earlier thought, offers structural positions that are in addition to those produced by tension and empathy, which tend to be in line with the dominant thrust of the story. It also responds from the vantage of textuality to the issue of viewer mobility and choice. Positions enabled by dramatic irony (we know more than the characters do) or the locations aligned with the many perverse threads (the middle) that run through and within Hollywood narrative film ground identifications with sites of knowledge such as those personified by fool figures, voiceover narrators, or the camera itself (in addition to any primary identification with the camera as the source of the image).[8] The obliqueness of the position may be one spur to identification, but shared knowledge provides a common ground that, though minor, appears to be the site from which intelligent viewing already arises.

Ida is an example of how this epistemological mode of identification might work. Like other female comic seconds, Ida brings to consciousness some of the narrative processes of the film—in fact, acknowledges that narrative ploys are already overtly conscious. Ida's knowledge doesn't suddenly propel us outside of the film, but we are no longer buried within its diegesis. Instead, I would suggest that through the presence and agency of female comic seconds who incarnate this inside-outside ambivalence, we occupy a space of both belief and incredulity, of acceptance and skepticism, not in relation to whether the film world exists but in relation to both the characters' actions and the audience's implied space in the film itself. Our identification is with what the secondary character knows as well as with the secondary character herself as repository of that knowledge. By virtue of a secondary character such as Ida, we are neither mere spectators nor total participants, but perhaps, like Ida, wise fools drawn in despite ourselves. Of course, we can and do accomplish this without such a character, but the character's presence draws attention to our narrative knowledge as if it returns from the text. This produces a sense of already being there—of viewer inscription in the text—leveraging the viewer in relation to the narrative's other complexities while seeming to also preempt or coopt viewer mastery.

This kind of identification based on shared knowledge and oblique positioning is more like McCallum's notion of the fetish, where Ida, as a fetish object, plays out our ambivalence in relation to the ontological status of the film text and its contradictory multiple drives.[9] Rather than being simply a substitute phallus or the signifier of disavowal, Freud's fetish, as McCallum demonstrates, is a means by which differences can be enjoyed. Our relation to Ida, which may be both identificatory and fetishistic, enables us to negotiate our more difficult relation to the rest of the film and its system of differences—to its dual style, its many desirable objects, the temporal and spatial disorder of its flashback structure, and the death that begins and ends the film. Ida is the part that makes the whole whole, that certifies the film's functioning as a whole. Although Mildred furnishes the nexus that links the plots, Ida provides the knowledge, tone, liminal ground, and humor that pull present and past together and make sense of the film's complex anatomy of virtue, ambition, greed, and crime.

To carry this idea of the female comic secondary character as mediator and site of knowledge even further, the ways Ida is imaged—her position on the margins, her relation to off-screen and safe spaces, and the temporal ellipses that interrupt her narrative—also produce in the persona of Ida a middle ground between the overvalued image of Joan Crawford and the audience who, like Ida, also occupies off-screen space. Ida is not only an audience double, she is also an audience prosthesis whose knowledge empowers us, through her, to step into the screen. If we assume that we consume films through identifications with images and narratives and if we understand identificatory mechanisms to be as much defined by a process of inserting oneself into a like narrative position as by any process of imagistic captivation, then Ida's affinities with our own position as audience and with our knowledge make her perhaps one of the film's most predictable identifications, a primary locus through which we mentally consume the film. In this sense, we are always tracking Ida anyway because Idaness is built into the film as a mode of its own consumption. And if we identify with Ida or share her perverse knowledge and are captivated by her blissful appearances, then the audience itself is also perverse in relation to the film.

What we know through Ida may well realign our investments in the film in relation to the source or reflection of our own knowledge. Our positions might shift, and our choices might be influenced by innumerable factors—familiarity, serendipitous associations, predilections, sexual attraction—in addition to the rhetoric of the story's narration, the shape of the story, and the moral and ideological forces aligned with particular characters. If we watch from the perspective of the perverse in the first place, then we might align ourselves with the film's perverse elements (and vice versa in that if we align with the perverse we watch from its perspective). At the same time, we also consume the dominant, not only from the dominant perspective produced by the cinematic apparatus but also from a perverse perspective whose relation to knowledge and alternative narratives assumes crossgender identifications and desires. And if our primary identification seems to be with the camera's perspective, because that is the lens through which we see the film, watching against what the camera wants us to see opens up the possibility of abandoning that central identification to permit what might be considered a multiple and nonhegemonic viewing practice that, I contend, has always been both possible and practiced because it is already inscribed in the film and because spectators are not always compliant receptacles. Therefore, we can identify with Ida and with Joan Crawford at the same time; as perverse viewers we can both identify with and desire Joan Crawford and anyone else even if the film's imaging practices do not foreground these characters. Although we might follow the dominant narrative, we do so from a position that already knows that its dominance depends on the perverse, the ancillary, and the multiple and present other possibilities the film also inscribes. Coming to watch these other possibilities consciously is a way of acknowledging a different reading that has always been a part of whatever reading we have done.

What we know through Ida may also be another mode of film consumption that is no longer, strictly speaking, identification, but is more of a fetishistic practice based on an epistemophilia. In other words, Ida provides a certain kind of knowledge in the film that is related to the shape of the plot, an astute understanding of character, and a sense of the generic conventions that govern Hollywood film. The knowledge Ida conveys enables us to locate her as perhaps the only available knowing subject in the film (we find out at the end that the police detective running the investigation knows the identity of the murderer). Although Ida knows what we know, her enunciation of that knowledge within the film works as a way to transfer an illusion of control to the viewer insofar as this shared knowledge allays audience frustrations about the characters' blindness to the obvious. This knowledge is not the kind of knowledge the detective has but rather a knowledge of tendencies, of human character and its narrative possibilities. Given the personalities of various characters—Veda, Monte, Mildred—as seen from Ida's more distanced vantage, certain narrative dispositions are likely, especially because we know at least one outcome to the story. And even though more than one character has a motive to murder Monte, and even though Mildred has been offered as the most likely candidate, careful attention to Ida throughout already points to the more psychologically plausible solution. Having this kind of knowledge both communicated and confirmed by Ida enables the audience to negotiate tensions around Veda and Monte's behavior (we know they are bad and we know someone else knows they are bad) while it both exacerbates and blunts the sense of doom enfolding Mildred. Ida's pronouncements are simultaneously cathartic and prophetic and provide a site from which the audience can both know and not know, can escape tension and be immersed in the film at the same time. Ida makes this ambivalence both sensible and productive. And she also makes it fun.

A Nose for Trouble

> Stella: We've become a race of peeping Toms. What people
>   ought to do is get outside their own house and look in for
>   a change.
>
> —*Rear Window*

As wheelchair-bound photographer L. B. Jeffries (James Stewart) watches the neighborhood from his apartment window, insurance nurse Stella (Thelma Ritter) arrives and cautions him that "the New York State sentence for a peeping Tom is six months in the workhouse," a warning that commences the series of admonitions Stella delivers in the course of Jeff's daily temperature-taking and massage. By her own admission a "homespun" philosopher, Stella has a "nose for trouble." "I should have been a gypsy fortuneteller," she tells Jeff as she narrates how she "predicted" the stock market crash by means of a General Motors director's kidney ailment: "When General Motors has to go to the bathroom ten times a day, the whole country's ready to go." "I can smell trouble right here in this apartment," she continues. "First you smash your leg, then you get to looking out the window, see things you shouldn't see. Trouble. I can see you in court right now, surrounded by a bunch of lawyers in double-breasted suits. You're pleading. You say, 'Judge, it's only a little bit of innocent fun. I love my neighbors like a father.' And the Judge says, 'Congratulations. You've just given birth to three years in Dannamora.'"

A self-proclaimed "maladjusted misfit," Stella edges around and through *Rear Window*'s investigation and romance plots as well as its coincident meditation on the relationships between watching, the drive to know, and the irresistibility of narrative.[10] Trying to pull the perverse Jeff away from his pleasurable voyeurism and into marriage with Lisa

(Grace Kelly), Stella initially voices the obvious parameters of normative romance and the ethics of civic respect. Her manner wry and perceptive, Stella is fool figure who openly recommends conventional behavior as her brand of quirky insight. As an older, spunky, no-nonsense functionary, Stella is almost but not quite maternal; her comic delivery makes the prosaic seem idiosyncratic and the ordinary unusual as she declares, using a pop psychology vocabulary, that not getting married is "abnormal," that "nothing has caused the human race so much trouble as intelligence," and that she and her husband are happy "misfits."

In the film, which Hitchcock called his "most cinematic" and visual, Stella is the aural—the word (Law) tested against the power of the image.[11] Although Laura Mulvey uses *Rear Window* as a quintessential example of a forced identification with male looking, as Tania Modleski proposes, the film is not so monolithically constructed. Although the film's structured pairings—Lisa and Jeff aligned with Thorwald and his bedridden wife, or Jeff aligned with Thorwald in his wish to rid himself of Lisa—the film also engages us with other points of identification. Pointing out the relative mobility of the women, Modleski suggests that at points the film constructs an identification with the endangered Lisa, whom we watch in Thorwald's apartment. Indeed, as Modleski observes, Lisa has the last look in the film, gazing at the sleeping and very passive Jeff. She notes, "We are left with the suspicion (a preview, perhaps, of coming attractions) that while men sleep and dream their dreams of omnipotence over a safely reduced world, women are not where they appear to be, locked into male 'views' of them, imprisoned in their master's dollhouse" (*The Women* 85). Jeanne Allen argues that *Rear Window* "affords the pleasure of critically engaging the analysis of the traps and lures of heterosexual romance as presented by the constructed persona (not the historical person) 'Hitchcock'" (33).

The seemingly inevitable binariness of the readings of gender and the look in *Rear Window* tend to read over Stella, who is perceived as a kind of tertiary extension of Lisa (or Jeff). Allen says she is "Lisa's helper" (38). But Stella, who is not romantically invested in Jeff, may embody more what Modleski suggests not so much as a wielding of power but as a mobile vector of consciousness—as a figure of the Law itself as a third term. In lacanian psychoanalysis, this Law, linked to the metaphorical power of the Name-of-the Father (in that a name works to secure a relationship that until recently was never sure) serves as the sense of prohibition and refusal.[12] This third term secures the other two, especially in terms of sexual differentiation. In other words, without three, two would not be oppositional. It is from the vantage of the third that the first two become visible. In a sense this is Stella's figurative function. Not the father and only mouthing prohibitions, Stella serves as a mobile vantage on sexual difference throughout the film, helping both Jeff and Lisa discriminate, mediating the difference (and distance) between seer and seen.

Because the "normal" seems to belong to Stella, who rails against what she sees as the recalcitrant bachelor Jeff's self-imposed celibacy, it seems both insightfully pragmatic and unconventional at the same time, just as the film's meditation on marriage, made through its many window-exposed examples, is also simultaneously cynical and romantic. But because the "perverse" Jeff is played by a stable, astute, homespun James Stewart, eccentric voyeurism seems somehow the right course.[13] Jeff's and Stella's positions as peeper and referee, respectively, make it evident that even if the female comic secondary character is eccentric in terms of film narrative and imaging, she does not necessarily always represent perverse or nonnormative values. Rather, she is situated in a figurative (and often literal) middle, arbitrating the conflicting values and ironies of law and romance.

We would expect that as a protagonist, Jeff would embody dominant cultural values because protagonists often were allied with the mainstream both because of the Production Code, which restricted to mainstream morality the "lessons" a film could offer, and because of the ideological alliances of formulaic film narrative. Hitchcock added his own twist to Hollywood's rectitude, of course; *Rear Window* deploys Stella's common-sense admonitions to signal the danger of Jeff's voyeurism, whereas his perverse vigilance turns out ironically to have been the judicious course.[14] Stella's "law" is an incitement to love; Jeff's perverse watching, though seemingly riveted on Thorwald (Raymond Burr), the suggested murderer, is also a species of narcissism as Jeff watches how another "traveling man" like him treats his woman wrong. The murder and its mysteries, of which we have only trace evidence, are the MacGuffin (Hitchcock's term for a misleading detail) that distracts us from the film's other business of satisfactory romance.[15]

Jeff's attraction to watching and Stella's attachment to the law represent the ethical foci of the film's two major plot lines: a detective (or oedipal) quest for proof of a murder that leads both to justice (the successful apprehension of a murderer) and the protagonist's quite literal fall and to a romance narrative wherein the female protagonist proves her worthiness as an intrepid adventurer and wins her man. Romance narratives are multiplied throughout the apartment courtyard (the despairing "Miss Lonely Hearts" hooks up with the composer, "Miss Torso" fends off suitors and waits for her GI husband, the newlyweds barely come up for air, and Thorwald kills his wife), but the detective narrative is a twist on the old story: Instead of knowing there's a murder and seeking the killer, we know the identity of the killer and seek proof that there was a murder. Stella's initial suggestion of romance as an antidote to voyeurism collides with Jeff's curious devotion to a vigilance that, until he is vindicated by finding proof of the murder, seems an eccentric avoidance of the beautiful Lisa, who almost literally throws herself at him.

The need to devise a narrative that accounts for Mrs. Thorwald's disappearance gradually draws all the characters (Jeff, Lisa, and Stella) into the pleasures of narrative speculation and the task of securing the evidence that proves that their window conjectures are indeed true. As the film continues, Stella becomes increasingly involved with Jeff's puzzle; she and Lisa act as his legs, investigating what is buried in Thorwald's garden; Stella watches with Jeff as Thorwald discovers Lisa in his apartment. Once she has been drawn into Jeff's attempts to account for the missing wife and her murder, Stella's fantasy and language turn from the commonplace to the macabre. Conjuring images of splattered blood and dismembered corpses, Stella becomes the plainspoken representative of the matter-of-fact morbidity indulged in by police; when Lisa objects, Stella points out, "Nobody ever invented a polite word for a killing yet." At the beginning of the film Stella's common sense might have come from a "looking in" on Jeff, but by film's end, she has lost her distance and she, too, is looking out at others. The trouble she predicts in the beginning indeed comes to pass not as trouble but as a necessary danger; the law against looking Stella invokes turns out to be its opposite, a law compelling looking as a necessary means to both justice and marriage.

Of course, we can also take Stella's warning against the dangers of voyeurism as narrative irony, an understated hint about the inevitable direction of the narrative's complications. In this more ironic context, Stella's increasing participation in Jeff's irresistible detective activities is very much in line with the more traditional functions of a secondary fool figure who wards off dangers, protects and insulates the protagonist, provides an epistemological vantage point for identifications, and ultimately holds things together. Not only does Stella literally care for Jeff's body and concern herself with his happiness, but she also speaks for Lisa throughout the film, from her initial observations of Jeff's "abnormal" disinterest to bailing her out at the end. Stella buffers Jeff from whatever is threatening about Lisa while enabling Lisa's insinuation into his routine. She ushers the multiple plot lines through the distracting dangers of the middle. At the same time, Stella tries to keep Jeff to the story, protecting him from his own curiosity, warning him of the hazards of too much looking, running errands, and ascertaining facts that cannot be gleaned from Jeff's window vantage point.

Stella's devoted service raises the question of what she is doing in Jeff's apartment at all hours; at a certain point, her presence is beyond the call of her nursing duties. Although she mouths normative strictures about happy marriage, the married Stella is ultimately as perverse as Jeff, spending her time in Jeff's apartment with Jeff hooked on watching Thorwald. More central to *Rear Window* than Ida is to *Mildred Pierce*, Stella functions as a framing element that transports, nourishes, counters, extends, and mediates the activities of the protagonist and his relationship with Lisa. Instead of occupying the margins as Ida often does, Stella's middleness is literal as she is often visually centered in the frame, eliciting Jeff's murder theories as she warns against them. In the film's narrative and visual triangulations between Jeff, the window, and Lisa, Stella literally steps in, first as a third-term substitute for Lisa, then, as Lisa becomes embroiled in the window watching, as a fourth term doubling Jeff, Lisa, and the police detective, Doyle. Her central secondariness—her occupation of both narrative and spatial middle—is a different kind of perversity from Ida's marginal incursions, bringing the issue of the relation between dominant and perverse literally to the center of most of the conversations, many of which are focused on the ethics and narrative possibilities of watching Thorwald. At the same time, by analogy she provides a running commentary on the voyeuristic pitfalls of watching film itself as she mediates between film and audience.

Stella thus is a mobile term who moves physically to wherever aid or response is needed. She works increasingly as an emblem of attention— as the character who, like Ida, represents both the film's internal audience as witness to Jeff and Lisa and its viewing audience who watches Jeff watch. Like the audience, Stella becomes embroiled in the narratives she watches unfold, but like the audience she is never caught completely within one window frame or another for long. Stella's transitions from scene to scene—from digging up Thorwald's garden with Lisa beyond Jeff's window, to standing beside Jeff watching Lisa climb through Thorwald's window, to watching Jeff and Lisa watch—mark transitions in the viewing positions the film constantly asks viewers to make.

These positions are tied to the series of progressive frames produced in the film: the windows that frame action within other apartments, the frame of Jeff's own window as we see him watching, the film frame that situates us beyond Stella, Doyle, or Lisa watching Jeff, and the sudden reverse reframing that occurs during incidents of the watched (such as

Thorwald) watching back. Each frame signifies an edge or ambivalent, liminal site that negotiates between image (or the "seen") and knowledge (or the interpretation and narrativization) of what is seen. Posed both uncertainly between image and knowledge—at the point before the former becomes the latter—and as the progressive site of perspective and control, the framing *Rear Window* so overtly acknowledges and examines is figured by Stella as the character who most mobilely and consciously moves from one frame to another and as the character who constantly reflects on the ethics of the watching they all indulge in. Stella's movements pave the way for Lisa to become equally mobile, a flux requisite to her courtship of Jeff, whose primary requirement for a woman is that she be transportable and adventurous (even though he markedly isn't).

The film's opening encounter between Stella and Jeff anticipates not only Stella's mediation as she moves around Jeff's apartment while he cannot but also the practice of watching and interpreting that occupies most of the film. Just as Stella spies Jeff watching and immediately applies a law to the activity, so Jeff, the other characters, and the film's viewers undertake the same process throughout the film. Stella's initial connection to the law also links her to the ultimate lens through which the murder narrative makes sense, the law that demands the "how" of the crime in order to act. However, this law, represented by both Stella and Doyle, who double each other as fourth terms, is as helpless and impotent as Jeff is without the romance narrative that provides motivation for movement and change. If Jeff's watching ends in justice for Thorwald, it also ends in justice for Jeff, whose voyeurism is rewarded with continued immobility and marriage.

As an agent of law and romance, then, Stella is ultimately the incarnation of the law's perverse ambivalence—its search for the truth via narrative, its helpless power, its double-edged operation that exacts a toll from all. The law's ambivalence is figured by Stella's combination of critical distance and discerning engagement with the process of unfolding a plot. Her place is quite literally in the middle. If the law requires both eyes and mouth, witness and story, then Stella is, as she remarks, the nose, the arbiter between them. The distant-close, droll-serious, normative-perverse character of Stella functions as a way to compensate for both the eccentricity of the protagonist and the inadequacies of a law that can only believe if it sees. Stella, who begins as a dominant culture apologist, functions to bring Jeff and the law together in the perverse site of the ironic immobility spawned by voyeurism and a drive to know.

Bye, Bye Birdie

> Moe: I have to go on making a living so I can die.
> —*Pickup on South Street*

That Thelma Ritter would portray a character who oscillates between matchmaking and crime watching is not the least bit unusual, given Ritter's mixture of the worldly wise (and weary) with the hopelessly romantic. Ritter's clown quality comes from the paradoxical combination of cynical street smarts with sentimental optimism portrayed through the pragmatic persona of the older, experienced, resourceful character who knows her own abilities and limitations. As Stella, Birdie Coonan in *All about Eve* (1950), Moe in *Pickup on South Street* (1953), Alma in *Pillow Talk* (1959) (all films for which she received an Academy Award nomination for Best Supporting Actress), and Isabelle in *The Misfits* (1961), Ritter occupies the knowing margins of a pathetic has-been-ness combined with expert perceptiveness communicated through asides, hustling sales talk, or a drunken stupor. With her Brooklyn, lower- to lower-middle-class affect, Ritter becomes the trustworthy representative of populist experience and insight, the middlebrow especially in relation to the more refined (if not necessarily more upper crust) leading characters she supports. At the same time, she has the attributes of a wizened jester, a magical persona whose knowledge extends into the uncanny and almost mystical.

As Birdie Coonan in *All about Eve*, Ritter plays the retired vaudevillian buddy of theatrical star Margot Channing (Bette Davis). From the moment Margot's friend, Karen Richards (Celeste Holm), brings a seemingly innocent starstruck groupie, Eve Harrington (Anne Baxter), to Margot's dressing room, Birdie is suspicious of Eve, uttering wisecracks and manifesting a dubious attitude. As Margot's old friend and factotum, Birdie has access to the inner sanctum—the safe private space of bathroom, girdles, and imperious star moodiness—but she also has the privilege of being able to speak frankly to Margot without worrying about her celebrity ego. After Eve first tells her story to Margot and friends in the dressing room, Birdie comments, "What a story. Everything but the bloodhounds snapping at her rear end." Chided for her distrust, Birdie chooses to apologize to Eve, but she is still unconvinced about Eve's sincerity or loyalty. Margot asks Eve to help her out as assistant and secretary, and Eve appears to take Birdie's place as Margot's confidante. But Margot and Birdie continue to communicate through a series of meaningful looks and

Margot Channing (Bette Davis), Birdie (Thelma Ritter), Eve (Anne Baxter), and Karen Richards (Celeste Holm) in *All about Eve*

Birdie's subtle but expressive body language. Her displacement as instrumental intimate makes Birdie even more of a mediator.[16]

Birdie ceases to appear after an hour of the film, at the point when Margot begins to lose both her stage roles and her temper. Birdie turns out to have been right about Eve all along. Her disappearance, which is unremarkable unless one is looking specifically for her in the film, signals the disappearance of Margot's perspective and judgment as Margot flails about desperately trying to regain her career. Connected to margins and safe, private spaces, Birdie functions not only as the film's cynical conscience and metanarrative acumen but also as the warning note in the all-too-predictable "golden bough" drama of usurpation. Given the film's flashback structure (it begins with an awards ceremony where Eve is lauded as the year's best actress), Birdie's ability to penetrate Eve's guise of candor and naivete seems canny and prescient, as her decidedly minority view matches suspicions the audience already might have.

Like Ida in *Mildred Pierce*, Birdie is marginal and forceful, but her function as insightfully distrustful aide is accomplished through underplayed disdain and a very subtly contained forcefulness, an enactment of superficial ambivalence and polysemy. Ida performs her fool role through sarcastic joviality, but Birdie enacts a semiotics of contrary wisdom through small movements of face and eyes, the set of her shoulders, and the way she enters and exits the room, all of which make apparent her cynical presence. As mobile and mediate in *All about Eve* as she will be later in *Rear Window,* Birdie signals her attitude through a passive-aggressive dynamic as she moves around and through the rooms in which Margot is seated and centered. In her penultimate scene in the film, for example, she enters Margot's room with her breakfast tray, sets the tray on Margot's lap, goes to the window, and pulls open the sheer drapes without ever looking at Margot. Withholding her glance suggests that she is withholding her opinion—that she knows her place and if some folks want to know the score all they need to do is ask. Her eyes are focused at a point ten feet beyond Margot. But withholding her look also means that when Birdie does look at Margot, the look has force, even if, as in this scene, Margot looks away. At the same time, Birdie's indirectness also permits Margot to ignore her, to hope she has no opinion or one in line with her own.

While Birdie ambiguously conveys her disapproval, she rarely confronts Margot directly. Instead, moving around the room, Birdie communicates her dislike through indirection; like her withheld glance, when the indirection becomes direct, it has a quiet power. Birdie's penultimate scene in the film builds to the revelation of her quite accurate perception of Eve's purpose in serving Margot. Margot first asks Birdie, "You don't like Eve, do you?"

> Birdie: You want an argument or an answer?
> Margot: An answer.
> Birdie: No.
> Margot: Why not?
> Birdie (*approaching her*): Now you want an argument.
> Margot: She works hard.
> Birdie: Night and day.
> Margot: She's loyal and efficient.
> Birdie: Like an agent with only one client.

At this point Birdie, cleaning an ashtray, moves away from Margot. The verbal dance performed by a Margot in denial who refuses to hear what she already suspects about Eve evades its denouement, snaking into another brief bout of indirection before Birdie makes a trenchant analysis that at first is addressed to the ashtray. Imaged in a medium close shot, Margot asks Birdie, "She thinks only of me. (*Pause, during which Birdie cleans the ash tray and looks the other way*). Doesn't she?" Birdie looks at Margot over her shoulder, and says in a slow and measured fashion,

Birdie (Thelma Ritter) in *All about Eve*

"Well, let's say she thinks about you anyway," as she goes back to cleaning the ashtray.

Her refusal to engage Margot directly at this point signals the centrality of the insight she is withholding. Ritter is like a singer who makes her audience want more by obviously holding back and who by holding back signals that there is more to give. She is a middle who refuses closure. When Margot asks her, "How do you mean that?" Birdie approaches the bed and tells her, "I'll tell you how. Like . . . like she's studying ya. Like you was a play or a book or a set of blueprints. How you walk, talk, eat, think, sleep." Birdie's speech builds in speed and passion until her list of single verbs indicates how invasive and calculating she thinks Eve is. As she builds toward actually verbalizing the perception that Eve is using Margot as a model for her own career, Margot interrupts, saying, "I'm sure that's very flattering, Birdie. I'm sure there's nothing wrong with it." Clearly refusing Birdie's insight, Margot's interruption prevents Birdie from being completely direct, leaving her still in the realm of suggestion. The unspent potential of her discernment characterizes Birdie's subtle force as Ritter conveys a character constantly containing that force, holding back, while her unimparted wisdom matches audience knowledge. This scene, in which the heroine refuses insight, not only cements the tensions of dramatic irony that began in the film's first scene but also aligns the audience permanently with a character whose disappearance suggests that the audience might well take over her role in the film as helpless but knowing observer.

With her performance of holding back, Birdie becomes a spot of heat and tension in the film; but attached to a minor character who disappears in the middle, such tension ultimately folds into Margot's anger. The relationship between Margot and Birdie is the baseline safe homosocial relationship in the film. That this relationship is threatened by the usurping Eve sets the pattern for the ambition and jealousy that characterize all the other relationships, including Margot's with Karen. When Birdie ceases to appear, the sense of reassurance and possible escape of the inevitable conveyed through her obvious acumen disappears as well, as the events of the film—the jealousies, rages, triangulations, and passions—careen out of control. Although Birdie is ultimately proved right, the pattern of ambition and usurpation doesn't stop as Eve herself is finally victim to another ambitious young actress studying her.

As repositories of knowledge, Ritter's characters often occupy the paradoxical position of being marginal and central at the same time. Stella triangulates the characters in *Rear Window*, and Birdie quickly perceives the truth of Eve in *All about Eve*. In *Pickup on South Street* Ritter plays another knowledgeable character, Moe Williams, who, though culturally marginal and a minor character in the film, is the only character who can identify and locate the major players in a cold war communist-spy-meets-pickpocket plot. The pickpocket (or "cannon"), Skip McCoy (Richard Widmark), lifts a wallet from the purse of a communist spy ring courier (the "muffin"), Candy (Jean Peters), who is delivering microfilm of a secret chemical formula to a communist kingpin. Because the formula is in the wallet, the FBI (who have been secretly watching the courier) go to the police to discern the identity of the thief. Moe, the ostensible purveyor of "personality neckwear," is the source to whom police Captain Tiger goes when FBI agents come looking for a lead on the pickpocket. Speaking in a stoolie jargon and working through innuendo and the cover of selling ties, Moe recognizes the modus operandi of McCoy, whose name she gives to Tiger along with seven others, betting him that the perpetrator they seek is among them. When the FBI agent selects McCoy, Moe also knows where to find him, a fact she's willing to trade for "double or nothing" in future dealings. She is so central a source of information that she must be killed halfway through the film, becoming the martyr whose death drives the pickpocket into patriotic respectability.[17]

Moe is the conduit to and double for McCoy in the film; just as McCoy is evasive and devious in his thievery, so Moe is evasive and devious in her information-selling, like Birdie, performing through indirection and subtlety, but this time performing her indirection through the coded criminal jargon she uses to avoid any straightforward acknowledgment of her activities. Like *All about Eve*, *Pickup on South Street* works toward revealing a truth known only by the fool character (and the audience), whose function it is to reveal that truth gradually and strategically —in this case not only the key location of McCoy but also the truth about the nature of her own activities, so like the activities of the spy ring, redeemed by the patriotic sacrifice she makes when she refuses "commie" Joey's (Richard Kiley) demand for information.

Moe appears in four scenes in the first hour of the film, once with each of the main players: Tiger, Candy, Skip, and Joey. Her willingness to provide information and the kinds of information she is willing to provide change, becoming increasingly direct. When Candy, the victim, is threatened by Joey, she tracks Moe down for information about Skip. But Candy is far more candid than the police, calling Moe a "stool pigeon," a term to which Moe strenuously objects: "What kinda talk is that, calling me a stoolie? I was brought up to report any injustice to the police authorities. I call that being a solid citizen." But Candy's apparent membership in the criminal fraternity cuts beneath Moe's coded pretense, and Moe willingly and openly sells Candy the information. In Moe's encounter with Skip, she is even more direct, all coded jargon dropped as she tries to warn Skip that the communists are after him and advises him that Candy is in love with him. In her final scene, an encounter with Joey, all bravado is dropped and Moe becomes a tired old woman, spunky to the end. "Even in our crummy line of business," she says, "ya gotta draw the line somewhere."

Moe does have a code of ethics. Even though she'll sell information about any pickpocket to the police (it's part of her duty as a "solid citizen"), she won't sell information to communists. The pickpockets understand her role and get irritated only if she sells them for too little, but the evil and desperate communist spies take information as literally a life-and-death matter, refusing the ethic of her small-time, cottage-industry capitalist economy in service of a more totalitarian ideal. The ethics for which she sacrifices herself become the conscience of the film; in a cold war, even the stool pigeon knows where to draw the line. Her death retroactively renders Moe less a pathetic clown and more an undaunted and uncowed heroine.

Playing the pragmatic stool pigeon, Moe dances around the ultimate truth of her own sacrifice, from the beginning announcing that she sells information so she can gather enough money for a decent burial ("If I was to be buried in potter's field, it'd just about kill me"). That the fool becomes the sacrifice combines the seer with the scapegoat, unmasking and ennobling Moe. Even as she speaks a tough street jargon, there is something both pathetic and dignified about Moe, who describes herself as "an old clock running down." Her ability to face facts and her own death (before Joey shoots her, she tells him, "I'm so tired you'd be doing me a big favor blowing my head off") make her almost a tragic figure, but it is precisely her ability to face death directly that makes her the film's most extreme case of knowledge and bravado, in a film where the sale of knowledge is already what is at stake and bravado means knowing where to draw the line. The mixture of information selling, ethics, and belief in love make Moe the film's moral center as well as a cold war heroine; through the rest of the film, Moe's example spurs Skip and Candy into doing the right thing. At the end, the police captain rewards her sacrifice by tracking down her sad coffin as it is being transported to potter's field and ordering her longed-for burial on Long Island.

Like Stella in *Rear Window*, Moe plays her part in the film's romance narrative between Skip and Candy, telling Skip that Candy is protecting him and advising him, "Stop using your hands and start using your head. The kid loves you," when she talks to him right before Joey's fateful visit. Ritter's roles as seer and matchmaker combine wisdom and love in a way that makes each an effect of the other: Wisdom is a byproduct of romance and romance a byproduct of wisdom. But although the fool character has wisdom, she seldom has romance; if she does, that romance is either a comic parallel to the main romance, as in *Pillow Talk*, or is sadly past, as it is in *The Misfits*. The fool's wisdom about romance comes from her own past experience and from her current state of observing from outside. Ida's outsideness was produced by her acknowledgment of a kind of hermaphroditism, whereas Ritter's characters are outside by virtue of age and class.

The Most Devoted Listener

> Jan: What am I missing?
> Alma: When you have to ask, believe me, you're missing it.
>
> —*Pillow Talk*

Ritter's humble heroine of *Pickup on South Street* turns into the dipsomaniac maid, Alma, of *Pillow Talk* (1959), who, through the fog of her morning hangovers, subtly suggests to the recalcitrant and resentful Jan (Doris Day) that there is more truth to Brad Allen's (Rock Hudson's) admonitions than Jan is willing to admit. Alma, like many of the characters Ritter plays, is the advising manipulator who rearranges the confused elements of a film's narrative middle so the proper parties can come together in the proper way at the proper time. Ritter's characters accomplish this rearrangement through a species of unconscious wisdom: They can see what others need but are incapable of correcting their own, often similar dilemmas. Unlike the fool figures who know and are in control of themselves (like Ida), Ritter's fools are convincing because they seem to be too much inside rather than outside. Their knowledge comes from some innate common sense rather than from some outsider vantage point. In this sense, Ritter's characters epitomize a middle muddle, whereas Arden's convey the coolness of someone perpetually on the outside. This difference between inside and outside actually has little effect on their functions as points of knowledge and identification. Arden's characters may offer audiences a position much like their own, seemingly outside the film text, whereas Ritter's offer the audience a position akin to their own in terms of narrative captivation. In both cases, the types are responsible for observing what the audience already knows, and both operate the actual mechanics by which romance plots develop.

In *Pillow Talk* Alma seems primarily subconscious (or unconscious). Interior decorator Jan is forced to share a party line with the womanizing Brad, who spends all hours crooning to various admirers over the phone. Jan's complaints to both Brad and the telephone company spur questions about Jan's happiness as a single career woman and insinuations that she has "bedroom problems." Alma, who spends half her time recovering from hangovers and the other half listening to Brad's phone romances, seconds and revises Brad's indictment of Jan as a "woman who lives alone." "You know," Alma says after eavesdropping on one of Jan's phone fights with Brad, "he makes pretty good sense."

> Jan: Have you no shame?
> Alma: No Ma'am. He's brightened up many a dreary afternoon for me.
> Jan: What did he say that made such good sense?
> Alma: If there's anything worse than a woman living alone, it's a woman saying she likes it.

Although Alma's paraphrase is not exactly what Brad said (what Alma attributes to Brad is her own more insightful conclusion), it is a formulation of the "lady doth protest too much" symptom that undermines the apparent rationality of Jan's complaints. Even though Brad is annoyingly patronizing and Alma still a bit unsteady, both seem to know better what is going on with Jan than Jan does. Although their incredulousness

at the idea of a woman liking being alone is a predictable patriarchal reaction to female independence, their understanding of Jan's anger as a
symptom of sexual frustration is an instance of the film's coded indirection around the sexual that exists almost as parody and constitutes the
pattern of suggestion and duplicity by which the proper partners ultimately come together.

In the late 1950s, the strictures of the Production Code that had limited the direct expression of sexual content had relaxed slightly. Like
Auntie Mame, *Pillow Talk* revels in Hollywood's outworn modes of encodement and indirection, focusing on the stylization of sexual "miscon-
duct" through the use of objects, music, and situational innuendo. Jan is
an interior decorator, and her relations with all the men in the film are
mediated in some way through decoration. Jan is decorator for Jonathan
(Tony Randall), her beau at the film's beginning, who tries to reward her
with a car. She ends up in a night on the town with the drunken son of a
client who gives her a ride home. Rex tries to get her to talk to him by
hiring her to redecorate his bachelor pad, which she does with a vengeance, turning its subtle bachelor appointments into garish signifiers of
cheap excess, complete with beaded curtains, a player piano, and a statue of a fertility goddess. All the cars in the film (except taxis) are sexy
convertibles (and it is winter). Brad, who is a composer, spends his time
singing the same song to each girlfriend, while Rex and Jan enjoy "Roly-
Poly," a ditty that refers in a roundabout way to a penis, while on a date.
Even the title song is full of suggestion.[18]

Most of the film's activities are as loaded as they seem, even though
they are arguably innocent on the surface. For example, although Brad is
too much of a wolf for a recalcitrant Jan to be interested in him, Brad can
keep her interested in Rex by using reverse psychology, predicting peri-
odically what Rex will do and warning her of his dangers. Although his
prognostications are designed to be untrue, thereby painting Rex in an
even better light, they are all quite true of Brad (and even of Rock Hudson when Brad implies that Rex is gay). Rex/Brad cleverly maneuvers Jan
into what appear to be compromising positions, such as his hotel room,
and then defies expectation by asking her merely to look at the view.
What is not verbalized but glaringly obvious are the sexual ideas Jan was
entertaining.

In relation to *Pillow Talk*'s ubiquitous innuendo, Alma's pronouncements are indirect in a different way. Although the film's various situations call for sexual conclusions—everything from the nature of Brad's
relations with his dates to the obstetrician's conclusions about Rex—
Alma sees sexuality as the proper end to a satisfactory courtship. An

expert on the romance narrative, Alma's practical advice has to do with love. Not only does Alma admire Brad for his romantic telephone interludes ("I'm one of your most devoted listeners," she tells him), but she also advises Jan to follow her feelings and get her man: "Don't just stand there making with the toast—go get him." When Brad tries to get to Jan through Alma by taking Alma out for a drink, Alma drinks him under the table while offering him advice on how to get Jan back: "You have an apartment. She's a decorator."

Although Alma deploys ideas of romance to get Jan to conform, her matchmaking urgings also encode the same sexual discourse presented by innuendo throughout the rest of the film. What Alma is interested in is not only the trappings of courtship but also the essence of the "bedroom problem." When Jan asks Alma what she is missing, Alma's answer—"When you have to ask, believe me, you're missing it"—not only suggests Jan's virginal innocence but also refers directly to the sexual terms that are missing from overt articulation. In this line, Alma both centers an unarticulated but ubiquitous sexuality and performs the relation between sex, situation, and innuendo that makes this film represent exactly what it—and Jan—seem to be missing. The film's various duplicities—Brad's masquerade as Rex, Jonathan's hiring a detective to track Brad—suggest that duplicitous and indirect language is the order of the day, but Alma's overt eavesdropping and unsolicited advice seem to break open the web of innuendo even as Alma, like Jan, seems largely unaware of her own missing sexual center. Focused on alcohol and the fantasy narratives of Brad's telephone flirtations, Alma is wiser about Jan's bedroom problem than she is about her own. Alma doubles Jan as the reluctantly courted woman in a comic romance involving the telephone, the bedroom, and ultimately the elevator.

Alma's most continuously comic routine in the film is her morning ride on the elevator, operated by a dour, resigned, middle-aged man. In Alma's first scene, after the elevator has risen in an exaggeratedly slow fashion, the door opens to reveal Alma clinging to the back hand rail. As she creeps out, she chastises the elevator operator: "Must you zoom up so fast? What are you, jet-propelled or something?" In the second elevator scene, Alma, again draped over the elevator's back handrail, chides him: "You don't have to break the sound barrier, you . . . you hot-rodder." The third time, she gets her umbrella caught on the elevator rail and, giving the operator a dirty look, calls him a "beatnik." Although all of this elevator play seems to be simply about her hangovers, the final elevator scene suggests that it has always been about something else. Inspired by Brad's Neanderthal abduction of Jan in her pajamas when he sees how she decorates his apartment, the elevator man zooms Alma up to Jan's floor. When Alma warns him, "if I ever get on my feet again, look out," the elevator man tells her she needs a man to look after so she won't have so much time to drink. Instead of getting angry, Alma responds by smiling up at him and telling him admiringly that he's "so strong." The elevator, like Brad's apartment, is a coded sexual situation; Alma's annoyance has to do with the elevator man's slow courtesy, his unwillingness to take the lead and sweep her off her feet.

Unlike Jan, Alma is the properly lusty woman, but her lust is the stock characteristic of the lower-class servant character who because of her age is deemed to be past romance but wise about it. That Alma is cast as more "normally" receptive than Jan, however, demonstrates that lust is a matter of degree and class; ladies like Jan may be cold, but they attract such prizes as Rex. But Alma's enthusiasm for Rex and her advice to Jan lure us away from her own sublimation of sexuality; while Jan focuses on her career and dead-end dating, Alma drinks. Although her alcoholism may make her an alcoholic stereotype, whose function, according to Richard Dyer, is to police boundaries (*Matter* 16), she works structurally to do more than that. Her role is to get Jan and Rex to exceed their boundaries to conform to the dictates of the heteronarrative. In other words, her eccentricity works to undo theirs. Alma has ironic insight, but she is also a part of the film's generally ironic reading of female desire as that which is known to individual women only with difficulty but is visible to everyone else. Just as Jan's prim propriety can captivate only suppliant males such as Jonathan and the inebriated col-

Alma (Thelma Ritter) and Jan (Doris Day) in *Pillow Talk*

lege-aged son of a client, Alma's drinking seems to make her merely a bystander while the elevator operator is quietly attached to her.

Unlike Ida in *Mildred Pierce*, who approaches a working equality with Mildred, Alma will never come close to being Jan's buddy, not only because of the pronounced class and age differences between them but also because Jan, curiously, has no women friends. Jan's iceberg independence (the primary colors of her wardrobe are ice blue and white) apparently extends to both men and women; only someone like Alma, who seems almost not present during her hungover arrivals ("You know I never get onto focus until 10:00," she says) can get in below Jan's defenses and even become someone Jan takes care of as she obligingly sets out tomato juice, Worcestershire, and tabasco for Alma each morning. Although Alma seems less in control and knowledgeable in this film than Stella is in *Rear Window*, she still operates the middle, pushing both Jan and Brad at the right moments, knowing how the romance narrative works and how to work it. Her own comic parallel to the confused indirection and duplicity of the characters is its own elevated example of how one thing is not always what it seems to be, how a cigar is not just a cigar, a couch a couch, nor an elevator simply a lift. At the intersection of romance and delusion, fantasy and crudeness, inebriation and sober insight, Alma's no-nonsense practicality—as James Naremore puts it, "there never was a screen character less likely to put up with fools or snobs than Ritter" (247)—makes her advocacy of Brad less the suspect fantasy of a bored domestic worker and more the insight of a wise character inhabiting magically the private space of the heroine when she needs her the most.

Ritter thus functions as the element that humanizes Jan and sets Brad on a more profitable tack. Her metanarrative consciousness and ability to assert the right observation at the right time make her the catalyst that meshes Jan and Brad, first in their hostility, then in Brad's (or Rex's) pursuit. Ritter plays a similar kind of character in *The Misfits* (1961).[19] As Isabelle Steers, landlady to the unfortunate, imminently divorced Rosalind Tabor (Marilyn Monroe), Ritter plays the wise, companionable, discriminating, but fallible friend, the fourth wheel in Rosalind's first inadvertent love triangle with Gay (Clark Gable) and Guido (Eli Wallach). From the beginning, when she intercepts Guido, a mechanic who has come to look at the damage to Rosalind's Cadillac (a divorce gift from her husband damaged in innumerable fenderbenders with Reno men who wanted to have a reason to talk to bombshell Rosalind), Isabelle functions as both ironic commentator and pathetic survivor. Emerging from her house with her arm in a sling, she asks Guido the time, saying that she has six clocks and none of them work. She negotiates with Guido about the price for the caddy and tells him that she broke her arm celebrating a divorce. "I misbehaved," she tells him, "I'm so sick and tired of myself."

Finding out that it is nearly time for Rosalind's divorce hearing, she coaches Rosalind on her testimony and gets Guido to give them a ride to court. When Rosalind complains that what she's saying isn't true, Isabelle counsels her, "Just say it, it doesn't have to be true. This isn't a quiz show, it's only court." Jumping into Guido's truck as an extra party, a status of which she's well aware, Isabelle takes the position she'll take before she disappears halfway through the film: the self-aware, ironically conscious character who knowingly occupies the role of the odd woman out, a woman who admires the cowboys, even though she knows their unreliable characteristics and protects the naive Rosalind as much as she can from the beguiling males. When Guido and his friend Gay run into Rosalind and Isabelle at Harrah's celebrating Rosalind's divorce, Isabelle sees quite clearly that the two men have already begun to compete for Rosalind. Sticking with Rosalind as the men propose a party at Guido's house in the country, Isabelle tries to warn Rosalind about cowboys—"they're as reliable as jackrabbits," she says, but they're "real men." She drives out to Guido's with Rosalind as the men go ahead in Gay's truck; the couples reshuffle, Rosalind stays with Gay, and Isabelle returns with loser, Guido.

At the second house party, we learn some of Isabelle's history; she is divorced and she wasn't "beautiful enough to go home" to Virginia. She also gives Rosalind her best piece of advice: "Dear girl, you've got to stop thinking you can change things." But Isabelle increasingly fades into the background, a puckish presence, enjoying the whiskey, the dancing, and the male competition but resigned to her ringside role. When the four decide to go to the rodeo to find a third hand for mustanging and encounter Purse (Montgomery Clift), Purse replaces Isabelle and becomes another contender for Rosalind's favors. Discovering that her ex-husband is attending the rodeo with his wife, Isabelle rushes off to become an addition to their vacation, delighted that they are going to spend a week as her house guests.

Isabelle's third-wheelness—her position of apparent excess and mediation—automatically makes her both wise observer and pathetic has-been. That she is aware of these positions tends to ennoble her. Her capacity for drink, parties, and enjoyment makes apparent her reasons for continuing as third wheel: Not only does she want to protect Rosalind, but she still likes a good time. Even if the cowboys don't dance with her at Guido's house, she happily beats the rhythm on her cast and drinks with the best of them. Her philosophy is clearly to go with the flow, take what pleasure you can get, and be aware that in the end, the cowboys will let you down.

This philosophy clashes with Rosalind's more idealistic sensibilities. Not only do Isabelle's age and appearance contrast with Rosalind, but her ideas about accepting others' flaws collide with Rosalind's naive insistence that people better themselves. Isabelle knows that Gay won't change from being a predator who prefers anything to "working for wages," but Rosalind, who wants a world of kindness and beauty, tries to domesticate him. Isabelle is willing to accept things—and men—as they are, but Rosalind wants a more softly romantic world where marriage is intimate presence and men act on empathetic principle. Isabelle goes with the flow; Rosalind tries to rewrite the story. On one hand, Rosalind filed for divorce on the grounds that her husband "wasn't there," although Isabelle points out that if "not being there was grounds for divorce, there'd only be about eleven marriages in the U.S. of A." On the other hand, Rosalind wants Gay to release the mustangs the men have caught because it is wrong to kill such beautifully wild creatures. Isabelle is like the cowboys but perhaps one step more aware; as such she functions as a mediator between Rosalind's world of ideals and the cowboys' bullheaded freedom.

In all of her films, Ritter portrays a stubborn survivor. The essence of Ritter's secondary genius is that she incarnates in a complex fashion the warring impulses at play in the rest of the film—and in general during Hollywood's 1950s and 1960s. She ambulates between the law and desire, home and exile, inside and outside, life and death, demonstrating how these oppositions might be negotiated and serving as a point for their mediation. Her almost genderless, ageless common folk observer status disqualifies her from the action she witnesses but also demands her presence as a perspective—as a synecdoche that encapsulates the crisis of the film, whether that is the usurpation of stardom, the sale of information, the problems of voyeurism, the dilemmas of courtship, or the clash of values. In her insideness and even though she often appears to be a third wheel, Ritter, though constantly moving, is centered in films. Even if she often disappears halfway through, her character embodies the terms of the film's dilemmas. Arden's characters exist on the margins, empowered by their slight distance but never moving to the center. Instead of embodying contradiction as Ritter does, Arden observes and comments on it. If Ritter's characters provide a site for audience engagement from the inside out, Arden's characters provide such a site from the outside in.

"I Don't Know What You Pay Me for
If You Utterly Ignore My Judgment"

Cudare: What would you do if youth came walking in through the
    door?
Stonewall: I'd put braces on its teeth.

—*Cover Girl*

In *Cover Girl* (1944), Eve Arden plays Stonewall Jackson, executive
assistant to magazine publisher John Cudare. Like Ida in *Mildred Pierce*,
Stonewall has power and responsibility, but she more constantly accompanies her boss and more directly tells him when he's gone wrong than
Ida did. Although Cudare is not the central character in the film—dancers Rusty Parker (Rita Hayworth) and Danny MacGuire (Gene Kelly) are
the heart—he does represent the institutional star-making force that,
although with good intentions, threatens to destroy the idyllic romance
of the young entertainers. Danny, Rusty, and Danny's buddy Genius (Phil
Silvers) happily put on shows at Danny's unpretentious Brooklyn nightclub, after which they order oysters to look for pearls. Danny is clearly in
love with Rusty, and the trio are a cheerful and satisfied cohort of lower-
middle-class, diamond-in-the-rough, lovable characters.

Searching for a "new face" to grace the fiftieth-anniversary bridal
issue of his magazine, Cudare, who says he wants "a girl with a story in
her eyes," really searches for the image of his long-ago love, music hall
star Mary Bell Hicks, who left him at the altar. Stonewall holds the auditions for the cover girl spot, and both Rusty and a co-worker try out.
Rusty's "friend," whom Stonewall interviews first, gives Rusty deliberately misleading advice, telling her to be lively when Stonewall has asked
for decorum and experienced when Stonewall is looking for fresh talent.
Rusty overdoes both, posing as a hyperkinetic model with experience in
advertising cold remedies. Vaguely interested in Rusty's co-worker, Cudare and Stonewall visit Danny's Brooklyn nightclub, where both women are performing. When Cudare sees Rusty, he knows he has found what
he is looking for because she looks just like Mary Bell and turns out to
be her granddaughter. Confiding the story of his past to Stonewall, Cudare sees Rusty as the fruition of his past dreams. But a frustrated Stonewall merely throws up her hands: "I don't know what you pay me for if
you utterly ignore my judgment. . . . I realize that while I was wading
through 10,000 girls, out of the whole 10,000 you choose a red-headed
nervous breakdown who specializes in sneezes. She told me so. That one
isn't a girl, she's a leaping thyroid." She adds in exasperation: "When I

think what I've gone through trying to find a girl while all the time she was in your desk drawer, I could just scream."

Although Stonewall is initially wrong about Rusty, misled as she is by Rusty's interview excess, she is right about Rusty throughout the rest of the film, whereas Cudare and his producer friend Noel Wheaton, a younger version of himself, are wrong. Stonewall applauds innocent romance, but Cudare puts Rusty on the path to stardom and tries to hook her up with rich producer, Wheaton. When Cudare and Stonewall are playing billiards, for example, Wheaton enters, complaining that he has "tried everything short of kidnapping" to get Rusty to star in his theater. Stonewall quips, "What's this side of kidnaping?" When Wheaton refuses her raillery with a "please don't be humorous," Stonewall gives them the low-down on Rusty: "You're humorous, both of you. You're both trying to do something you'll never do, lure a girl away from a guy she loves with things. Well, it won't work and I'm just dame enough to be glad of it. What do you think of that?" With these last lines, Stonewall takes a shot at the cue ball and misses, tearing the felt, and, with as much dignity as she can muster, walks away.[20]

Even though she is a competent and trusted assistant in *Cover Girl*, Stonewall, as the billiards scene shows, is also the butt of the film's humor. Part of this contradictory positioning is an effect of genre. Although female secondary characters are wise, wisecracking, and generally unassailable in dramas, they combine the position of "she who knows" with the role of *trompeur trompée*, or trickster tricked in comedies. Serious dramas in general, such as *Rear Window, Mildred Pierce, Pickup on South Street*, and *All about Eve*, deploy their secondary characters as comforting vantage points that frame its central action, combining the slightly comic distance necessary to provide a different perspective with meta-commentary on the film's action and shape. In comedies, both male and female comic secondary characters comment on, mirror, amplify, and unwittingly parallel the misunderstandings, misdirections, and errors that have created the protagonists' temporary dilemmas. They both note the foibles and narrative probabilities of the other characters and are themselves often guilty of the flaws they perceive, providing a level of comic reflection and repetition. That the main characters' anxieties become visible as slapstick and burlesque around the comic secondary characters is part of what makes film comedy work as comedy because in themselves, the main characters are rarely funny.

Although both Stonewall and Genius serve as comic reflection in *Cover Girl*, their differing modes of comedy are linked to Hollywood's gender politics. If female seconds are often masculinized, serious, and sardonic, male comic seconds are often feminized, tending more toward the burlesque. Genius, like other male comic seconds such as Donald O'Connor, is vaguely feminized by his softer appearance, his focus on Danny, his lack of overt power and the muscular markers of conventional masculinity, and the absence of any female love interest. His feminization serves both as a heterosexualizing gloss on the buddy couple and the register through which parody and burlesque play as a kind of drag performance of the masculine qualities of the primary characters. Genius circulates backstage, shouting mock encouragements, greeting showgirls and stagehands in a spoof of an important personage, and performing a number where he lampoons the male recipient of female favors. His burlesque of the male boss comes through a mincing, somewhat feminized lens and serves as a burlesque of all of the self-important male characters in the film, most notably Cudare and Wheaton, who are both romantically impotent. The feminine quality of the burlesque is not only a way to taunt the self-importance of masculinity but also a signal of the male secondary character's minorness and his access to more feminine insight and sensitivity.

While Genius is feminized, Stonewall's masculine qualities also serve as a way to mock the powerbroking of Cudare and Wheaton, but as direct commentary rather than parody or burlesque. Genius is a buffoon; Stonewall is a "serious" character who becomes the victim of others' excess. Stonewall's name, height (she is taller than any of the male characters), and function as arbiter of female beauty make her the trustable confidante and strong functionary of Cudare. Her facial expressions when prospective cover girls begin to vamp her register the weary why-are-you-bothering-to-flirt-with-me expression that shows she is accustomed to being treated as if she were male. Stonewall's is not a drag performance; rather, she is drag's opposite: the woman often treated as if she were male but who does not present herself as male or take seriously feminine masquerade. Stonewall doesn't hide her ability to command, and her femininity is secured by the constant undermining of her authority. Although she displays a certain hermaphroditism not unlike Ida's, and although her lack of acknowledged allure enables her to function quite easily as a buddy to Cudare, her role is to provide a common-sense balance against which the other characters' excesses play. The comic misfortunes that befall her befall common sense, befall the normative impetus toward truth and decency she represents in the face of the male characters' selfish sentimentalism. In this way, her comic calamities figure the misadventures that plague the loving couple whose togetherness common sense would impel.

As types rather than protagonists, both Stonewall and Genius contrast with the handsome, talented, and powerful primary characters, but they also function as sites for the comic displacement of anxieties. For example, backstage at Danny's after the show, Stonewall is far more aware than her oblivious companions of the extent to which they are in the way. Stonewall continues to suggest that they leave, but she is also the one the waiters and showpeople run into, until at the end of the scene, as they have just gone off screen into the kitchen, Stonewall collides with a waiter who comes on screen with her hat on a tray. Stonewall's awareness of the intruder status of the rich Manhattanites is a metaphor of their status as interlopers in the idyllic courtship that they are now trying to interrupt. Her endeavors to get them all out of the way and her symbolic kitchen beheading figures a warning that, of course, goes unheeded until the end of the film.

The film's climax comes when Genius and Stonewall get together to push Cudare into doing the right thing. Although Wheaton's courtship of Rusty is a wrong turn, Genius and Stonewall's association provides a correction. That the sidekicks will save the day is figured in their two parallel encounters in which their mock affection leads to the reestablishment of true love. The first encounter, backstage when Cudare and Stonewall bring Wheaton to see Rusty perform, occurs when Genius comes up behind Stonewall and says, "You were wonderful tonight" and kisses her. When Stonewall gives him one of those Eve Arden, you've-got-to-be-kidding looks, he says, "Oh, I beg your pardon. I mistook you for somebody else" and kisses her again. Mistaking someone for someone else is the gist of the film's misdirection as Cudare, who has mistaken Rusty for her grandmother, compounds his error by encouraging Wheaton to live out his own failed dream. At their second encounter during the film's climax—the wedding day of Rusty and Wheaton—Genius arrives at Cudare's to see whether Rusty is really happy and to bring the pearl Danny finally found in his oyster. Stonewall answers his question: "Oh, she's very happy. She lost ten pounds, but of course, it's very becoming and then, of course, if she thinks about it too much, she can always go out and get a little tight, which she's doing quite often lately." Having gotten his answer, Genius asks how he can leave without passing all of the wedding guests, saying "I'm a back door character." Stonewall tells him to take the door on the left, thanks him for coming, then kisses him. When he looks desperate, she says, "Oh, I'm sorry, I thought you were somebody else," and kisses him again.

Genius's concern tells Stonewall that Danny still cares for Rusty; she becomes a catalyst that prods the others to repair the damage. She chides

Cudare, telling him not to "be so stubborn. You've made a mistake, admit it. You've still got time." As the three of them—Rusty, Cudare, and Stonewall as maid of honor—go through the wedding procession, they engage in a sub voce conversation. When Rusty says that she can't leave Wheaton at the last minute, Stonewall tells her, "Your grandmother could and did. What's the matter, your family getting soft?" When a perplexed Rusty wonders why Stonewall has brought up her grandmother, Stonewall urges Cudare, "Go on, tell her. Her grandmother got her into this. It's up to you to get her out." After another of Cudare's flashback reminiscences, Rusty gracefully bows out of the wedding, thanking Stonewall and running to meet Danny in the oyster bar.

Although Cudare and Danny are the film's movers and shakers, Stonewall and Genius are its true shapers. Seeing the human desires and the romantic design to which the others are blinded, they deploy their persuasive powers to get the main characters to do the right thing. Although the desires and ambitions of the primary characters provide the motivations for the film's confusions and misdirections—in a sense its wrong turnings and perversities—like Stella in *Rear Window*, the sidekicks are the representatives of the normative, enforcing through their more subdued, comic, and seemingly perverse positions the normative narrative of proper heterosexual mating, a narrative the audience knows from the film's beginning. Not only does the audience know that Rusty will end up with Danny, they also know this will be accomplished through the actions of the secondary characters. This preknowledge of the secondary characters' intervention through their insight aligns the audience with such characters, even though both Stonewall and Genius become the butts of jokes. The fact that female comic secondary characters in particular are the repositories for that knowledge makes them key—a resolution in reserve until the narrative's "right time" to end when the romantic elements are ready to be properly aligned. As repositories of knowledge, comic sidekicks are indispensable to Hollywood's conventional comedy.

We understand the sidekicks' roles by their type, by the fact that neither fits the stereotype of the conventional lead. Each is too much something—too tall, too direct, too uninhibited—and cartoonish with large, expressive eyes and plastic faces whose range of expressions can mirror the absurdity of events. Although most Hollywood characters, including bankable stars, are also types, secondary characters are more conscious of their own typing, betraying a level of conscious performance of type reflected in the way they deliver their lines and the level of sheer performance their commentaries require. Female comic secondary characters never merely state something, they deliver. Their timing and manner are such that each side comment is a central performance and artful presentation. When Genius acknowledges that he is a "back door character" or Stonewall makes her understated reactive faces, both are consciously performing a secondary type as secondary—as privileged to comment, as free to be scandalous, and as licensed to tell the truth we long for that no other character really wants to hear. This doubling—type performing type—produces another level of comic excess as it hooks into the film's play of dramatic irony and epistemophilia. Marked as unlike the protagonists they aid by class, age, and gender differences, female comic secondary characters work less as a vision of verisimilitude—less as a reflection of real-world female relations or employer-employee relationships (which are always idealized)—and more as a marker for audience knowledge and narrative operation. It is precisely because they are self-consciously types that they work as shorthand engines of narrative, embodying synecdochally both the anxieties and the epistemophilia that drive narrative tension and curiosity.

Classed with Necessities

As the Hollywood studio system winds down in the late 1950s and early 1960s, the conventional female comic secondary role becomes more rare. Both *The Misfits* and *Anatomy of a Murder* (1959) slightly alter the conventional role of the secondary character. Isabelle Steers is far more pathetic and buried in the film's Reno ambiance than Ritter's previous characters. From 1961 until 1968, when she made her last film, she continued to act the part of the comic secondary in comedies such as *The Second Time Around* (1961), *For Love or Money* (1963), *A New Kind of Love* (1963), *Move Over Darling* (1963), *Boeing Boeing* (1965), and *What's So Bad about Feeling Good?* (1968). But her more memorable films of the 1960s were dramas in which she played completely serious roles such as the mother of the prisoner in *Birdman of Alcatraz* (1962), for which she was again nominated for an Oscar for Best Supporting Actress, and her last film, *The Incident* (1968), in which she played one of the subway car riders victimized by young hoods.

Arden, who starred in her own television series, *Our Miss Brooks*, in the 1950s, appeared primarily in comedies from 1960 until her last film, *Grease 2*, in 1982. But Otto Preminger's *Anatomy of a Murder* plays out how the conventional secondary character begins to fade as a force in serious drama, as Eve Arden's character Maida Rutledge, secretary to defense attorney Paul Biegler (Jimmy Stewart), becomes as much an audience as a wisecracking observer and becomes more clearly entangled in the project of rehabilitating another secondary character, the alcoholic but wise has-been lawyer Parnell Emmett McCarthy (Arthur O'Connell), Biegler's mentor. Maida still retains Stonewall's valuable executive qualities but much more openly participates in the cooperative transformation of the primary secondary character, McCarthy, who is less a comic and more a pathetic double of the protagonist. As in *The Misfits*, the secondary characters form a more collusive and interinfluential network than they did in the films of the 1940s and earlier 1950s, approaching the interdependent, tag-team configuration in which they begin to appear in the 1960s and after.

Anatomy of a Murder centers around Paul Biegler's defense of an army lieutenant, Frederick Manion, who was arrested for shooting Barney Quill, a man who raped his wife, Laura (Lee Remick). A former district attorney who was defeated in the last election, Biegler has recently devoted his time to fishing, leaving the law office in the capable hands of his secretary, Maida, and playing jazz piano, drinking, and reading law in the evenings with faithful friend McCarthy. Most of the film centers on Biegler's courtroom defense of Manion and his attempts to gather evidence, and the film's major subplot is the rehabilitation of the lovable McCarthy, whom Paul invites to help him on the case. Asking whether he can give up booze, McCarthy seems unsure until prodded by Maida, who asks him why he doesn't know whether he can quit drinking and encourages him when he says, "I might be a real lawyer again." Through the rest of the film, Maida protects McCarthy, refusing to tell Paul where he has gone when McCarthy takes the car and disappears. The first time Paul asks, she tells him, "My word is my bond." The second time, Paul tries to sneak the inquiry into a series of orders:

> Paul: Phone the army psychiatrist.
> Maida: Will do.
> Paul: Where is Parnell?
> Maida: Won't do.
> Paul: You're fired.
> Maida: You can't fire me until you pay me.

Maida's familiar insubordination is based not only in the fact that she's "been around" but also in her good-natured attempts to keep Biegler's office running in the black. When she announces to Biegler that there is no money to pay her salary, she also asks what he did with the last check. When he responds that it went to necessities, she knowingly suggests that an outboard motor for his boat was one of those. "I wish I could be classed with necessities," she sighs. She is also a source of opinion and information for Biegler. He asks her what she thinks of the seductive Mrs. Manion, and she warns him at the beginning that as a professional soldier, Manion probably won't pay him: "Those professional soldiers never have a dime. I ought to know, I was married to one." She also does detective work, going to the manicurist to gather information on Mrs. Manion and Mary Palant, the manager of Barney Quill's resort hotel.

In the courtroom scenes that constitute a large portion of the film, Maida serves as audience, a constant and reassuring face appearing behind Biegler and most often between Biegler and Mrs. Manion, who is seated to his right—again, a secondary character who is literally situated in the middle. Even if we are not consciously aware of her, she is almost always visible in medium long courtroom shots of Biegler from the perspective of the bench. Maida figures the film's audience as well as the trial gallery as the film records her entrances to the courthouse and carefully keeps her centered in medium long shots. The consistency of her appearance backs up Biegler's already reassuring persona; our trust in Biegler (and Stewart) and in the homespun manner in which he wins points against the slightly pretentious district attorney Ludwig (Brooks West, Arden's real-life husband), and the bright and snide young emissary from the attorney general's office, Charles Dancer (George C. Scott), actually provides the foundation for the film's ultimate irony. Although Biegler prevails in the case with a defense of temporary insanity, his client and his wife drive their trailer off in the night, sticking Biegler with the bill and a bit of doubt about his client's innocence. But as Biegler and a sober McCarthy stand over the barrel of cans and abandoned high-heeled shoes left by the Manions, Biegler's last line is, "How in the world are we going to face Maida?" Though minor, Maida is the cynical arbiter of good sense in a cynical world.

As in *Rear Window,* Stewart plays a character who is somehow humbly wiser than those around him. Like Stella, Maida tries to keep the Stewart character on track, but like Stella, she becomes a willing accomplice to his projects despite her own doubts—in this case about money or the character of his client's wife. And like Stella, Maida is often centered in the visual field, coming between Biegler and Mrs. Manion. But unlike Stella, Maida's figuration of a normative direction no longer prevails; instead, Maida represents a normalcy that has been decentered and sidelined in favor of the more cynical and ironic truth of human dishonesty. Biegler wins the case despite Maida's doubts. When they are awaiting the verdict, Maida comments, "I don't know what I'd do if I was on that jury. I really don't know. Do you?" Like the highly sympathetic judge

in the case, played by Joseph Welch, a real attorney who figured prominently as a lawyer in the Army-McCarthy hearings, Maida tries to bring
an even keel to Biegler's more private proceedings.[21] But despite their best
efforts, one suspects at the end of *Anatomy* that justice has not prevailed,
that Maida's subtle warnings were on target, but that at least McCarthy
has a new lease on life, which is ultimately what matters most. The end
of *Anatomy* is finally quite normative; Biegler asks Parnell to become his
law partner, and the two ride off into the sunset. Their evocation of Maida
situates her as the eccentric limiting factor, an absent normalcy that circumstances and desires have ultimately defeated. But Maida's position
at this point again locates her as the audience whose appreciation of the
film's ironies can come only from Maida's site of cynical wisdom.

Although Maida Rutledge's role seems to be more minor than that
of Ida or Stella, Maida still performs all of Ida's functions. Although these
functions are somewhat subordinated to the relationship between Biegler and McCarthy, Arden's role demonstrates how the specifically female
comic second still works as the site of knowledge, mediation, common
sense, humor, and insight in drama as well as in comedy. The female
comic second fades into the background in *Anatomy of a Murder*, but the
fact that she still performs the same functions and occupies the same
middle position in relation to characters and audience argues for the value
of such a character type as part of Hollywood's character economy and
demonstrates a fixed relation between the actress, the character type, and
the character's role.

Ending up as the almost mundane purveyor of normalcy, the female
comic second seems to have collapsed into a pragmatic operator. The
chaotic possibilities of a disorganized middle have been marshaled and
contained by the female comic second into a few lines of misdirection
easily salvaged by communication. This is not to say that the middle or
its ethos has disappeared but rather that it has become increasingly contained in the figure of the second herself, who comes more and more to
police normalcy in the face of an absurd world. That the "abnormal"
paradoxically polices the "normal" is a way of producing the appearance
of freedom through cooptation. The secondary character simultaneously signals tensions and delivers resolution that subordinates any sense
of risk to the status of a circumstance that is easily fixed. The stolid character of these secondary types also belies their complication, however.
Although they are synecdochal of middleness, like protagonists, they are
complexly constructed in relation to other characters. They, too, have
their middle.

4 Reliant Constructions

No Such Thing as a Solo

In 1942 Paramount made *Holiday Inn,* an Irving Berlin musical starring Bing Crosby and Fred Astaire, premised around the dreams of singer and composer Jim (Bing Crosby), who wants to become a farmer and quit his nightclub act with dancer Ted (Fred Astaire). When farming turns out to be too much work, Jim decides to turn the farm into a nightclub open only on the holidays, providing a showcase for Berlin's package of holiday tunes from "White Christmas" to "Easter Parade." A romantic comedy vaguely reminiscent of *A Midsummer Night's Dream, Holiday Inn* features the blonde love interest, Linda (Marjorie Reynolds); the brunette love interest, Lila (Virginia Dale); a vaguely sleazy agent and manager, Danny Reed (Walter Abel), who looks after Ted; and a mammy character, Mamie (Louise Beavers), who attends to Jim. Among Berlin's seasonal songs is a minstrel number in honor of Lincoln's birthday performed in blackface, inspired by Jim's last-minute efforts to hide Linda from Ted, who is looking for a new dance partner (although all the waitresses and even the band are also in blackface, and Linda's identity isn't much hidden when her black face is contrasted with her blonde pigtailed hair). Based around questions of value, integrity, and style of life, *Holiday Inn* endorses Jim's desire for hearth, family, and high-quality entertainment.

In 1954 *Holiday Inn* was partially remade as *White Christmas* starring Bing Crosby, Danny Kaye, Rosemary Clooney, and Vera Ellen. As a substitute Astaire, Kaye is just as frenetic and ambitious as his precursor, but Crosby, still low key, has become a powerful and generous star. Still a romantic comedy as most musicals are, *White Christmas* follows the efforts of Kaye to get Crosby married so that he (Kaye) can have some time off. As part of these efforts, he gets Crosby to follow the Haynes sisters (Clooney and Ellen) to Vermont, where they are scheduled to appear at an inn owned by the guys' former commanding officer, General Waverly. Abandoned for lack of snow, the inn and the general aren't doing too well until the boys decide to bring their show to the inn for rehearsal and for a special secret reunion of the corps who served under the general. In all of this, the various mating confusions of the four main stars are abetted by the composite helper figure of Emma, the inn's housekeeper (Mary Wickes). All trace of blackness has disappeared. Not a soldier, a servant, or a dancer is black, and the minstrel number has been transformed from blackface and pickaninny pigtails to silly attempts at minstrel jokes ("Mister Bones") and red-and-green-clad dancers banging tambourines and singing "Mandy."

The question here is not only what happened between 1942 and 1954 that made even the questionable traces of stereotyped blacks disappear from the screen but also how the mammy character, Mamie, could be replaced by the spinster geek, Emma. The black mammy and servant stereotype began to disappear from Hollywood film in the 1950s, at least as portrayed by black actresses. The three most prominent black actresses who consistently played secondary roles—Louise Beavers, Hattie McDaniel, and Butterfly McQueen—either died (McDaniel) or retired (McQueen) by the early 1950s or appeared only sporadically, as Louise Beavers did, in a few movies (five between 1950 and 1960).[1] Never lead players like Dorothy Dandridge, the mammy and servant figures appeared in more movies than Dandridge because their demeanor fit better into stereotyped utility roles. But when these black characters began to disappear as a feature of Hollywood cinema, these actresses also disappeared, and their roles were subsumed into the fool figures we have been looking at or, as in the case of *Auntie Mame*, into a Japanese houseboy, an Irish maid, and a geek, who both elide and contain racial, ethnic, and sexual difference. Although it might be easy to attribute this minor change to biography, changing social conditions, or the shifting configuration of the studio system, the move away from clearly delineated class and racial positions also indicates a more conservative, difference-denying tactic that comes to characterize, perhaps ironically, much of mainstream 1960s Hollywood film.

Servant figures and children, unless they function as buddy characters, are tertiary rather than secondary in the sense that they occupy less screen time than secondary characters, and they are often subordinate or secondary to secondary characters. They furnish another tier of characters who are often less individualized than stereotyped but who still play an important role in promoting the flow of information or augmenting the charms or foibles of the main characters. The populous variety of such characters produces a visual counterpart to the multiplicities of the narrative middle. Providing myriad differences and alternatives and contributing the illusion of filmic and social depth, these characters are organized by class and narrative function. But like secondary characters, they also signal the breakdown of pretense and the illusive solidity of categories of the dominant—whiteness, femininity, middle-classness, heterosexuality—announcing the emergence of the far less organized difference that subtends narrative.

By producing a breach in pretense, secondary and tertiary characters such as Ida and Lottie reveal the ways these categories are both a cooperative effort and the effect of a masked and unorganized variety of unstable positions. Often this breach is purposeful, but often it seems more incidental and symptomatic, a byproduct of the seething substratum of multiple possibilities that contribute to and undermine a veneer of categorical order. Although this surface versus depth model might be slightly misleading, Hollywood cinema actually produces the illusion of a surface-depth relation both literally and figuratively. Its use of deep space and greater depth of field provides a sense of literal space, whereas the variously disproportionate time accorded each type of character makes some characters recede into the hidden depths of the film. Spatial metaphors govern the relation between major and minor, whereas temporal and spatial metaphors define the relation between the narrative middle and the beginning or end; the middle is fleeting, temporary, and less important in relation to what seems to be the disturbed stability of the beginning and the resolved stability of the end.

Focusing on this fleeting depth, on the relations between minor characters, makes visible the presence and operations of a variety that I'll call, after Derrida, *différance,* which coexists with and underwrites the binary differences that superficially shape Hollywood cinema's conventional plots and star system. This *différance* comes from Derrida's notion of the play of production and generation that enables and structures difference. This differing, as Derrida puts it, means "to temporalize or resort consciously or unconsciously to the temporal, and temporalizing mediation of a detour that suspends the accomplishment or fulfillment of 'desire' or 'will' or carries desire or will out in a way that annuls or tempers their effect" ("Differance" 36). In relation to secondary and tertiary characters in mainstream cinema, this sense of differing works as a mediating detour, a quality that puts off the return to structures and ideological categories. The relation between difference and *différance* is analogous to the difference between a point on a square that is defined in relation to a fixed and locatable axis and a point in curved space without a fixed Euclidean axis (Reimannian geometry), where the point can gain significance only in relation to other points in the curve and not in relation to a more universal location. The usually ignored or taken-for-granted secondary and tertiary female characters' differences are relational as well as socially inscribed, at least until such *différance* surfaces as variety. They function to embody and displace anxieties about stars' femininity, heterosexuality, and even racial "purity," pointing toward the *différance* that plays in and through delusions of controllable binary difference organized around gender, class, race, nationality, and sexuality.

The relations between primary, secondary, tertiary, and even quaternary characters demonstrate that the middle itself has a middle, a middle occluded in some films—such as *Cover Girl*—that deploy the secondary character as a containing blind. Sameness and threatening chaos regress infinitely and have perhaps less to do with identity than with structures of repetition, enframement, and persistent slippage between categories. One effect of this is the revelation of how bourgeois femininity is fabricated from multiple, contributing, and contradictory elements and how, at these points, the conventional alignments of race, class, sexuality, and gender give way momentarily to a play of varied and multiple differences that seem to have been there all along. But gender is not the sole category brought into play; white femininity repeatedly requires the presence of nonwhite others as its guarantee, and the reproduction of white heterosexual femininity smooths over the perverse appearance of homosexual hints in moments of slippage. However, these points of contrived instability are also symptomatic attempts to control disorganized and unaligned difference by making femininity's constructedness an open secret. The lure of femininity's artificiality distracts us from the fact that this same phantom femininity still glowingly endorses patriarchal gender ideology. Given the gendered gloss through which narrative operates (or is perceived as operating), it is significant that the ground that shifts is associated openly with issues of femininity and its constructedness. As the site of displaced anxieties about patriarchy and masculinity, femininity is programmed to come apart. But as the site of patriarchy's anxious symptom, it also threatens to betray too much of the chaos that underlies everything. That femininity is constantly being constructed replays a reassuring reorganization of chaos into the "other." It is thus no surprise that when femininity comes apart, it is made up of various "others."

The studio system's casting (which tended to use the same actors and actresses for the same kinds of roles) and practice of character economy (which used a few tightly organized characters to convey community) used these tiered character hierarchies as a shorthand for social and familial structure. At the same time, such tight organization complemented a culture that clung to the fantasy of an oedipal or patriarchal organization such as the family and the small town that seemed to provide meaning during a period of rapid technological and social change. Before the stereotype disappears, however, tertiary black characters such as those played by Butterfly McQueen appeared in concert with secondary fool characters; their screen association may provide some clue not only to why Mary Wickes can replace both Louise Beavers and Walter Abel but also to what, other than vague social realism, is at stake in including the black servant figure in the first place. These tertiary characters invite a glance beyond both primary and secondary characters, revealing a complicated net of interconnected relations by which each character, no matter how minor, contributes to the construction of all the characters, from the most idiosyncratic to the most stereotyped. From the vantage of the tertiary, the sense of independence and fixed centrality belonging to focal personae dissolves into a plethora of intertwined social and cultural positions, and the secondary by itself tends to preserve social distinctions. The interrelation of characters demonstrates the degree to which constructions of gender, race, and sexuality depend on multiple positions within a complex and reflexive hierarchy. They also signal the ways classical Hollywood films regularly contemplated the instability of dominant categories before reasserting them.

Home Girls

The Women, for example, features a brief scene between Butterfly McQueen as a maid (not even included in the credits) and Joan Crawford as Crystal Allen, the lower-class, fortune-hunting temptress who is seducing protagonist Mary's husband. In this scene, which is a behind-the-scene presentation of the preparation for another scene, the interactions between Crystal, another salesgirl, and the maid reveal the extent to which Crystal's pose as a high-class adventuress is a contrived construction of both class and femininity. In the stockroom behind the perfume counter in a department store where Crystal works, Crystal rushes to prepare for a date with Stephen, Mary's husband. After ordering one employee to wrap something quickly, Crystal turns to the maid (Mc-Queen), who has entered asking, "Was you asking for me, Miz Allen?" In the bossy, bitchy style typical of Crystal's underside in this film, Crystal tells the maid, "Been scouring the whole store for you. Why don't you run to my apartment and cook dinner?" When the maid says she's got a date, Crystal tells her to break it; when the maid warns Crystal, "But I'm noted for the bad way I cook," Crystal replies brusquely, "If you throw a lamb chop into a hot oven, what's going to keep it from getting done?" After this interchange, the shopgirl, a wisecracking fool type who is onto Crystal's airs, asks Crystal what happened to her "hot date." "It's hotter than ever, dear," Crystal responds, "I'm having him dine at my place. It's about time he found out I'm a home girl." "Home girl, huh," replies the other salesgirl, "Why don't you borrow the quintuplets for the evening?" "Because I'm all the baby he wants, pet," Crystal rejoins, revealing how much this contrived domesticity is really a pretext for a seductive anti-domesticity.

Crystal's self-production as a "home girl" depends on the maid as the agent paid to produce the illusion of her domesticity. Both the maid and the other salesgirl are under no illusions about Crystal's "home girl" qualities, and, for the maid, constructing Crystal's image is an economic opportunity. "How much will you pay me?" she asks and tries hard to bargain Crystal up from two to three dollars. Reluctantly accepting two dollars, the maid asks, "Will I find anything in that icebox of yours?" and the other salesgirl answers, "Yeah, cobwebs and a bottle of gin." But if both the maid and the salesgirl rib Crystal, what function does the maid's blackness have, given the fact that she is the one enlisted to help produce Crystal's illusion? In other words, why does this scene need a black maid at all, one who appears in no other scene in the film? It is clear from this scene that Crystal has a social and economic power over the maid that she does not have over the other salesgirl, who is an "Ida" to Crystal's "Mildred." As this structure is reflected in more minor characters and particularly around a "bad apple," the secondary figure's wise insight, though still mirroring audience knowledge, becomes more sardonic and more about exposing Crystal's ambitions. As a part of this dynamic, Crystal's bullying is linked to white privilege and to the need to find someone over whom she can assert her power. Although both Crystal and the maid belong to classes lower than the film's other featured characters, Crystal's contrast with the black maid establishes a racially moored, classed pecking order in the stockroom that not only reflects a similar class disparity between Crystal and the society ladies but also establishes Crystal as white with its relative—and in this case demonstrably un-deserved—privilege. The physical contrast between Crystal and the maid makes Crystal look taller (mostly because McQueen is shorter), forcing the maid to look up to her. The racial difference between the maid and the two salesgirls also distracts from questions about the relative beau-ty of the two white women. Although the other salesgirl is blond and quite attractive in contrast to Crystal's dark, angular look, in compari-son to the maid's modest appearance, Crystal seems glamorous. But the scene does not entirely permit Crystal to leverage off of the maid; the maid's return gibes, unwillingness to help, and own romantic pretensions produce an ambivalence around Crystal that comes from both her will-ingness to take advantage of racial inequities and her inability to domi-nate completely the person she exploits.

This small backstage scene is part of the first series of scenes in which we are introduced to Crystal, who until this point has been the mystery woman who was wrecking Mary's marriage. Charming at the counter and brusque in the storeroom, the hypocritical Crystal is unmasked by both maid and associate; her lower-class behavior, lack of domesticity, and unprincipled ambition revealed through her rude exploitation of the maid produce her desired image as a gracious and capable hostess. In her ef-forts to arrange the masquerade, she undoes any claims she might have had to decorum and decency, revealing herself as calculating, unprinci-pled, and ungenerous. And that she employs—actually takes crass advan-tage of—the maid (and one who readily confesses her poor culinary skills) shows both her lack of class and the careless and cobbled-together char-acter of her version of the "home girl."

Showing the precarious constructedness of class is not a random endeavor in *The Women*. It is important that Crystal be so undone from the start because the film depends on the fairly overt manipulations of audience sympathy: Crystal needs to be a scheming charlatan so that we can sympathize with the silly Mary. In other words, in *The Women* the woman whose class and gender pretensions are the most dangerous must also be the most openly contrived—one who not only constantly reveals the meanness beneath her pretense but also one whose machinations depend on openly exploitive relationships with others. Crystal's treat-ment of the black maid is in overt contrast to Mary's congenial relation-ship with her white household staff, where as a pampered favorite Mary can pretend, in the best traditions of humble gentility, that the cook has some power over her. Desperately deploying a black freelancer instead of a stable white immigrant European staff, Crystal's version of the *grande dame* is imaged as desperate and inferior, even though the contrast might also suggest that noble Mary's domestic tranquility rests equally on the labors of others.

In either case, the conversation between Crystal and the maid denaturalizes the quotidian production of femininity (a commonplace production that, when revealed as a production, denaturalizes the femininity it produces), suggesting the exploitive constructedness of all versions of femininity in the film. White bourgeois femininity is largely unstable and must be tended constantly, as is evident in the number of times the beauty salon serves as a setting for both revelation and a series of wacky procedures and exercises designed to make feminine beauty look like the production it is. The backstage of the beauty salon, like the back room of the department store, is the site for a greater class and racial diversity—much like the "women only" as-if-off-screen settings of the films discussed in chapter 2—than other, more personal boudoir scenes.[2] No one in *The Women* is securely either feminine or a lady; all must work at it and all bear some mark of affectation that disappears quickly in fights (some of them quite physical) over men.

The moment when Crystal employs the maid to be a surrogate "home girl" is the point in the film when the contrivance of both class and femininity becomes most obviously a concoction as the elements of a crassly bartered domestic surrogate in combination with racial difference draw attention to the cold-blooded and self-consciously deliberate manipulations of Crystal's endeavors. Although this revelation of the power relations that contribute to white femininity depends partly on the racism inherent in the scene, what makes Crystal's brash contrivance stand out is the way in which both the maid and the other salesgirl openly penetrate Crystal's guise while denigrating Crystal (who frankly doesn't care because she knows that only appearances in front of the more powerful count). Like the maid, the audience also penetrates Crystal's pretensions, making both her class and femininity quite precarious. We expect Crystal to slip at any moment (which she does, notably in front of Little Mary), and the tension around the insecure construction contrasts with other, more stable renditions of femininity in the film that, though also quite openly constructed, are naturalized in relation to Crystal.

This brief scene, which shows up the vulgarity of the villain, is actually more a symptom or signifier of the constructedness of femininity and class than it is an accident or a device deployed simply to vilify Crystal Allen. Butterfly McQueen appears again with Joan Crawford in *Mildred Pierce*, as the maid, Lottie; in this film the socially ambitious daughter, Veda, deploys Lottie to remind her mother of her working-class background. By having Lottie wear Mildred's waitress uniform, Veda not only makes Lottie Mildred's stand-in but also forces Mildred to confess her job as a waitress. Making Mildred Lottie (and vice versa) not only shows the similarity in their jobs but also accounts for Veda's "Crystal Allen" treatment of her own mother, whom she wheedles and bosses in turn. Throughout the film, Lottie provides a comic version of both Veda and Mildred's pretensions in her awkward attempts to play the sophisticate. But she also functions as an unwitting mediator between classes (Veda and Mildred) and between the competing versions of dangerously independent femininity (Mildred and Ida) that make up part of the film's dilemma, something she can do because she is black and is therefore invisible unless she imitates whiteness. Her imitations are innocently parodical, and her presence as echo, reminder of origins (when Mildred was a waitress), and signifier of affluence (they now have a maid) is enabled by her blackness, which signifies a history of exploitive relations and at the same time gestures toward the instability of Mildred's restaurant empire. Lottie both moors the restaurant and signals its vulnerability by presenting a constant reminder of origins and mocking the pretentious forces that will ultimately destroy Mildred.

Early in the film Mildred is depicted as both industrious and beautiful in direct comparison to Lottie. Mildred has gotten her waitress job and is working at night baking pies to augment her income. In a scene in

Lottie (Butterfly McQueen) and Mildred (Joan Crawford) in *Mildred Pierce*

which she and Lottie are in the kitchen finishing the night's pie production, Mildred lists the dozens of pies they have made, and Lottie says, "I
don't know how you keep it up, Mrs. Pierce. Honest I don't. Now I sleep
all morning, but you go down to that restaurant and work and work just
like you been sleepin' all night, only you ain't." "Keeps me thin," Mildred
replies. "Beg pardon?" Lottie asks, then looking first at one side of her
body then the other, she adds, "Don't do nothing for me." Because both
Mildred and Lottie are in the same shot, Mildred in the foreground right
and Lottie slightly behind her on the left, the physical comparison between black and white, tall and short, thin and slightly plump is obvious. Because Lottie makes the comparison between Mildred's industry
and her own more normal pace, it comes off as both admiration and a kind
of witnessing that augments Mildred in relation to others, like Lottie, who
labor at the same tasks as Mildred.

In another scene, when Mildred returns from an extended vacation
in Mexico, Lottie greets her in the parking lot of her restaurant. "My, Miz
Pierce, this is a day for rejoicing, it certainly is," she welcomes Mildred.
"You look wonderful," she goes on, "You've been away for so long."

> Mildred: Yes, I've been to Mexico.
> Lottie: Is that a fact? Oh, it's nice to have you back. I don't know what
>   we would have done if you'd stayed away longer.
> Mildred: Thank you, Lottie. It's nice to see you, too.
> Lottie: Likewise, I'm sure.

Performing the courtesy of the white middle class but with wrongly
gauged, overly effusive compliments, Lottie's out-of-key courtesy is not
so much a reflection on Lottie as a reminder that in some ways Mildred
is "likewise" a pretender who hasn't gotten it all quite right, even though
the contrast between Mildred and Lottie makes Mildred look like a sophisticated lady. In this scene, Lottie is also a substitute for the missing
Veda; Lottie becomes a mock version of the daughter, who should be
welcoming her mother back but who is instead the reason for her mother's absence. When Mildred enters the restaurant, Ida replaces Lottie, and
the subject of the conversation is ultimately Veda.

In the immediately postwar *Mildred Pierce*, revealing the constructed
quality of class and gender is more than a plot device used to sway sym-
pathies or show the superficiality of patriarchy's gender demands. Even
with a more traditional female protagonist, a femininity that must constantly be fabricated and negotiated works as a cover for a much more
sinister idea of perverse females who prefer freedom and industry to the
confines of conventionally feminine roles.[3] Mildred is far too ambitious

and independent even as she deploys a feminine masquerade; she succeeds where the men around her fail. Perverse independence like Mildred's persists among the secondary characters, whose class difference disallows the more smoothly arranged compensations of social masquerade; Ida's brasher independence neutralizes Mildred's menace by providing an even more overt version of autonomy. Even though Mildred is an aggressive, self-reliant, and powerful character, her femininity is never brought into question, not because she is so traditionally feminine that there can be no doubt but because the threats Mildred poses are negotiated both through the narrative, which returns her to her husband at the end, and through Ida, who works on many levels to dissipate displaced anxieties about Mildred's aggressiveness and determination. And given what Thomas Schatz calls "the undercurrent of anxiety about traditional notions of sexuality and marriage, which in a postwar milieu necessarily raised questions about women in the work place, housing, and the economy in general," *Mildred Pierce* was already a dangerous movie to produce (*Genius* 421). The Breen Committee objected to several versions of the script in which Veda actually had an illicit affair with Monte.[4] Focused on sexual impropriety, the Production Code Administration ignored the perhaps more threatening specter of Mildred's and Ida's version of independent women who were quite able to succeed on their own—in fact, succeed better if there were no parasitic men around to sell them out.

Mildred Pierce is partly about what happens when women become independent and successful and how easy such a transformation can be. Both Mildred and Ida prove that women can be both successful and independent. Both shift economic classes, and Mildred crosses into high society with her relationship to Monte. Ida also complicates the film's categories by incarnating a deviant cross-class alliance instigated by Mildred's rise to fortune and brought into issue by Veda, who eschews the "grease" that founded her mother's wealth. Ida becomes the displaced representative of Mildred's previous lower-class status, not quite lower class herself but not quite as wealthy and aspiringly upper class as Mildred and certainly Veda. To the extent that Ida operates as a way to deflect attention away from any question about Mildred's femininity or class status, Ida seems to embody femininity's opposite—not masculinity, but the dissociation between traditional femininity and biological femaleness—as a feature of both minority and the fool function.

But even Ida's version of dissociated femininity is itself constructed and negotiated through the presence of Lottie with her caricature of upperclass affectation. In relation to Lottie's somewhat naive imitations, Ida appears urbane and sharply commonsensical, whereas Lottie appears as a mere caricature of the upper class. That Lottie is a black woman seems to naturalize her caricature, however; because she is black in a racist context, her imitation of "white" manners appears as only an imitation. Therefore, Lottie's parody is ambivalent. On one hand, it seems to be the innocent product of a well-meaning but slightly inept retainer, and on the other, its very ineptness pointedly suggests the ultimate class masquerade of both Mildred and Veda, who were at one point socially inept themselves. Lottie's position as a maid also deflects attention away from Ida's helper status, making Ida look both more like Mildred's equal and more like a lady than she actually is. Using racial stereotypes and racist assumptions as a third-level element through which the class and femininity of white women are secured is a way of both naturalizing the labored construction of white femininity and securing femininity itself as a white phenomenon, illustrating quite aptly Barbara Christian's claim that "Each black woman image was created to keep a particular image about white women intact" (qtd. in Doane, *Femmes Fatales* 243).

This securing function is apparent in scenes with Lottie in which the social distinctions between the women threaten to collapse, first in the scene where Veda dresses Lottie in Mildred's waitress uniform and second in a complex scene where Lottie moors an intricate quadrangulation between herself, Mildred, Ida, and Veda. This latter scene takes place just as Mildred is being forced out of business by her partners, Wally and Monte, and during a large birthday celebration for Veda at Mildred's mansion. Lottie is pouring champagne and exhorting another maid to be careful because the champagne is "Perrier-fils 1927." When the other maid asks whether that is "better than '28," Lottie explains that "it's the newest we could get." In a room off to the side of the party proper, Lottie answers the telephone, at first very hesitantly as if the phone were a strange contraption, then in the more sophisticated fashion she was taught: "This is the Beragon residence. Who should I say is calling?" The caller is Mildred, asking for Ida. During this scene Lottie is standing in the foreground, slightly off center to the right; she walks off to the left toward the party to get Ida. The film crosscuts to Mildred's office, where Mildred is standing in exactly the same position as Lottie, screen right, with the business party in the same relative position as the birthday party. As Mildred tells Ida she'll be late, the film crosscuts to Ida, who is also standing in the same relative position. Ida asks Mildred, "What's going on there? Are you in trouble? You sound funny." As she hangs up the phone, Veda and Monte enter from the left, the same direction as the troublesome business conference in Mildred's scene. Ida tells them, "Something's going on. I'm worried. I think she's in some kind of

Lottie (Butterfly McQueen) in *Mildred Pierce*

Mildred (Joan Crawford) in *Mildred Pierce*

Ida (Eve Arden) in *Mildred Pierce*

business trouble." Monte replies archly that "it happens in the best of families." Catching on to his involvement, Ida tells him snidely, "Don't look now, but you've got canary feathers all over your face." But Veda joins in with a more symptomatic response: "Business and making money. That's all mother thinks about" as she exits with Monte.

This scene illustrates graphically the ways in which Lottie not only triangulates Mildred and Ida's relationship by serving as the human link in their communication but also mediates Mildred's relation to the businessmen who hover in the background in Mildred's office. The parallel cut scenes—Lottie with her back to the party and Mildred in the same place with her back to the businessmen—make a visual connection between Mildred and Lottie and between the businessmen and the party that turns out to be quite canny because both threaten to destroy Mildred. This is not an instance of Lottie bolstering Mildred's image, as in the pie scene; it is more likely that Mildred will again become like Lottie, resembling her more in terms of class and task than race. But Lottie also performs different versions of the black retainer, suggesting the essentially slippery pose of all positions, especially when Lottie is visually replaced by Ida after a cut. Dressed to the nines, Ida takes Lottie's place on the screen, where like Lottie she mediates for Mildred. But Ida uses her canny understanding to signal Monte's guilt and her genuine concern for Mildred to show up Veda's frivolous and spoiled version of feminine wiles.

Each rendering of the feminine—from Lottie's caricature to Ida's handsome command to Mildred's worried sacrifice to Veda's flippant flirtation—not only depends on the others but also threatens to collapse into the others, apparently as a result of economic upheaval. But the alibi of the film's plot is not the frame through which this collapse is made immanent; rather, when the minor is an operative point of exchange, the distinctions that moor up class, sexual, and racial difference fade in favor of the more disorganized, dissociated play of details, masquerade, and minor attributes that suggest similarities *in* differences instead of similarity *and* difference. Because of changes in economic standing, Veda might become Mildred (even as she is who she is because of Mildred), who might become Lottie, who became Mildred by way of her waitress uniform. If they lose their wealth, they might also become capable-but-spinsterish big sisters like Ida, out of the marriage market and all hope of position. We see this other kind of more varied play only if we pay attention to Ida and Lottie; focusing only on Mildred and Veda produces a narrative of oedipal competition and maternal self-denial in which those who constitute the links between them, such as Lottie and Ida, fall out as merely functionaries.

Given the example of Butterfly McQueen, the tertiary black character functions as contrastive support for insecure constructions of both white femininity and the middle class. This in itself is not a new insight, but what may be less obvious is the way the tertiary black character also catalyzes the transformation of the white woman from masculine and aggressive to feminine and domestic via the presence of the secondary fool figure. By themselves, the characters Butterfly McQueen plays would only provide contrast, as in the pie scene in *Mildred Pierce*. In concert with wisecracking fool figures such as the salesgirl in *The Women* or Ida, the black figure becomes more than contrast in combination with the secondary white female's alternate version of a more hermaphroditic, independent, yet lower-class version of womanhood. The black figure also works to secure the secondary character's whiteness, while the secondary character's brash independence certifies the more dependent femininity of both black and white figures, the black figure's version of femininity then working as support for the femininity and racial purity of the central white female character. The black character is tertiary not only because of Hollywood's interpretation of social reality but also because she works as a third term that negotiates the sexual difference between the primary and secondary female characters and catalyzes and figures the production (and deconstruction) of multiple versions of gender and class. Racial difference provides the visual and aural differences that separate and distinguish the white women from one another.

Roly-Poly

The black servant figure who moored white domesticity fades, but the symptomatic appearance of black figures does not entirely cease. No longer servants, black figures become representatives of a joyous teeming sexuality that characterizes night life, jazz, and a certain freeing of bourgeois restrictiveness. With a black orchestra, stiff white people can loosen up. Less organized differences, which had been announced by the breakdown in class, gender, and sexual markers between women, become sexual liberation, the unrepression of "primitive" desires in white people whose movie courtships required much game playing and misdirection. The unleashing of these differences in the atmospheric presence of black characters becomes the pretext for enjoyment and the release of pleasure.

In 1943 the enthusiastic black orchestra that opens Dorothy Arzner's *Dance, Girl, Dance* represents the low-culture illegitimacy from which the girls must escape; in the 1959 *Pillow Talk*, Jan and Rex/Brad find their romance catalyzed by the three-piece black band in a piano bar. In *Pillow Talk* the black trio provides both an excuse to launch into more overt sexuality and the environment that renders visible the main characters' complex layerings of identity, especially as the characters are invited to disclose their "real" desires. If Butterfly McQueen's appearance in a film often showed up characters' pretense, in *Pillow Talk* the black figures actively invite and witness the revelation of the white characters' underlying "authentic" selves. Rather than articulating only with the film's female characters, as the black tertiary characters of earlier films often did, *Pillow Talk*'s black singer, Mary (Perry Blackwell), effects a complex doubling of all of the film's main characters.

The piano bar scene occurs an hour into the film—the literal middle—on Jan and Rex/Brad's third date when piano player Mary invites Jan and Rex/Brad to join in the group sing. The scene begins with the song "Roly-Poly," ostensibly about a fat man but also transparently about a big, fat male organ. Mary invites Jan to sing the song, and although Jan initially refuses, claiming she doesn't know the words, Mary gives her the sheet music and Jan takes over the solo. The rest of the bar patrons sing along awkwardly as Jan and Rex, drawn in by the song's irresistible fun-loving cadence, attempt clumsily to flirt and play patty cake. At the end of the song, Rex continues when everyone else stops. In the post-"Roly-Poly" conversation, Rex performs the homosexual signs that as Brad he had previously warned Jan about: the crooked little finger when he drinks, his interest in decorating and dip recipes. Jan, unable to let this go any further without clarifying their relationship, asks Rex directly whether his interest in her is merely platonic, and Rex takes the opportunity to give her what he calls a "direct" answer: a long kiss. Overwhelmed by Rex's osculatory expertise, Jan retires to the ladies room to the relieved strains of "I need no atmosphere." While she is gone, Mary continues to sing and watch the comedy that ensues when Jonathan and his detective enter and Jonathan tells Brad that he is on to him. He orders Brad to put Jan in a taxi and then go to Jonathan's Connecticut summer house, where he can finish the music for the musical Jonathan is financing. Jonathan retires to watch Brad from outside, and when Jan returns, Brad asks her to go with him to Connecticut, making sure all their outward actions comply with Jonathan's demands. Mary witnesses all of this, and as Jan and Rex/Brad leave the bar, Mary sings "You lie, you dog, and you'll be sorry," a prophecy that in the short term proves correct.

As the all-purpose double and romantic ally to Jan and Rex, Mary serves as witness, mood-setting catalyst, and repository of truth. *Pillow Talk* has been sustained all along by dramatic irony—by the audience knowing more than any of the characters, including Alma. The "Roly-Poly" scene is the first occasion in which any character has witnessed what the audience knows as the audience comes to know it: Jan's romantic response to Rex/Brad and Brad's knowledge of Jonathan's knowledge of the trick Brad has been playing. As a black figure who cannot interfere with what is going on, Mary is an interesting on-screen audience correlative who can, but only in a limited fashion, both shape and react to the unwinding of events. By getting Jan to sing "Roly-Poly" Mary gets her past a certain frigidity; by selecting such fitting music as "Trip to the Moon," Mary provides both atmosphere and commentary on what is going on between Jan and Brad. When Jonathan threatens Brad, Mary makes appropriate faces, and when Brad suggests that Jan go to Connecticut with him, Mary raises her eyebrows and begins to sing "You lie." Mary's witnessing of the romance drama is neither casual nor accidental; the film constantly intercuts Mary's reaction shots to each new revelation, from the kiss to Jonathan's threat to Brad's attempts to circumvent him. The question here is why this is necessary.

This scene, which is in the center of the film, begins to nail down the flying identities and prevarications of the main characters. It is the first turning point in the Brad-Jan romance narrative, reversed later when Jan finally finds out what Mary already knows. The scene works as a nodal point, a site of convergence in which Mary provides an alternative stewardship to Alma's inebriated observations. Mary sees beneath Jan's pretense and invites her to sing a fun, indirect, but sexually explicit song. She provides a far superior version of petty Jonathan, whose lack of natural intuition forces him to engage a detective to gain knowledge Mary already has about Rex's duplicity. Jonathan acts out of a sense of property disguised as courtliness; Mary, like Rex, is a musician who works with the soul instead of the bank book, so that ultimately, like Alma, she is aligned with Rex in an effort to get Jan, whose decorating career places her on the line between property and art, to swing in the direction of art. In this capacity, then, the black figure works as the ultimate representative of soul, art, and freedom in relation to Jonathan's capitalist proprietorship while representing frankness and honesty. In *Pillow Talk*, the world of color—the deep colors of the piano bar, the garish colors with which Jan decorates Brad's apartment—wins out over the sterile whiteness of Jonathan's office and Connecticut house and the sedate pastels of Jan's apartment.

As a site of romantic insight, Mary can act as a catalyst; part of the function of blackness in this scene is a holdover from the mammy character's quiet wisdom and perceptiveness that gives her a certain privilege to sense the mood and possibilities. That Mary is black tends to suggest this quality; her facilitation of the romance confirms it. In a more racist register, Mary's blackness enables the other characters to discount her presence so that she is able to witness very private events without being noticed. Her insight then permits her to comment on the action, but her position as outsider suggests that any comment she makes must be indirect. In addition, the restraints on her commerce imposed by race and by her position as bar entertainer make her analogous to the film's audience, who knows what is going on and, like Mary, can have only a limited reaction. The implicit connection between audience position and blackness is ambivalent. On one hand, it enacts the limitations of the audience position; on the other, it links the audience with perception and artistry, with the patience, canniness, and disdain Mary enacts. Because Mary appears only once in the film, she is more minor than Alma, whose persistent wisdom continually matches audience knowledge. Because Mary is not an intimate but an observant stranger, Mary must be indirect, although her indirection is tied to the general indirection that typifies the mating rituals in *Pillow Talk*. Mary's position in the film's middle (and at the beginning of the unraveling of Brad/Rex's identity) suggests her dual functions as the one who represents the apex of confusions and who stimulates the beginning realignment of the parties. It is as if Mary's racial difference provides the element that can spur discernment among a confused mass of white people.

Pillow Talk's Mary signals the unmasking of disguise rather than breakdown in categories, in part because class and gender are never at issue in the film. What is openly at issue is sexuality: Jan's with her "bedroom problems," the fictional Rex's with his homosexual behaviors, and Brad's propensity for the obstetrician's office into which he ducks several times to escape unwelcome encounters.[5] Unlike earlier Hollywood fare, *Pillow Talk* does not expose the symptomatic constructedness of categories but rather substitutes identities and multiply directed desires (Rex's homosexuality) whose overt constructedness is the means to an end. What might be the film's "unconscious," akin to the moments in earlier films where class and gender seem to come apart, is not any underlying instability or difference but rather a foundational truth about the real desires that drive the characters' masquerades. Having apparently taken control of any insecurities lurking beneath the surface, *Pillow Talk* thus reverses the anxieties around the layered structure of manifest stability and underlying instability, making the manifest the openly unstable and the latent the site of truth. The deliberate quality of the characters' masquerade also makes masquerade, as the ostensible site of instability, a site of greater will and control, however; thus, there is no real breakdown of categories in the film. Where Butterfly McQueen signaled dispersion and instability in *The Women* and *Mildred Pierce*, Mary catalyzes the redistribution of secure sites and the ultimate revelation of their hidden "truths."

In *Pillow Talk*, then, the black character takes on a slightly revised position. While still representing the mammy's insight, she has become more urbane and jazzy and more clearly the representative of the Dionysian soul at the heart of all battles against Apollonian propriety. Although this is essentialist, it is precisely Mary's racial difference that produces the contrast necessary to break the tug of warring values (and suitors) and move beyond stasis. If anything, Mary's singular blackness signals a difference, a shaking up and moving on that will break the chain of masquerade that in itself can lead nowhere, even if Mary contributes only a small opportunity and a large measure of lyrical commentary. She is a familiar who offers no threat, a facilitator who is, within a logic of miscegenation, outside the white folks' mating pool, who, because she is black, automatically knows more about romance than any of those stiff, white characters. But these functions depend largely on racist stereotypes, which clearly in the late 1950s have not disappeared, even if African-American mammy figures and servants seem to have. That Mary can know what the others cannot see results from nothing other than a belief in the primitive wisdom of the black retainer.

"I Don't Have a Very Clear Picture of What's Going On"

Points of contrived instability such as Brad's masquerade as Rex in *Pillow Talk* may also be symptomatic attempts to control disorganized and unaligned *différance* by making the construction of various categories an open secret. The lure of contingency in one site distracts us from the fact that in another site, another category might not be quite so stable. In *Pillow Talk*, that category is more likely to be masculinity, which seems secure with Rex/Brad because of his homosexual masquerade but is less secure with Jonathan. The fact that Brad suggests Rex may be gay lures away from Jonathan's more stereotypically gay mannerisms; played against what has become public knowledge of the actors' sexualities, *Pillow Talk*'s complexly layered joke displaces all instability away from the males into its symptomatic relocation as a question of femininity—in this case Jan's sexuality. Because we think we know what Brad's sexuality is (we "know" both the character's heterosexuality and the actor's homosexuality, insofar as sexualities are knowable), the apparent answer to questions of male sexuality displaces questions about sexuality onto Jan, whose sexuality no one seems to know.[6] But although she may have "bedroom problems," these, too, are superficial. Attending to them, as Rex does, leads to the reassuring truth of her heterosexual desire. For although Rex may be effeminate when Jan is independent and frigid, when Rex becomes the masculine Brad, Jan becomes the compliant and receptive woman. *Pillow Talk* is thus a closed circuit in which uncertainty (which, it turns out, is less uncertainty than simply a lack of knowledge) leads only to the knowledge we already know.

This recirculation of categorical stability seems a feature of late–studio system Hollywood, a system that was by the late 1950s extremely insecure, well on the way to the collapse of its thirty-year filmmaking practice. The secondary players who provided the pool of familiar minor faces were less and less on contract; films became more package deals cast out of a sea of freelancers. This seemed to inspire a much larger variety in the faces that appeared on the screen and, superficially, at least, would account for the disappearance of regular secondary figures. But studio politics is the least interesting reason strong female comic seconds began to disappear. We might map the reasons for their disappearance by tracking another instance of the overt construction of femininity, this time in the 1958 *Auntie Mame* where *différance*, or at least variety, seems to be an open secret, much like Brad/Rex's real identity. In contrast with the scenes from fifteen or twenty years earlier, where the black character is the site of displaced gender production and instability, in *Auntie*

Mame the black figure has been transformed into the white geek Agnes, and the femininity at issue is hers. Even so, the film's comically overt construction of femininity seems to open a window to the lurking *différance* that is pressed into service.

Agnes Gooch is the character whose femininity is openly construct-ed. Sporting orthopedic shoes, thick glasses, and utilitarian couture, Gooch, as Brian O'Banion so tactfully puts it, is "an offense to the hu-man eyesight." Part of the variety Mame gathers around as her house-hold—Ito the Japanese manservant, Norah the Irish Maid, and O'Banion the Irish poet—Agnes Gooch is nothing if not modest, unprepossessing, and Brooklynesque. Needing a substitute to send with Brian to a dinner with Warner Brothers, Mame decides to transform Agnes from a geek to a lady. Removing Agnes's glasses and clothing and plying her with alco-hol (which Agnes says makes her a "different girl"), Mame enlists Ito and Norah to set out the makeup and clothes by which Mame will take "the sow's ear" and turn her into a "silk purse" acceptable to the opportunis-tic Brian. Mame's Gooch-girl project demonstrates the elements through which femininity is constructed and shows that this construction re-quires the cooperation of a variety of disparate characters: the delighted Ito (who says he'll be "Charlie of the Ritz"), the dubious Norah, and not least, the snobbish Brian. It also has its own queer import; when Mame is literally undressing Agnes and exclaims that she "does have a bust" and pretty eyes, Agnes stops and says, "I don't have a very clear picture of what's going on."

After Mame rushes Agnes upstairs in a flurry of canted camera shots accompanied by chants of "live, live, live," first Ito, then Norah, then Mame descend the stairs in anticipation of the now-transformed Agnes, who can't see and who doesn't know how to hold herself up in high heels and tight strapless gown. Mame orders her to hold her stomach in, to stick her chest out, and to put her chin up, and Agnes descends to regal mu-sic, falling the last few steps where the spiral staircase turns. The impe-tus of the entire episode is toward the production of an obviously bogus feminine masquerade worn precariously by Agnes, who, as Mame ex-claims, tapping into a wealth of vastly different connotations, is "com-ing out." But this deliberate production of feminine masquerade does not only turn on getting rid of Agnes's glasses and orthopedic shoes or im-proving her posture as she descends the staircase; it also requires that Mame suggest to Brian that Agnes comes from a wealthy banking fami-ly, an intimation that instantly turns the clumsy and myopic Agnes into a feminine ideal.

Mame's reconstruction of Agnes as a lady shows not only that femininity is very much a construction and that its terms extend well beyond the body but also that attending that site of construction is a fairly disorganized panoply of differences, here defined in ethnic and class terms but already not necessarily aligned with social or gender stereotype. If we penetrate the veneer of femininity as a desirable construction for Agnes (which it probably isn't because it leads straight to pregnancy), what we find is that all femininity is contrived and, more interesting, that when it is contrived a disorganized and perverse *différance* comes into view. We see the scurrying Norah and Ito, temporality is disturbed and elided, the screen is filled with frantic and directionless movement, and the camera is canted and disoriented. But shifting to the geek as the object of transformation signals a shift from locating potential instability in the main characters' class or gender to displacing this instability into the variety from which it already seems to emanate—from *différance* itself. This displacement of instability is about neither liberalism nor insight but is defensive. As we shall see, it is a way to disarm *différance* altogether and reestablish an insidious sameness in its place.

Agnes's openly manufactured femininity is a tool for fighting off regimentation and the imperatives of sexual difference in the film as Mame uses Agnes's feminine masquerade as a way not only to protect herself from the lascivious Brian but also as a way she can be present to protect her nephew Patrick from the insidious charms worked on him by the same kind of contrived femininity—that of his wooden, snobbish, metaphorically blind, wealthy fiancée, Gloria. Femininity is an openly constructed decoy or ruse that, by consciously imitating petty dominant cultural caricatures, draws attention away from both Mame's own unquestioned and questionable femininity and from her ulterior motive of preserving the marginal, humane, teeming, heterogeneous bohemian world that has defined her persona. Mame deploys the constructedness of femininity not only with Agnes but also with herself as a way to lure attention away from and thus preserve a more threatening, joyful, and emancipated existence that can survive only in the margins and underneath the veneer of a false ideal.

In preparing for her first meeting with Dwight Babcock, Patrick's trustee, Mame decides she needs to have a "Madonna" look, complete with a "halo" made of a braided switch. In consultation with Vera, Mame is deliberate about the relation between how she presents herself and the impression she wants to make. Manipulating quite openly conventional versions of femininity, Mame calculates not only what version of femininity is appropriate but also how to construct her appearance and behavior so as to produce the correct impression. All this production is in contradistinction to her hangover and to the comically unfeminine gymnastics necessary to becoming feminine as she wildly tries to braid her switch with one end of it in her mouth. Mame's self-presentation to Babcock is drolly calm and demure in comparison to the frantic panic of its preparation.

Because Mame is able to construct herself variously as hostess, Madonna, actress, working girl, southern belle, high society dame, and widow, femininity clearly becomes a wieldable tool that has very little basis in biology or personality. If, on the heels of McCarthyism, *Auntie Mame* provides a comically cynical exposé of femininity's contingency and through this the possibility that sexual difference is unstable, it also shows that masculinity and patriarchy themselves are equally constructed, unstable, and untrue. What Mame worries about throughout the film is that Patrick will be constructed in the wrong version of both masculinity and patriarchy (and such also were the fears of his father that Mame would pervert Patrick from good old-fashioned patriarchal ways)—that Patrick will emerge under the tutelage of Babcock as a priggish, conservative bore (which he almost does). The varied influences of his childhood and the diversity of Mame's household are hedges against narrow notions of propriety, racism, and conventionality. Because *Auntie Mame* is already in the minor register, its contemplation of gender as a construction or the purposes to which it is wielded are not surprising. This constructedness, however, works as comedy rather than calculation or manipulation precisely because the film is already set in a world of disorganized variety— of *différance* as a foundational condition of human existence.

The crucial tertiary character in *Auntie Mame* is Ito, the servant who anticipates Mame's needs, approves her plots, and can take on any of a number of roles from valet to chauffeur to collaborator in Mame's ruses. Ito is a Western stereotype of an Asian male, vaguely feminized, often associated with women's clothing as he carries dresses, undresses the inebriated Vera, and delights in Gooch's makeover. Ito is not imaged as a manly man like Babcock or Lindsey Woolsey, nor as a servant does he operate in the world of public affairs. Instead he announces and enables private affairs; one of his first lines in the film is "Madame having affair now," referring to the cocktail party going on around him. Ito is the operational part of Mame; his exoticism adds to the variety of Mame's menage but also, along with his apparent joy in service, distracts from the ways Mame's pleasures are enabled and supported by her staff and the racism of Ito's characterization. In many ways Ito stands in for the men who are absent in Mame's life; like nephew Patrick, Ito is a child man who does not threaten mastery but nonetheless provides a pretext for Mame's mastery interpreted as open-mindedness. Ito's quasifeminine rendition augments Mame's own femininity. Not too feminine in a traditional sense, Mame's various feminine masquerades are aided by contrast with Ito and with the more masculine Norah, who acts as the household's grumpy old man. Ito also stands for all the varied racial differences absent in the film, which are displaced into a vaudeville of quirkily talented characters and figures of different nationalities (none of the others are black or Asian). Racial and national differences, represented by Ito, are domesticated into a variety that enables Mame to sample Hinduism along with "natural food" and eat caviar out of a carved-ice Buddha. This domestication situates all diversity not only as Mame's energetic arrangement but also at her service. On one hand, at least *Auntie Mame* presents diversity during a point of rigid suspicion in American history; on the other, it is clear that Mame is the great cultural imperialist. But finally, its overt play of *différance*, like *Pillow Talk*'s overt masquerade, recaptures difference for the white bourgeoisie—as its hobby, as its plaything, and as nothing dangerous at all.

Tiny Echoes

This *différance*, signaled by a tertiary character and made overtly operational by the combination of tertiary and secondary, is actually grounded in the literal play of a fourth term—children—whom we probably notice even less than we do tertiary characters such as Lottie and Ito. The very young, the very old, the nonwhite—anyone not in the white bourgeois mating pool—serve as voices of truth, caution, and insight, and like tertiary black characters, they signal the potential visibility of *différance*. However, they do so by repeating on a different scale the character of the relationships already outlined between the protagonist and the female comic second. Ito and Lottie (with her childlike voice) function as hybrid servant children—as sort prefools; actual children with their unsexed status and "innocent" inquiries are inadvertently wise fools. The "out of the mouths of babes" license children have for speaking directly aligns them with the fool side of the equation. For example, little Mary from *The Women* questions her parents' silly actions and adds moments of necessary common sense. Mame's Patrick keeps her on an even keel until he threatens to become too "even" for her taste. Tomboy Kay (Jo Ann Marlowe), Mildred Pierce's younger daughter (in many ways the most blissful character in the film) brings both Mildred's and Veda's pretensions into perspective long before Mildred meets Ida (who in some ways takes Kay's place when Kay dies). Kay, who according to her father is "twice the girl that Veda is and always will be," is a fresh, unpampered, happy child who plays with kids in the street and is a no-nonsense, wisecracking observer of her sister's airs. In the first scene in which Kay appears, we see her from the back as she is bent over to hike a football on the street (and she hikes the football directly toward the film's audience). She tackles the ball carrier before going to the sidewalk to join prissy Veda, who is walking home from school. Veda tells her, "You act like a peasant" and her answer is, "Ah pretzels, what do I care?" When Veda tells her that she'll care when she gets interested in boys, Kay responds, "I got over that when I was eight."

Kay is indeed a precursor to Ida and a fool figure in her own right; she is Veda's Ida. Hermaphroditic, plain-spoken, open, and ingenuously charming, Kay is well aware of who she is. When Mildred exclaims over the condition of Kay's clothes, Kay answers, "I know. I know. I shoulda been a boy." When Kay accompanies Veda upstairs to try on a new dress, Kay comments on Veda's figure:

Kay: You ought to do something about your sit-down.
Veda: What's wrong with it?
Kay: Sticks out.
Veda: It's the dress. It's awful cheap material. I can tell by the smell.
Kay: What do you expect? Want it inlaid with gold?
Veda: Well, it seems to me if you're buying anything, it should be the
    best. This is definitely not the best.
Kay: Oh quit, you're breaking my heart.

Deflating Veda's vanity and her arrogance, Kay moors the conversation in common sense, providing a perspective on Veda that is similar to the audience's. But in this scene with Veda and Kay, there is an even more subtle commentary on Veda that breaks down even further Veda's class pretensions and shows the role of these small-scale comic seconds. While Veda is trying on her ruffled dress in front of a mirror, Kay is sitting on a bed, playing with a black doll with pickaninny pigtails. Just as Veda adjusts her dress and complains, Kay somewhat unconsciously adjusts the doll's dress. The very subtle comparison between Veda and the pickaninny doll made through the medium of Kay echoes the connections later between Mildred and Lottie and among the four women. The presence of the specifically black doll encapsulates the complex power relations telegraphed through the presence of a black character as an ambivalent site of contrast and a symptom of the fragility of categories.

What this scene suggests is that Mildred's relationship to Veda (almost courtly service) is the opposite of Kay's relationship to the doll (absent-

Veda (Ann Blythe) and Kay (JoAnn Marlowe) in *Mildred Pierce*

minded care) but that Kay's relationship to Veda is the same as her relationship to the doll. If we transpose this scene onto the birthday party
scene at the end of the film—where Ida replaces Kay and Lottie replaces
the doll—Mildred's relationship to Veda is again the opposite of Ida's relationship to Lottie, but Ida's relationship to Veda is the same as her relationship to Lottie. In both scenes, Mildred is literally not present; in both
scenes Veda occupies the background left side of the frame (the side of
trouble). What this almost mathematical comparison suggests is that Veda
and Lottie (doll) occupy a similar position of object in relation to Ida/Kay;
that this relationship is reversed between Mildred and Veda, suggesting
that Veda regards Mildred as an object (a Lottie, a doll), especially as she
dressed Lottie in Mildred's uniform; and that Mildred needs Ida/Kay to
relate properly to Veda. Clearly, both Ida/Kay and Lottie/doll are necessary to provide the appropriate model, to enable and mediate a more suit-
able relationship between Mildred and Veda. Unfortunately, their mediation fails as Veda becomes a selfish, superficial social climber and killer.

Kay's screen presence is magnetic; for a very minor character, Kay is
very compelling. But Kay is the film's sacrifice. As Mildred begins her restaurant career and begins to date Monte, Kay gets pneumonia and dies.

This may well foreshadow the tragedy of Mildred's course, but it also suggests that the natural and unprepossessing is killed by ambition and the desire to become what one is not. But that Kay seems replaced by the adult version of the tomboy, Ida, suggests that only one such character can persist (but that there needs to be one), and Ida becomes the composite of the best friend and ignored dead daughter who still vainly tries to preserve Mildred from the imperious demands of the selfish and superficial Veda.

In another scene early in *Mildred Pierce,* Kay and Veda perform a mock nightclub act, which not only foreshadows Veda's later nightclub career but also pokes fun at the kind of femininity such display requires. Dressed in a tablecloth and a turban and with makeup smeared across her face, Kay sings and dances a mocking version of a tropical song. This is similar to a scene in *Philadelphia Story* (1940) involving Virginia Weidler, where as Dinah, the imperious Tracy Lord's (Katharine Hepburn) younger sister, she performs another mocking song designed to make the interloping reporters from *Spy* magazine (Jimmy Stewart and Ruth Hussey) believe that the wealthy Lords are very idiosyncratic. In both cases, the performance of the song is precocious but also a parody of adult dilemmas. Like nonwhite characters, children can mock; presumed to be either innocent or ignorant, they are the *enfants terribles,* the fools who unknowingly utter wisdom beyond their capacity. As innocent, they are not quite like Ida or Stella, who are quite conscious and deliberate in their commentary. The inadvertence of nonwhite or child parody or commentary displaces its source to those who receive it—not those in the world of the film who seem unable to penetrate the status of the speaker, but the audience, who can perceive the truth and applicability of what these characters say even when the primary characters don't.

Just as the tertiary black character both negotiates difference and figures the collapse into (or emergence of) *différance* in dynamic combination with the secondary character, so these children and other fool figures negotiate the distribution of knowledge. With secondary fool figures, the primary tension and locus of identification is dramatic irony, where the audience, like the secondary fool figure, knows more than the characters. In other words, knowledge is distributed unevenly between audience and the diegetic world of the film, and the secondary fool figure mediates the two in a conscious and almost deliberate way, saying to the characters what the audience might like to say and signaling to the audience that the diegetic film world is not entirely blind. The deliberateness of this action makes the secondary character an operator, one who wields a certain amount of epistemological power as it makes knowledge itself a signifier of both power and frustration because its distribution is deliberate (and not accidental or serendipitous).

The presence of tertiary and more minor fool figures reduces this knowledge and power dynamic to a minor key, where truth becomes something available to all—even the smallest child—and insight is natural and innocent instead of calculated and withheld. The inadvertent fools are safety valves in the tensions of dramatic irony. They let escape as if by accident, truths the other characters can't see. Little Mary in *The Women* certainly functions as the innocent incarnation of wisdom as her common-sense observations provide the information necessary to end Crystal's reign. Kay commences a critique of Veda that leads the audience in its estimation of her character, easing us into the frustrating problem of Mildred's blindness toward this daughter and suggesting a deflating approach no other characters in the film take. Kay's common-sense wisdom is reiterated in Ida, but with Ida's self-consciousness, such wisdom takes the less edenic form of indirect barbs and wisecracks that signify the level of tension and frustration Veda's adult behavior produces. Kay and Ida are not doubles, although they occupy similar positions in the structural relation between the female characters; they are different versions of the same function, and are interdependent, Kay paving the way for Ida (and vice versa because Ida actually appears on screen first) and Ida continuing Kay's place. Kay's innocent insight enables Ida's adult perspicacity; Kay's open tomboyishness culminates in Ida's hermaphroditism.

The tertiary and minor secondary characters are thus parts of both the field of *différance* and the dynamic that produces and secures the primary and secondary characters. Their visual differences in age, size, gender, and race provide both contrast and the constitutive difference at the heart of appearances. For if Mildred appears to be a successful white woman, she is at heart also a lower-class failure. If Mary Haynes is a noble white society matron, she is at heart also a vindictive child. But more even than this metaphorical difference or self-contradiction is the difference against which these central characters define themselves: the lower class, less solidly feminine characters who surround them. Thematic self-contradiction makes these primary characters interesting, but the more radical differences that produce them are foundational and omnipresent, appearing symptomatically as tertiary characters, children, fools, and the like.

The Trouble Ain't with the Turkey, Mr. Jim

The character of foundational omnipresence does shift as Hollywood relinquishes the studio system. Children and a black mammy play a key role in the transposition between the 1943 *Holiday Inn* and the 1954 *White Christmas*, one that echoes the shift from Mamie to Emma, from blackface to stylized minstrelsy, from the black servant to the geek, and from multiple holidays to a focus on Christmas (which is really a focus on the men's loyalty to a father figure), from multiplicity to a staunch singularity where the stability of the end is guaranteed by middling characters' obvious ability to manipulate *différance*. In *Holiday Inn*, Mamie (Louise Beavers) has two small children, Vanderbilt (Shelby Bacon) and Daphne (Joan Arnold). The children, who appear as the Old and the New Year at the New Year's Eve party and who also sing a portion of the "Abraham" emancipation song, participate in a recurring bit with their mother around the question of identity and proper place. When Linda arrives at the inn to seek a job and ends up buried in a snowdrift with Jim, Mamie enters, followed by her two children. When Mamie turns and sees the children following her, she asks them, "Is your names Mamie?" Answering "no," they back up a couple of steps and continue to follow her. Jim asks Mamie to take Linda upstairs for dry clothes. As Mamie shepherds Linda, the two children follow and Mamie again turns to them and asks, "Is your name Miz Linda?" They answer "no" and fall back, only to follow again after a few seconds.

This comic repetition at first seems to function as a way to remind the children of their place and to gently chastise them for being nosy. But the question of who they are not is more than a loving rebuke. The place of the children, linked to their very names, is a question of proper social place. Their unwillingness to stay where their mother thinks they belong is a symptom of social displacement throughout the film, a displacement that works finally as a way to locate and settle into the proper place figured through the literal but minor out-of-placeness of the black children. What Daphne and Vanderbilt do wrong is attempt to go places beyond the confines of the kitchen, to enter a society beyond the aspirations of black children. But that is the problem with everyone in the film, except Mamie (who also steps out of her place to talk sense into Jim, even though such out-of-placeness is exactly her place). Jim, a successful entertainer, wants to be a farmer, which he is terrible at. Lila, who was engaged to Jim, wants wealth and show business fame, so she goes with Ted. Linda, who comes to Jim's inn on a tip from Danny, is "discovered" by Ted and goes on tour with him, even though her heart is really with Jim. Lila marries a Texas millionaire, only to find him a fake. These social displacements and misled ambitions are paralleled by the film's slapstick physical comedy of misdirection as Jim hides Linda from Ted by steering Ted down the wrong hall, locking him into rooms, and attempting blackface masquerade.

Mamie sets all this indirection right when she tells Jim what's wrong with him over his uneaten Thanksgiving dinner.

> Mamie: The trouble ain't with the turkey, Mr. Jim. It's you. Why you close the inn and sit around like a jellyfish with the misery? Cause some city slicker stole your gal and you ain't got fight enough to get her back. Excuse me. (*She giggles when recognizing how far she has stepped over the line*). What kind of keepin' is that? Nothin' but tricks. If you went to Hollywood and told Miss Linda how much you loves her and misses her and told her that the way a lady likes to hear it told, I'll bet you she'd be the quickest ex-movie star that ever exed.
> Jim: You're crazy, Mamie.
> Mamie: I'm crazy? I knows Miss Linda. I knows her like I know my own kids. Why she ain't the fancy type no more'n you are. What she wants is what you got right here. You could melt her heart right down to butter, if you'd only turn on the heat.

Voicing what the film audience already knows about Linda, Mamie sets Jim right at the film's denouement, but such common-sense knowledge can come only from a mammy character with her intimate license to speak. Because Mamie has already demonstrated her acute knowledge of proper place with her children, she is the appropriate person to police others' propriety. And because Mamie is a mammy, it is her job to effect such policing within the household before deviations cause trouble outside. Her question to Jim is really something like, "Is your name Ted?" And of course, she is right about Linda, who is happy to be rescued by Jim on the Hollywood set dressed to look just like his Connecticut farm house as she embarks on a film based on his inn. This metacinematic moment at the end of *Holiday Inn* multiplies the problem of proper place because if Jim takes show business to the farm, show business takes the farm to Hollywood, and the only distinctions possible are those that Mamie makes and can make because she has both racial and class difference and because she knows how to differentiate. But despite its happy ending and solid class ordering, *Holiday Inn* is steeped in a politics of disruption and displacement—Linda, Lila, and Ted's unexpected appearances at the inn, Jim's musical sabotage—that its narrative never quite overcomes.

Michael Curtiz's 1954 partial remake of *Holiday Inn*, *White Christmas*, certainly does overcome displacement by shifting the entire problem of the film from a question of proper place in a somewhat confused fatherless world to a project of oedipal reverence in a world that gravitates inevitably toward the father in his snowless Vermont ski lodge.

Moored by Bob's (Bing Crosby) and Phil's (Danny Kaye) experiences in World War II, *White Christmas* is more centered than *Holiday Inn*. Bob and Phil seem to have grown up from Jim and Ted, no longer fighting over the same girl or getting unmanageably drunk (as Ted does). Instead of being traveling performers, Bob and Phil are successful producers, headline entertainers with power and influence. Instead of philandering Bob's girlfriends, Phil tries to procure one for him. Both men have become insecure with women and much more comfortable with each other, functioning as a couple with their easy familiarity, awareness of the other's habits, and attempts to trick the other into doing what is good for them. Because the women are going north to Vermont, Phil persuades Bob to follow and have a vacation in the ski lodge where they are entertaining, only to find that the lodge is owned and operated by the favorite commanding officer, General Waverly, who, as Phil observes, has become a "janitor." From the moment the two men spot the general, the impetus of the film is to rescue him from the ignominy of a bad investment, which Bob and Phil do by bringing the entire division to the inn in a big Christmas reunion, topped, of course, by a generous snowfall.

White Christmas is no longer about the son's proper place, as in *Holiday Inn*, but about the father's. In this openly oedipal scenario where the men pay homage to their symbolic father, Emma, the housekeeper and Mamie replacement, functions as the safety valve for all potentially negative observations about the general, preempting any criticism from beyond the family circle by making it first herself. When Bob and Phil ask how the general got the inn, she responds, "He got it in a shrewd business move," as she hands the general the garbage to take out. When the girls ask her whether she can talk the general into paying them only half salary, she says, "Not Lighthorse Harry. Advance, advance. He's advancing himself right into bankruptcy." She calls the inn a "Tyrolean haunted house" and says they are using the ski tows to hang out laundry.

But Emma also worships the general, hovering behind him in almost every scene. In fact, she acts much like a wife but with a little too much masculinity. When the general tells her, "I get along fine on my own without you," she tells him, "It took 15,000 men to take my place." She holds the chair while Betty is sitting down and stands, just as the general does, like a maitre d' in the inn dining room. Emma's tall, gawky appearance, her wry witticisms, her taking the privilege of speaking, and her lovingly belittling remarks about the general certainly reflect the perspective of a masculine character overly endowed with a servant figure's common sense. But Emma's observations are less aligned with audience knowledge than Ida's and function more to preempt any criticism of the general. In one of the few moments of dramatic irony in the film, when Emma hears only part of Bob's telephone conversation, the audience knows more than Emma. She functions less like a fool figure (Mamie is more of one) than as the comic hermaphroditic figure who tends the general and the couples with the avidity of a sheepdog. She and the general (a homosexed couple like Bob and Phil) even have a "daughter," Susan, the general's granddaughter, a dutifully lifeless teenager who fills out the familial triangle. Where Daphne and Vanderbilt always wanted to go beyond their place, Susan is the model of the demure, bland place-keeper whose role is to stabilize (like the third leg of a tripod) whatever is unstable in the three pairs. It is not as if her absence would make things fall apart, however; her complete docility is a pale echo of Mamie's nice but curious offspring.

Mamie emerged from her place to tell Jim his and thus solve the romance problem of *Holiday Inn;* Emma, the geek, causes problems by not quite knowing hers. Mamie is comforting, but Emma is a thorn in the side, precisely because she knows neither her place nor her gender. Emma does act true to her housekeeper type (which like a mammy with less intimacy still goes out of place to police behaviors), eavesdropping on phone conversations and inadvertently causing a rift between Bob and Betty that is healed later by chance. Hearing only a part of Bob's telephone conversation with a television variety show host, Emma jumps to the conclusion that Bob and Phil are going to humiliate the general to get free publicity for their show. When she tells this to Betty and offers the disappointed adage "Stick your nose into other peoples' business, find out things you wish you hadn't," Betty takes advantage of an invitation to perform in New York and leaves the show. Only by helping Phil and Judy keep the general away from the television broadcast does Emma undo her damage, which is in fact undone by Betty's watching the show in New York. The film ends with hundreds of soldiers at the inn, performing a show in honor of the general, who is further blessed by a healthy snowfall.

The shift from Mamie to Emma is a symptom of a shift from chaos and heterogeneity to oedipality and sameness. The 1940s film permits a much wider range of racial, class, and gender differences signified almost prosaically by the fact that it has a full range of holidays. The 1950s film closes down racial (and holiday) variety to a species of homogeneity. The impetus of *White Christmas* is toward sameness: Bob and Betty resemble one another, as do Phil and Judy and all of the white, faceless soldiers who come to honor the father. Class is no longer an issue (somehow hundreds of white men can afford to travel and bring their families to resort hotel at Christmas without difficulty). In this economy of same organized around the oedipal, Emma, the female man, the equivalent of the black mammy, is her functional opposite, eliding difference, whereas Mamie, even if she ultimately supports a white hegemony, presents the image of an omnipresent racial and social difference.

But what does this move from heterogeneity marked by the presence of the black mammy character to a homogeneity mean? Is it a McCarthyesque retreat into the security of a white oedipal sameness undisturbed by the small breaches of category that characterized earlier films (even directed by Curtiz)? Does it represent a nostalgia for a fantasmatic white homosociality that obliterates the reality of social unrest, the burgeoning civil rights movement, and the insecurities of the cold war? *White Christmas* has no looseness, no play of category. Its only moment of gender play comes in the drag scene early in the film in which Bob and Phil roll up their pants, tie bows on their heads, and wield the girls' sky-blue ostrich feather fans while lip-synching to a recording of "Sisters." Although in these post–*Gender Trouble* years one might be tempted to argue that such drag shows the constructed nature of femininity and gender in general, I suggest that in *White Christmas*, this drag, which is easily penetrated and shows both men's resident femininity (Phil's more than Bob's), secures the regime of homosociality that governs not only Bob and Phil's relationship with one another but relationships between all the main characters in the film. The film is dominated by figuratively "same-sex" couples: Bob and Phil, Betty and Judy, and General Waverly and Emma. Furthermore, Bob, Betty, and the general line up as versions of the same (the stoic commanders), as do Phil, Judy, and Emma (the manipulative busybodies). So, at the end, when Bob pairs off with Betty and Phil pairs off with Judy, what they have done is pair off with homologues. They may look like heterosexual couples, but their pairing still follows the film's ineffable logic of sameness.

One could argue that the seeming irrelevance of biological sex in this homosocial scheme undoes gender categories quite effectively. In *White Christmas* there is no guarantee that sex and gender will match, which disrupts the sex and gender system even if it doesn't show gender's constructedness. One might go so far as to claim that the film is quite queer in seeming to endorse same-sex couples. This might be the case if the occasional misalignment between sex and gender produced anything other than that same old homosocial sameness that already underwrites patriarchy. The secondary and tertiary characters of *White Christmas* simply do not lead to any moments in which the category of white middle-class American masculinity is not secure. In this context, Emma, whose hermaphroditism might bring categories into question, actually figures the cycling between same sex and gender that typifies the film, organizing both masculinity and femininity in literal service to the master. Emma embodies and contains any threatening gender and class slippage that might be imputed to the film's couples.

So what happens between 1942 and 1958 is that blackness as a mediating term is elided and displaced into other registers of difference— the geekiness of Gooch and Emma, the Asian Ito—in a general move from a flirtation with *différance* through *Mildred Pierce* to the resounding reassertion of white bourgeois patriarchy in *White Christmas* to *Auntie Mame*'s thematizing of heterogeneity as an eccentric and superficial hobby. If the minor has been made major in Auntie *Mame,* threatening *différance* has also been domesticated under the guise of the domestic servant. The danger of the extracategorical has been tamed by cocktail parties and by an artful homogenization that casts that very same bourgeois homosocial patriarchy as the enemy of a variety that has become the avocation of the wealthy. *Auntie Mame* thus dramatizes the colonization of *différance* and the disappearance of the sidekick and the third wheel from their crucial roles in Hollywood film, ushering in a new era of ensemble comedy, superficiality, and chained variety that take the place of old Hollywood's deeper structures and more profound symptoms of disturbance. To resort again to the surface versus depth model, if *différance* was the covert secret of the 1940s' openly patriarchal films, then films in which difference seems to occupy the surface are certain to be patriarchal to the core. The flip-flop in the deployments of secondary and tertiary characters and *différance* in general is part of a way to revivify the father, who, like *White Christmas*'s general, is certainly dying and needs all the help he can get. The appearance in the late 1950s, 1960s, and 1970s of ensembles of caricatured minor characters in everything from *Auntie Mame* to *M*A*S*H* may seem to herald a new liberalism but may just as well work to secure an order that is already lost and is no longer secure enough to withstand an Eve Arden or a Thelma Ritter, who are relegated in the 1960s to less aggressive roles. Ritter died in 1969, Arden played fewer parts (seven between 1960 and 1982), and Mary Wickes became the geeky second par excellence, performing in eleven films and innumerable television shows.

But even that is a predictable analysis. The 1960s' and 1970s' realignment of secondary and tertiary characters as multiple versions of some random and quirky diversity, as in *Auntie Mame* but without its campy sensibility, reveals the end of the surface versus depth metaphor, where all becomes surface, and the differences that produced and occupied depth become simply accessories, elements of a variety that is neither perverse nor a detour but is more like a commodity variety that seems level all on the surface. This also suggests that somehow the chaotic middle itself has also disappeared, replaced by a chaos redistributed through the entire story that no longer works as a site of genuine disarray but only the simulacrum thereof to cover an ever more secure homogeneously oedipal foundation that has not been shaken but only reorganized and remasked.

The middle, then, seems to have spread, becoming deeper and wider. But what has overtaken the edges is not a real middle but its simulation as variety and choice. If the "inside" middle is now outside, what is inside? What produces the tensions of narrative? When the stuff of the middle is valorized—when variety is a visibly operative part of the text— narrative works through rearrangement rather than revelation. This is as true in *The Women* as it is in *White Christmas* and *Auntie Mame.* The difference between earlier and later versions of this narrative is that the middle itself shifts from being a covert and artfully revealed characterological *différance,* as in *Stage Door* and *Mildred Pierce,* to the potentials of temporal or spatial mistiming. The middle becomes unpeopled and instead is a site for structural misdirections that derive from failures in the circulation of knowledge. *Auntie Mame* illustrates the pleasures occasioned by the knowing control of misdirection; *White Christmas* and *Pillow Talk* derive their middling tensions from serial misunderstandings. Although this might suggest that classical Hollywood fool figures such as Ida and Stella should be even more important, it actually shows what their disappearance enables (or even what sparks their obsolescence). With no one to distribute knowledge, knowledge becomes the problem. Narrative shifts to the realm of epistemology (or an epistemology of epistemologies) from the realm of organizing chaos, event, and *différance,* and the audience is hailed as the fool.[7]

5   From Sidekick to Associate

Variety Pack

The 1991 film *Soapdish* spoofs two television institutions: the serial drama and the ensemble cast. Literalizing the adages that life follows art and truth is stranger than fiction, *Soapdish* parodies the calculated plotting, histrionic celebrity, and media tie-ins that make it less and less possible to discern the differences between media, commodity, life, plot, television, and film. Its parody of the soap opera format makes comic a forty-year truism about television's serial quality. The interactions between the film's ensemble cast—a large and varied company far from the economical five- or six-player focus of classical Hollywood—parodies the ensemble as the idiosyncratic variety pack soap opera and sitcom casts had become. Within its parody, *Soapdish* provides one sterling, hyperbolically wise, almost traditional secondary character in the figure of Rose Schwartz (Whoopi Goldberg), the soap's head writer, star's best friend, and prime manipulator. A reminder of Hollywood's glory days, the character of Rose with her improbable layerings of identity (black woman with a Jewish name) demonstrates the evolution of the female comic second from wise (cracking) white buddy to wise black (or other visibly marked as "diverse") persona. Like her predecessor female comic secondary characters, Rose evades class and sometimes gender and sexual categorization and wields a magical power and savvy beyond the immediate comprehension of the plethora of one-gag stereotypes that people the scene. She represents a hybrid of the conventional Hollywood female second with the racially diverse tertiary figure in a system governed by variety instead of structured through class, gender, and racial hierarchies.

Goldberg's version of the female comic second evolves through the primordial brew of television as its various forms—the serial, the sitcom, the variety show, the ensemble cast show, and the celebrity guest show—rebound into Hollywood filmmaking. Characters such as those played by Goldberg reappeared in the 1980s after the female comic second faded from Hollywood cinema in the 1960s. With the advent of television, secondary character types became stars both in television, as with Eve Arden's success with *Our Miss Brooks,* and in Hollywood films, as Rosalind Russell's performance in *Auntie Mame* illustrates. As a stock film character type, female comic seconds disappear into the ensemble cast (again as they do in *Auntie Mame*) to reemerge thirty years later transformed into composite figures whose marginality is figured on the body but whose roles are more powerful and central. The temporary disappearance of the female comic second can be explained in terms of television's formulas and Hollywood's shifts in genre; her reappearance in the 1980s occurs via the redistribution of power within ensembles, a redistribution that correlates with the celebrity of figures who mark themselves as marginal, contradictory, and comic, such as Goldberg, Ellen DeGeneres, Carrie Fisher, Mary Kay Place, and Kathy Najimy, actresses who are known as much for their standup comedy, screenwriting, and cartoon voices as they are for their screen appearances. As before, female comic second-ness is linked to particular actresses, but the signs of secondary wisdom change from being lower class, independent, and narratively perverse to being smart, physically different, or literally perverse—and young. As the narrative middle transforms into a veneer of variety and the middle's tensions become a matter of miscue, misdirection, and mistiming, the female comic second either disappears into the group or becomes even stronger and more central.

The shift in the qualities associated with female comic seconds is not merely a change in personae as aging stars make way for new faces. The reconfiguration of the female comic second is the result of large-scale cultural shifts to a commodity logic, the advent and popularity of television formulas, and shifts in race and gender relations in the United States. That the female comic second reappears at all has as much to do with the tenacity of dramatic convention as it does with the compensations of particular configurations of power such as late capitalism and fading patriarchy in relation to which the female comic second begins to operate. If the classic Hollywood sidekick was a wise and comforting denizen of the figuratively middling and perverse, then the contemporary sidekick is a safety valve, a way for the energies of seeming rebellion and difference to expend themselves in the service of normativity. These new seconds provide a seeming example of escape and power in difference but end up being the channel through which a very liberal humanity triumphs. This is not to denigrate the humane but to suggest that the neo–comic second is a figure of liberalism in its attempts at inclusiveness and its David-like endeavors against various dehumanizing government, corporate, and class Goliaths. Such characters no longer figure the narrative middle but instead convey an outsideness, a sense that they have always been audience to a story in which they might appear only as interlopers from outside. This whiff of outsideness suggests both a shift in the nature of the female comic second and a shift in narrative itself. Narrative shifts from being a structure leading to a sense of closure and meaning to a big series of short, chained events or episodes that provide the appearance of openness and choice, which necessarily overwrite cultures where the illusion of choice alibis meaninglessness.

Television, the Ensemble, and the Sitcom

In the mid-1950s, as television gained impetus and as major studios began to lose their hold over the actresses, actors, and directors that had enabled the efficient production of film, some comic secondary film characters became television stars. The May 1948 decree in the case of *The United States v. Paramount Pictures* forced the studios to divest themselves of their vertically integrated systems of production studios, distribution companies, and chains of theaters; the decay of the system freed some contract personnel to pursue careers in other media. Although major stars were still tied to studio contracts that often constrained them from television appearances, more minor personalities (such as Eve Arden, Lucille Ball, Spring Byington, Phil Silvers) and vaudevillian radio stars who had had minor film careers (such as George Burns, Gracie Allen, and Jack Benny) quickly pursued starring careers in the new medium. While Hollywood suffered from the zealous probings of the House Un-American Activities Committee, labor disputes, and antitrust suits, television technology, which had been waiting in the wings since the 1930s, was propelled forward by the postwar needs of the electronics industry, providing a new venue for a variety of shows including comic serials like those that had been broadcast since the 1930s on the radio.[1]

Part of the humor of 1950s sitcoms was the way they made visible

the popular radio serial peopled with minor Hollywood stars, capitalizing on the idiosyncratic personalities associated with the performers who
regularly played minor or comic characters in film. The reliable return
of the same humorous behaviors—Eve Arden's double take and snide
rejoinder, Lucille Ball's slapstick, Gracie Allen's "logic," Jack Benny's wry
understatement, Phil Silver's garrulous conniving—made television
shows weekly hits, drawing audiences who had enjoyed many of these
performers on screen and on the radio. The shows were mainly predictable; Gracie Allen acted true to Gracie Allen, Jack Benny continued his
stinginess, Lucille Ball turned the most routine tasks into comic disas-
ters, and Eve Arden remained the perpetual spinster. Still as economically
cast as 1940s films, television sitcoms of the 1950s imitated the character structures of Hollywood, but their short, serial format and reliance
on personality made the supporting cast more an ensemble of types than
active characters in their own right. Even if straight-"man" Vivian Vance
occasionally offered a resistant caveat or Rochester made an apt observation, television's sidekicks did not manifest the wise alterity of Hollywood's female comic seconds. In the television sitcom, there was no
longer any sense of a hidden middle or liminal space; all was up front,
and sidekick characters supported characters' foibles in a shorthand,
sometimes parodic manner. In his analysis of Jack Benny's servant Rochester, Alexander Doty shows the homosexual subtext subtending their
humor, and Vivian Vance's hamming of the supporting aspect of her role
was necessary to offset Lucille Ball's comic hyperbole (*Making* 63–79).
Part of this was because of sitcoms' far shorter format and live production. Part was also because audiences knew without any development
what the various roles of the characters were, so those roles could be
accomplished through a shorthand that permitted the show to focus on
the foibles of main characters—back to typage and *commedia dell'arte.*

Television's reliance on a supporting ensemble is reminiscent of films
such as *Stage Door* and *The Women* in which featured players stood out
against the texture offered by a varied but undeveloped backdrop of minor characters. However, it also represents a larger shift in both television and film in which the standout idiosyncrasy of Ritter and Arden is
transformed into a quirky ensemble where character interactions function much more as an exchange of detail and less as the elegantly dynamic
and repeated architecture of primary, secondary, and tertiary characters.
If the 1943 *Holiday Inn*'s evolution into the 1954 *White Christmas* meant
a shift from the scattered but delineated diversity of a show-biz apothe-
osis to the tired homogeneity of the dutifully oedipal sons, the shift from

1950s films to 1960s film and television was a move from a focus on a central oedipal (or familial or national) dilemma to the escapades of new sons, still under the sign of the father but accompanied by larger, more diverse and whimsical ensembles of minor characters that supplanted the wise fool. Superficial variety took the place of the more profound threats and challenges of the narrative middle and the perverse, becoming itself a version of the perverse where characteristics such as accent, body trait, and habit or behaviors that defy expectations (such as elderly women being mischievous scamps or men being effeminate) translate the perverse's threats of alterity into simple and totally demystified idiosyncrasy. Just as the geek (Emma, Agnes) supplants the politics of racial difference with a safe and homogeneous asexuality, so the ensemble takes the place of the singular fool, fragmenting and distributing the fool's qualities among many characters so that the fool's functions are fulfilled, not by one character with strength and an independent view but by a series of caricatures whose very lack of depth makes them more like comically functional furniture.

Television's episodic serial form—"in which one or more characters ran through the series, but each episode was complete in itself" (Barnouw 130)—is itself partly an effect of this shift in narrative as well as the source of some of the redistributions of the middle as variety. Although serials had existed almost since the advent of cinema, mostly as adventure series, and had been a regular and popular attraction of radio, television combined the visual with the serial and domestic. The sustained serial of the television soap opera became popular in the 1950s, and episodic serials began to appear in prime time; it is this form that finds it way back into film. Although the artistic hierarchy of screen and tube was still in place in the 1950s (and arguably still is today), television began to influence Hollywood in subtle ways, including crossovers in film style, narrative organization, stars, properties (such as Paddy Chayevsky's *Marty*, a 1953 teleplay made into an Oscar-winning film in 1955), and ultimately production as studios such as Fox, Warner Brothers, and Columbia began to make telefilms. By the 1960s both film and television style seemed subject to the vagaries of a very visually oriented pop culture that substituted a logic of commodity variety for the symmetrical economies of classical Hollywood. In addition, the 1960s shift toward youth culture as an exploitable market motivated film's deployment of the televisual forms familiar to the first generation that had grown up watching television. The rapid pace of episodic variety in film simulates television's integration of commercial and program in a thirty-minute format.

Where Did the Fool Go?

Post–TV era ensembles rendered the secondary more diverse and superficial, but the fate of the classical Hollywood wise fool secondary character is illustrated by the kinds of roles available to both Thelma Ritter and Eve Arden in the 1960s. Although both actresses were aging and thus moving into slightly different character categories, no younger actresses emerged to take the same kinds of roles. Sidekicks still existed, but, like Vivian Vance, they were no longer wise or perverse.

Arden appeared in only two films in the 1960s: *The Dark at the Top of the Stairs* (1960) and *Sergeant Deadhead* (1965). Ritter appeared in *The Second Time Around* (1961), a western starring Debbie Reynolds and Andy Griffith; *Birdman of Alacatraz* (1962), where she played the serious role of the prisoner's mother (and for which she garnered her sixth Academy Award nomination); *How the West Was Won* (1962); *For Love or Money* (1963), another mother role, this time as a comic matchmaker; *A New Kind of Love* (1963); *Move Over Darling* (1963), again with Doris Day; *Boeing Boeing* (1965); *The Incident* (1967); and *What's So Bad about Feeling Good?* (1968). Ritter still continued her comic secondary role in some films such as *Move Over Darling*, but these roles progressively disintegrated until she became the exhausted accomplice to Tony Curtis's ensemble of stewardess girlfriends in *Boeing Boeing*.

In *Move Over Darling*, a remake of Cary Grant's *My Favorite Wife* (1940) (and originally to have starred Marilyn Monroe), Ritter plays the exceedingly common-sensical mother to James Garner, whose wife (Doris Day) was lost in an airline crash in the Pacific. After being declared officially dead, Day returns home, revealing her presence to her mother-in-law, who immediately faints and then instructs Day to hasten to Monterey, where her husband is about to enjoy a honeymoon with his new wife. In this predictable comedy about preventing the consummation of a now-bigamous marriage, Ritter turns out to be the directing spirit that straightens things out as she finally has her son arrested for bigamy when he fails to inform his new wife of his other wife's return. Ritter is more in control in this film than she has been in others, functioning as a harbinger of the role the female comic second will come to occupy in the future.

Ritter's next role, in *Boeing Boeing*, illustrates the demise of the comic second figure she had been playing for so long. Ritter plays maid and factotum to a journalist, Bernard (Tony Curtis), working in Paris. His "routine" includes dating three different stewardesses from three different airlines (British United, Lufthansa, and Air France), taking advantage of their different schedules to make it appear as if he were the devoted—and monogamous—suitor to each. Ritter's duties include removing the previous girlfriend's clothing and effects and replacing them with those of the next arrival and keeping track of the nationalistic dietary regimens of each of the paramours (kidneys for British United, sausage and sauerkraut for Lufthansa, croissants for Air France). Given Ritter's performances in servant roles in the past where she was feisty and inevitably insightful, in *Boeing Boeing* she is surprisingly tired and whiny, complaining at every juncture, threatening to quit, and growling under her breath. Although at first this grumbling is comic, it becomes tiresome because it doesn't change until she finally walks out near the end of the film.

Part of the reason Ritter is so static and stale in this film is the film's repetitive structure, which is more like the repetitive catastrophes of *I Love Lucy* than the sustained architecture of a complex plot. Again, whether this episodic repetition is possible because of the model of television, is a feature of 1960s culture, manifests a shift in larger narrative structure, or all three, its effect is to eliminate the taut perverse functioning of an actress who had consistently played wise fool characters. *Boeing Boeing*'s comic premise is the Bergsonian situation of the human caught in the machine; Bernard is slave to airline timetables because for some reason he wants to date three women simultaneously (three identical blonde women who evince variety only through caricatured nationality). Because events are constantly moving, there is little time in the film for the moments of peace and reflection—or moments of alternative action—where the more traditional comic second operates. But there is also little sense of a larger world beyond the schedule machine. As in many formulaic sitcoms, there is no possibility of escape from the ludicrous dilemmas the characters devise, and it is exactly this outside or alternative and safe space comic seconds embody.

Bernard's routine is destroyed by the three airlines' acquisition of a newer, faster plane—a Boeing 707—which makes the stewardesses' schedules begin to conflict. In addition, one of Bernard's acquaintances, Robert (Jerry Lewis), arrives in Paris and moves temporarily into Bernard's apartment. Most of the film is thus the machine gone awry, and Bernard is kept busy preventing the various girlfriends from encountering each other and keeping Robert from taking off with one of the women. The constant repetition of the same potential catastrophe might provide an occasion for inventive intervention from a servant figure, especially if she is comic and savvy, but the film's automatonic, claustrophobic quality gives such a character no purchase, no alternative view to contribute, even though we might expect such a perspective from Ritter because of her performance in previous films. If Ritter were to act like the typical wisecracking comic second (as she did in *Rear Window*), the fragile fabric of *Boeing Boeing* would collapse because one word from the wise woman would demolish its absurd structure. Ritter's appearance works to present the illusion that *Boeing Boeing* is indeed a complex comedy, its inclusion of the fool a guarantee of its sophistication. But the feebleness of this nod toward an older, more intricate structure ends up revealing the film's serial poverty and one-dimensionality precisely through Ritter's static, reactive performance.

Boeing Boeing is the structural equivalent of the character ensemble typical in television and increasingly popular in film. Although it does not have a large and diverse cast (on the contrary, three indistinguishable blonde women, two brunette men, and Ritter), its redundant episodic plotting varies only slightly by the gag deployed to keep the women apart (e.g., taking one out to a restaurant, having one take a bath, having one take a nap, switching rooms). Each gag is analogous to a caricatured character, providing a seeming variety in repetition, demonstrating spectacularly the utter homogeneity of an impoverished set of ploys. In this brand of 1960s episodic comedy, perverse alternative has been subsumed into the plot repetition as variety rather than perversity.

Perverse Variety

Later in the 1960s and into the 1970s, the variety ensemble of characters began to enact a more perverse alternative. Not only did more traditional comic secondary characters begin to emerge on television shows (Rose Marie [Rose Marie] and Buddy [Morey Amsterdam] on *The Dick Van Dyke Show* [1961–66], Rhoda Morgenstern [Valerie Harper] on *The Mary Tyler Moore Show* [1970–77], and Endora [Agnes Moorehead] on *Bewitched* [1964–72]), but the variety ensemble itself began to function more perversely—that is, as a more eccentric counterpoint to the norm. But this structure transformed eccentricity into an alternative situated in opposition to normalcy. In comedies, thus, eccentricity became an oppositional antagonist.

One example of this is Endora, Samantha's witch mother on *Bewitched*. Her superhuman powers accounted for by her witchness, Endora appears mostly as a foil to the pretensions of the annoyingly human husband, Darren. What *Bewitched* makes clear is that the female comic second is indeed a different species and representative of a different and more powerful order. Henceforth, on television the wise fool figure is marked as ethnically, racially, or otherwise distinct from the other characters on the show.[2] Although *Bewitched* is not an ensemble comedy but more like the earlier *I Love Lucy* and *Donna Reed Show* with their economical casts centered around a domestic unit, *Bewitched*'s juxtaposition of worlds (the domestic and the domestic occult) spawns a wise fool whose role is to represent the enjoyment of species superiority while constantly being topped by the virtues of a very clumsy patriarchalism. Through Endora, *Bewitched* both valorizes the nuclear family and presents a glimpse of empowerment beyond.

The Mary Tyler Moore Show also presents a strong female comic second in the character of Rhoda Morgenstern. Focused around Mary Richards (Mary Tyler Moore), a single career woman trying to succeed at being a television producer, the show's ensemble includes her co-workers at the television station (a paternal boss, a wisecracking writer, and an inept newscaster) and her neighbor, Rhoda. Rhoda, marked as Jewish New York in Minneapolis, is the one who has Mary's ear when she's not at work, the one who gives Mary advice, can attack pretense, and is reminiscent of the single, snide comic fool of classical Hollywood. Rhoda contrasts with Mary's other neighbor, Phyllis (Cloris Leachman), a superficial, pretentious snob whom Rhoda loves to annoy. But Rhoda, like Endora but unlike Hollywood's wise fools, can never be more insightful than the show's star. Instead of representing what the audience knows (though to some extent such characters accomplish that in their observations about other characters), they contribute mainly a cynical viewpoint, often considered and rejected by a more naive star who continues to believe in the virtues of humanity.

The phenomenon of Rhoda in the early 1970s signaled the translation of the female comic second from Hollywood to television, but television never had the sense that Hollywood had had of the place and value of the female comic second. The popularity of these secondary characters on television (characters who were popular because they were secondary and played specifically minor roles) spurred networks to develop spinoff programs starring characters such as Rhoda in *Rhoda*. Unlike the successful *Our Miss Brooks*, where the writers had the sense not to let Constance Brooks get married (and hence continue her sideshow manners despite her stardom), Rhoda married in the first season. Being married or a star doesn't allow a secondary character type to function properly, especially if the show is trying to capitalize on just that quality. To make the show interesting, the writers first focused on the intriguing secondary character of her sister (Julie Kavner) and, when that didn't work, made Rhoda single again.

In the 1980s, the comic second was still marked as different until a couple of 1990s sitcoms revived a more traditional version of the Ida figure, made more prominent and more extreme but nearly as powerful. *Cybill* (1995–98), borrowed largely from Jennifer Saunders's British sitcom *Absolutely Fabulous*, presents a female duo as the focus of the show but reverses its comic valence from that of shows such as *I Love Lucy* and *The Lucy Show* or even *Rhoda* where the secondary character is pretty much a mildly comic dupe (although Julie Kavner in other contexts is a great secondary character). *Cybill*'s dynamic is more like that between Mary and Rhoda on *The Mary Tyler Moore Show*, except Christine Baransky has a much larger part. Although the plots tend to focus on the activities of the more mundane star, Cybill (Cybill Shepard), Maryann provides much of the character humor; her eccentricities in drink and dress (reminiscent of *Absolutely Fabulous*'s Patsy) and her sustained death wish for her ex-husband, Dick, provide a fertile ambiance in which everything becomes funny. Both Maryann and *Ab Fab*'s Patsy (Joanna Lumley) are depicted as astute practitioners of feminine masquerade, so much so that Patsy is mistaken for a drag queen when she visits New York. These two comic "seconds" are actually quite directive, both more assertive and influential than the shows' ostensible stars, but their knowledge does not produce any dramatic irony or site of epistemological identification because their knowledge seems to come from out of a drunken stupor. In fact, *Ab Fab* even satirized the couple's gendered roles as one morning Edina (Jennifer Saunders) acts like the wife to Patsy's husband, exclaiming, "Why can't I ever be the man?" This shift to the couple seems to bring to the fore the lesbian affinities of these pairs. Paradoxically, bringing a lesbian figuration into the open also dispels it on one level. By acknowledging what might have seemed like a secret discerned only by the clever viewer, the very acknowledgement of the coded lesbian dismantles it as something that might have been but because it is brought up isn't. At the same time, making visible a literal "perversity" indicates the ways in which perverse has become very much the subject of a surface variety rather than a site of chaos and transformation.

Television learned how to redeploy the female comic second, but it still hasn't quite learned that a secondary type cannot be a star unless the show exploits the secondary qualities for their own sake. The sitcom *Ellen* (1994–98) is a case in point. Starring Ellen DeGeneres, whose career as a standup comic had already established her as a secondary type, the show tried to find a way to locate that secondariness so that it would function as a center. The show was generally off center until the writers decided to make the character's lesbianism the show's known secret. The coming-out year enabled the show to situate Ellen in a position of middling uncertainty for almost an entire season, a position that proved to be the most successful of the series. Definitively announcing her sexual orientation returned *Ellen* to its former difficulties because its largely suggestive functional margin had been erased. And Ellen had become in effect a romantic heroine, a position that is deadly to a secondary character.

Increasingly in the 1990s openly queer—and mainly male—characters began to occupy the site of the comic secondary. What had operated as the perverse in Hollywood cinema became a literalized version of the perverse in 1990s sitcoms. Carter on *Spin City,* Josh on *Veronica's Closet,* Bob "Bulldog" Briscoe (Dan Butler) on *Frasier,* and Jack on *Will and Grace* are all versions of a secondary that instead of being peopled with wise fool figures is populated by literally queer males. This shift has everything to do with the change in the nature of narrative from metaphor (or sustained hierarchy) to metonymy (or variety organized serially). In a traditional metaphorical narrative, the middle in its chaos and confusion is feminized as the ground on which the ultimate decisive actions must be taken. The serial form of metonymical narrative transforms gender into sexuality as all *différance* becomes superficial and wisdom becomes parody.

Marginal Materfamilias

As television's site of the perverse is increasingly literalized (populated, for example, by openly gay men), and the ensemble continues its hold on television sitcoms, the figure of the female comic second in both film and television reappears as an almost mythical but still minor figure who hints at an alternative power and fronts an ensemble of types. Although superficially this redistribution does not seem to differ much from the workings of interrelated secondary and tertiary characters in Hollywood film, it lacks the elegant architecture of classical Hollywood's economy, merely disbursing the various roles, qualities, and foibles associated with the secondary among a broader group of characters whose functions are no longer determined solely by the social hierarchies of race, class, and age. At the same time, the female comic second is marked by some overt racial, ethnic, sexual, or physical difference that accounts for both her inclusion in the gang's variety and her marked power. The fool figure's more literal differences materialize her perverse force (or, in the case of the superficial seriality of episodic narrative, produce her as perverse), equating her with the imagined knowledge and efficacy otherwise attributed to sites marked by differences in sexuality (and sometimes ethnic or racial differences). This revivified fool has greater power because she has become other and therefore culturally marginal instead of being a representative sample of *différance* derived from the structural exigencies of the narrative middle.

The classical Hollywood female comic second embodied an eccentricity that threatened to make the story fall apart and represented an alternative that nonetheless worked in the service of the normative. In contrast, the more contemporary other is a different story altogether. Although there are various ways to understand the notion of the other—sartrean, lacanian, hegelian—the important distinction here is the difference between a perverse character who is not really different in any way but who threatens the possibility of deviation and the other who incarnates some difference in relation to which other characters define themselves. The perverse second of classical Hollywood negotiates similarities and differences (mainly class, gender, and sexual) that incarnate an already-digested form of alterity that helps define primary characters but does not function as any form of otherness (except class) against which those characters define themselves. The more contemporary version of the unassimilated other is the site of projections; she is stronger, wiser, and more patient than either the primary character or the ensemble. These strengths also lend these newer secondary characters an aura of unapproachability, peripherality, and selflessness covertly linked with maternity. They are also often connected to the Law as they embody order and sense, which also links them to the paternal. No longer perverse, the new female comic secondary character is a surrogate parent, the repository of common sense, repressed or sacrificial desire, and control. Her otherness is marked not only by physical or identity difference but also by her occupation of a role (such as writer, doctor, psychologist) that situates her as someone with the power to shape and diagnose.

In the comic atmosphere of *Soapdish*, Rose Schwartz (Whoopi Goldberg) is the female comic second who plods doggedly through the film's parodies of soap operas and ensembles to keep star Celeste (Sally Field) together while offhandedly engineering the return to a reformed nuclear family. Located on the set of the fictional soap opera *The Sun Always Sets*, *Soapdish* unwinds a soap-operatic layering of familial misrecognition, reunion, and revelation that extends comically into the lives of its stars. Soap heroine Celeste Talbert encounters her niece, Laurie Craven (Elisabeth Shue), who has gotten a bit part on the show. After the live revelation of their relationship, Laurie lands a recurring role. On a later show, Celeste reveals that Laurie is really her daughter, born out of wedlock. The success of these on-air disclosures catapults Celeste into even greater popularity, which frustrates producer David Barnes (Robert Downey Jr.), who is attempting to woo a minor but very ambitious actress, Montana Moorehead (Cathy Moriarty). Montana will allow Barnes's advances only if she becomes the show's star, so Barnes decides to submarine Celeste by rehiring her irritating ex-lover and co-star, Jeffrey Anderson (Kevin Klein), who, it turns out, is also Laurie's father. While Celeste energetically tries to prevent any romance between the blissfully ignorant Laurie and Jeffrey, Downey's efforts backfire as Celeste reveals Jeffrey's paternity on screen, and Rose takes the stage as a Viennese physician to reveal that Montana was formerly Milton.

Soapdish has an ensemble cast of idiosyncratic characters including Rose, *The Sun Always Sets*'s head writer; the show's horny casting director, Betsy Faye Sherrin (Carrie Fisher); hapless wardrobe assistant Tawny Miller (Kathy Najimy); the permanently scared director (Paul Johannson); a bank of writers that includes character actor Ben Stein; and the incisive network executive for daytime programming, Mr. Edwards (Garry Marshall). Rose is Celeste's best friend but also almost a supernatural power; she has the political sense to get along with David and the insight to know where and when events are transpiring. She is able to twist staff meetings away from David and get Mr. Edwards to go along with her without even seeming to try. She also seems to have a sense about how far one can push a script before it becomes total nonsense, objecting, for example, to David's revival of Jeffrey Anderson's character because his earlier departure from the show occurred because he had been decapitated in an auto accident.

Rose's competence and seeming omnipresence make her very much like the female comic seconds of the old days; like Ida in *Mildred Pierce*, Rose is a friend and advisor. But her powers extend way beyond those wielded by Ida. Rose has influence in the world, and her authority over Celeste comes from her ability to suggest to Celeste what she should do. Unlike most of the other characters, Rose is not afraid of Celeste but sees her the way the film's audience views her: as a neurotic, spoiled, childish figure who embodies the unreasonable effects of celebrity. In this way, too, Rose incarnates the female comic second of yore combined with echoes of the mammy figure—a kind of supermammy—voicing what the audience perceives. But because many of the cast members of the soap opera also see Celeste's prima donna behaviors, Rose's power comes from the fact that she alone can manage them. Because *Soapdish* is itself pretty histrionic, Rose becomes the one calming sensible figure in the film and the only one of two (she and Mr. Edwards) who have any sense of the larger world beyond television.

Rose herself is a compact set of racial and ethnic contradictions (a set that parallels Whoopi Goldberg's own contradictions). A black woman, she bears a name marked as quintessentially Jewish (and itself a Yiddish reference to blackness). This clash (or match) of name and body registers as comic, but because such comedy contrasts with her competent, calm, and controlled—almost stoic—manner, the overall effect is of something larger than the combination of racial and ethnic stereotypes, a kind of omnipotent otherness produced as the effect of being able to wield the signifiers without reflecting the signifieds. In other words, Rose demonstrates the power of someone who is beyond stereotypes because she can manipulate them. This intimates an ability to wield culture itself, a power that redefines the female comic second as being far more omnipotent than previously. This power is necessary because the ensemble cast needs such a figure to bring order to the chaos of variety.

The reinvention of a far more powerful female comic second is not quite so teleologically determined, however, although such figures emerge only after the appearance of the variety ensemble. Characters such as Rose relate to several different formations at the same time: the ensemble, the search for the paternal, the civil rights movement, and the watering down of primary characters. In ensembles, what was in classical Hollywood a female comic second has become a composite parental, sometimes hermaphroditic figure who simultaneously balances chaos and compensates for the heroine's all-too-obvious flaws while enacting a marginality made literal through appearance, identity, or behavior. The perverse, transmogrified to the marginal other, allegorically enacts the threats of everything from the redistribution of wealth and opportunity to mainstreaming multiculturalism and to the myth of the other's power. But that such secondary figures are both comic and clearly in the service of the status quo replays a constant drama of domestication. Although this drama would not work if there were not the threat of a power that exceeds the normative, white, male American aegis, figures such as Rose show not only the superiority of the margin but also its practical powerlessness in the larger scheme of things. Rose may know all, but she still works as a soap opera writer, still has to comfort the spoiled Celeste, still is not the star, and still serves the network. Her behind-the-scenes functionality compensates for Celeste's dysfunctionality, and her command of entertainment politics makes her the unvanquished queen of the soap set, where she reigns unruffled over the crazy behaviors of her colleagues.

Why does the character of the female comic second change after the 1960s? In fact, why does she even reappear? One reason may well be to negotiate the racial, gender, and sexual differences that have become sites of dispute in American culture. Reinventing the female comic second as black or gay (or if we see some versions of the supporting character, as Patricia White does, as already encoded as gay or lesbian, coming out) enables the inclusion of black or other figures without having to center them. According such figures power not only plays out a cultural drama whereby the marginal seem to have gained power but also defuses such power in the service of the whole. It also dramatizes the power such marginality is imagined as having—at least enough to knock a complacent bourgeoisie from their comfortable assumptions. Female comic seconds as other become a means by which threatening otherness can be controlled and remarginalized while the feared power of the other is dramatized and delimited.

Another reason for the reappearance of the female comic second is that celebrity personas have become even more commodified, working within the economy of expanded choice and variety that governs shopping. Although Hollywood stars have long been figures to be admired and adulated, the increased availability of images (on television and the Web and in the explosion of print media) renders them consumable objects to be grazed among the many other admirable celebrity objects made constantly available. Whoopi Goldberg, Glenn Close, and Mary Kay Place all have dedicated Web pages managed by fans who mount pictures, news items, television schedules, filmographies, biographies, sound bites, and other miscellanea out of a fan fervor. Because of the increased availability of film reruns on cable television, it is possible to see actresses over and over again in vehicles from different times (in one week, one might see a rerun of *Norma Rae*, Whoopi Goldberg as Guinan on *Star Trek: The Next Generation*, Glenn Close in *101 Dalmatians*, and Mary Kay Place in a television movie.) Stars, even secondary players, have become ubiquitous choices not only within filmic ensembles but within the range of available images.

This commodified variety emphasizes yet another mode of identification in which viewers, like shoppers, choose from among a menu of attractions, flitting from one to the other, savoring their superficial attributes, and moving on. Although filmic identifications are still affect-

ed by narrative, the cinematic apparatus, and other elements that structure alignments, the vantage of the epistemological site associated with
the female comic second becomes the vantage of the shopper and perhaps
increasingly more a matter of spectatorship than identification. The female comic second's knowledge has become a connoisseurship, a capable and discerning eye that shops without necessarily investing. The
newly powerful female comic seconds become a point from which the
ensemble is shopped and consumed, but they are also stars to be consumed. This commodity model of identification suggests that in some
ways, some modes of filmic identification must have become quite weak
and superficial, but the opposite is probably the case. With variety as a
decoy, the sites of desire for, desire to be, and knowledge of are even more
bound in the narrative, in part by the very operation of the shopping variety that appears to give viewers the choice to range over a number of
possibilities, in part by the illusion of availability offered by increased
media saturation. The model of overt consumption masks a process
whereby viewers' desires are locked into filmic narrative and image because at the same time, the illusion of scanning and shopping appears to
prevent such a cathexis, to leave viewers free to flirt rather than fall in
love. But various degrees of love are also what motivate fan Web sites,
stalkers, lookalikes, and collectors whose devotion, though perhaps not
much different in kind from the manias fanned by Hollywood studios,
ranges over a much broader field of opportunity, beyond any single film
and somehow beyond the star apparatus itself.

   A sense of a central story disappears as ground but reappears as a
frame organizing variety (kind of like *Love Boat*), where perversity becomes a matter of a mismatch between gender and desire. The perverse
in this narrative is literalized as the "perverse" of literally queer characters who are most often male because male desire for males is both more
perverse and more typical (in that it literalizes patriarchal homosociality) and, in dominant cultural stereotypes, more entertaining. On one
hand, this seems to go along with political strides made by gay activism;
on the other, the open appearance of gay characters seems to signal some
shift in the underlying structure of narrative itself so that what used to
be material from a threatening middle has now become just another part
of a narrative that edges across the surface, peopled by all kinds of variety. The off-screen world, represented in classical Hollywood by the female comic second, has become just another site of variety; the perverse
is another commodity, but the female comic second reemerges in her hybrid form as shopping guide, the realtor of this strip mall landscape that
somehow dwarfs protagonists and other minor characters alike.

The Associate

In their new form as marginal but powerful other, female comic seconds sometimes become full fledged protagonists in their own right, starring in their own feature films precisely because of their charming and potent secondary charisma. This potent other has become a commodity working through culture the same way it works within the film: as a site for projections, self-definition, and the mediation of fears. Whoopi Goldberg in particular has parlayed the enigmatic second into a comic career (or parlayed a comic career into a position as a powerful second). The films in which she stars—*Jumpin' Jack Flash* (1986), *Corinna, Corinna* (1994), *Eddie* (1996), *The Associate* (1997)—present the story of how the potent second improbably but triumphantly wins a position of influence by means of the very qualities that make her secondary: the tendency to speak her mind, her insight, her strategic deployment of racial and class categories, and, most importantly, the position of the minor itself. The example of Whoopi Goldberg illustrates the final turn of the other, the paradoxical transformation of the secondary into the center of attention.[3] The ambivalence that attends this centering of what is still clearly minor is attractive because of the license permitted by her secondary qualities but also because of the ways in which her centrality enables her to manifest her strength, hermaphroditism, otherness, and wisdom in a way that permits her effective intervention rather than continuing the tradition of secondary characters only giving unheeded advice. If change cannot come from the center—from the status quo, the establishment, or the megacapitalist media—then it can come only from the eccentric extraordinary individual who is extraordinary because she is secondary and who can effect change because she indeed is the subject of a different story. The perverse, which has become just another part of variety, has also become a site of potential salvation in a cultural imaginary where dominant culture has become a vortex of self-serving deception. Goldberg's particular trajectory exemplifies how the sidekick becomes something else—an associate, someone whose relation to power has changed from helper to wielder, someone who knows the relative power of primary and secondary and deploys that relation to her own (and others') profit while becoming (again paradoxically) a part of the establishment herself. As with classical Hollywood's exemplary seconds, these qualities seem to be a part of Goldberg's persona, and with the advent of television and the expansion of media they now go anywhere, detached from the intricate character dynamics and narrative exigencies that originally sustained them.

Whoopi Goldberg began her career in alternative theater and stand-up comedy—on the margins. Her first film role was as Celie in Steven Spielberg's *The Color Purple* (1985), a central character who survives in her own individual fashion; her next role was as an offbeat computer operator who hooks into an international spy scandal in *Jumpin' Jack Flash*. By the time of her Oscar-winning supporting actress role as psychic medium Oda Mae Brown in *Ghost* (1990), Goldberg had perfected her irreverent comic persona as one that could range from masculine to feminine to butch, from street black to class-free being, existing both as within specific cultural sites and as almost timeless and wise in a world of change. This range enacts her control over various ethnic, gender, and sexual stereotypes, placing her both within and beyond them. On one hand, Goldberg's performance of stereotypes illuminates their quality as stereotypes and brings them into question; on the other, her ability to extend, elaborate, and complicate stereotypes so they become individual renders her both wise and powerful. In *Jumpin' Jack Flash*, for example, her character sports a large baseball shirt, suspenders, and high tops, hardly the typical style statement of stereotypical black urban females. The costume sets her apart from the stereotype while her behavior—a mixture of hip street smart and bourgeois—makes it difficult to locate her as a part of any group. Indeed, in the film, she is very much a loner with friends but a person with such extraordinary empathy that she can become the trusted contact person for a desperate spy.

Jumpin' Jack Flash establishes Goldberg as both offbeat and exceptional, and *Ghost* extends her intermediary function from computer contact to actual spiritual medium through which the dead can communicate with the living. As an ex-con working the spiritualist game, Oda Mae, whose talents lie in her capacity to impersonate, gains the real ability to converse with the spirits when the ghost of Sam Wheat (Patrick Swayze) enters her spiritualist parlor. Trying to warn his girlfriend, Molly (Demi Moore), of impending danger from those who murdered him, Swayze convinces a reluctant Oda Mae to talk to Molly, feeding her details about their life that no one else could have known. The film goes through the obligatory dance of disbelief, frustration, and gathering danger as Sam convinces Oda Mae to impersonate a rich fictitious depositor (whom the murderer is using as a front to launder drug money) to withdraw the laundered money and get the murderer in trouble with the drug lords he works for. Playing the depositor, Whoopi Goldberg as Oda Mae performs the multiple and conflicting roles in such a way as to show both her control over the layered positions (poor, rich) she masquerades but also to reveal their ultimate independence from any of the positions either the character Oda Mae or Goldberg herself might have.[4] Oda Mae may be a flim-flam artist, but she becomes the reluctantly kind vehicle for Sam's connection with Molly, allowing Sam to inhabit her body so he can touch Molly again. Thus becoming quite literally a hermaphroditic medium, Oda Mae registers as both male and female, black and white, poor and rich, a human who exists somewhere beyond most other humans. Although some critics see the scene of embodiment as a potentially lesbian scene and its truncation as another example of Hollywood's homophobia—and this may well be the case—I also see it as an expression of the queer (and perverse) range Goldberg's manipulations of gender, class, and race can enact. Oda Mae's incarnations are performances, although they are less a gender (or class or racial) drag that reveals the instabilities and constructed quality of cultural identities (although they may accomplish that as well) and more emanations of a control of categories from a position beyond them.[5]

This character in control of the performance of cultural identities is the character Goldberg plays in many of her subsequent films. She is the sage other who defies type. In *The Player* (1992) Goldberg appears as homicide detective Susan Avery, a part she begged director Robert Altman to play. Again combining and mastering the multiple stereotypes of straight-arrow cop and black woman, Goldberg knowingly haunts producer Griffin Mill (Tim Robbins), representing a suspicion of his guilt that matches the knowledge the audience (which has witnessed the murder) already has. Goldberg's low-key portrayal of the folksy detective (played in a way similar to the way Peter Falk plays Columbo) both disarms and irritates Griffin, who can't tell whether she knows something and is toying with him or is as she seems to be: the rube admiring his Oscars and wearing socks and clogs. Although she appears in only three scenes, the scene in which she and her two assistants, Willa (Susan Emshwiller) and Paul (Lyle Lovett), bring Griffin to the station to look at a mugbook is a classic scene of manipulative indirection as Detective Avery and Willa carry on a discussion about tampons, Paul swats flies on the computer console, and Susan whirls a tampon by the string while asking Griffin whether he "fucked" the girlfriend of the man who was murdered. As Griffin becomes the increasingly nervous, resentful citizen with something to hide, the three detectives begin to laugh, demonstrating resoundingly their control over the situation and their superiority over the rich, influential Griffin, who is doing a very bad job of concealing his guilt.

Goldberg also occupies the margins of the starship *Enterprise* as the character Guinan, the ageless survivor of a destroyed species, in *Star Trek:*

The Next Generation (1987–94). Manning the bar in the spaceship's recreational 10 Forward, Guinan dispenses cryptic but wise advice to crew and captain alike. Her relationship with the captain, it turns out, extends into the past in a time travel adventure when she first meets Picard and his crew in nineteenth-century San Francisco. Her monochromic costumes, headdresses, and eyebrowless visage represent both her species difference and her high-priestess wisdom, delivered not sanctimoniously but with the idiosyncratic matter-of-fact comedy she has established as the secondary character's mode. Goldberg combines the comforting wisdom of the screen mammy (and all its attendant racial mythology) with a refusal to be anything other than central in her own right, turning the marginal place of the other into the place of greatest power, restraint, insight, and common sense. Although she certainly doesn't command the way the paternalistic Picard does, she is in many ways his equal. She isn't a Starfleet officer, she has a license to speak, she has extra senses, she extends beyond the world of the ship, and she is, apparently, immortal.

The film that perhaps best illustrates what is at stake in the 1990s development of the female comic second into a star is the film *Boys on the Side* (1995), in which headliner Goldberg plays Jane DeLuca (again the unlikely mix of ethnic signifiers), a lesbian musician in love with white real estate agent, Robin (Mary-Louise Parker), who, unbeknownst to Jane, has AIDS. Answering an ad Robin had placed for someone to drive to California with her, Jane falls for the white, Carpenters-loving Robin but reveals that desire to Robin only late in the film and quite indirectly through a Carpenters' song she sings after Robin gives her a piano for her birthday. On their trip to the West, Robin and Jane stop to have lunch in Pittsburgh with Holly (Drew Barrymore), a friend of Jane, and find, as they arrive at her apartment, a raging battle with drunk boyfriend Nick, who is abusing Holly. As Robin capably calms everyone down, Holly knocks Nick on the head with a baseball bat, and when he seems unharmed, the women tie him to a chair and leave town. When they find out later that he has somehow died (and after Holly starts back to Pittsburgh), the three head west, stopping in Tucson only when Robin comes down with pneumonia. At a motel during the trip, as Jane begins to chide Holly for her choice of men, Holly tells Jane that she is well aware that Jane has again fallen for an inaccessible white woman, which she apparently had done before with Holly. Holly's opinion throughout the film is that Jane's attraction to the unavailable is a symptom of self-hate. Jane remains stoic, verbally noncommittal, and steadfastly self-denying.

In her role as informer, Holly also reveals to Robin that Jane is gay, giving her analysis of Jane's self-abnegating proclivities. When Robin gets sick in Tucson, Robin's doctor finally discloses Robin's HIV status. The three women settle down in Tucson, sharing a house and working, until Jane reveals to one of Robin's prospective dates that she is HIV positive and Robin asks her to move out, saying to her, "You're the one who's in love with somebody you can never have." Holly, who is pregnant and has begun dating police officer Abraham Lincoln (Matthew McConaughey), confesses the Pittsburgh manslaughter, goes to trial, and serves six months in prison as Abe cares for the baby. When Robin's mother (Anita Gillette) comes for a visit, she tells her daughter, "You get whoever you end up with. Whoever is willing to stick by you and fight for you and it ain't always who you expect, but you just have to make do." From that point the relationship between Jane and Robin becomes clearer, Jane telling Robin that she is "holding her," and Robin asking Jane (on what she thinks is her deathbed), "It was me that you loved wasn't it? . . . Well, I loved you too." At the very end of the film at a welcoming home party for Holly, Robin attempts to sing a song that acknowledges Jane's love, a song Jane finishes for her as the scene dissolves to Jane scanning an empty room and ending up at an empty wheelchair.

As Sharon Willis rightly observes, *Boys on the Side* comes from Jane's perspective, as the final scene of the film indicates, suggesting that somehow, with Whoopi Goldberg, not only does the secondary become central, but we are now seeing from a minor point of view, a view from the side, an eccentric perspective that, fulfilling a desire for the secondary, reveals the secondary to have been a site of unfulfilled desire. Wanting to track the secondary thus becomes a kind of desire for desire—a very lesbian position according to some lesbian theories of desire.[6] Although she is central to the film, Jane is, like other secondary characters, evasive and difficult to follow. Her desire is imparted indirectly rather than directly: through point-of-view lingering on Robin, through the provision of enigmatic stoic expressions from Jane as she contemplates Robin, and only once approaching the sexual when Jane chides Robin into voicing crude terms for "down there."

The desire economy between Jane and Robin is a desire for desire, a desire for a failure of satisfaction that affects both Jane and Robin. If Jane falls for straight women who won't love her back the same way, Robin has fallen for the impossible American dream: the husband, soapbox colonial, and two children ("You could have been Donna Reed in another life," Jane tells her). Although Jane's predilections seem to suggest that the lesbian is self-hating—a claim Holly makes continually about Jane—it also suggests that her desire is for the perpetuation of longing and for the particular role of the faithful, self-sacrificing, ever-desiring one. Even if Holly claims Jane is "anti-lesbian," Jane seems instead to have dignity and comic strength, standing up to both the abusive Nick and the prosecutor handling Holly's case. When Nick asks her what sex is like without a dick, Jane responds, "I don't know, you tell me." When the snarling prosecutor asks her point blank whether she is gay, she responds, "Yes I am. And I'm sure you hear that from women all the time, but in my case it happens to be true." When Holly's baby turns out to have a black father, Jane says to Abe, "Don't look at me." Instead of pushing Robin into unwanted romance, Jane protects her and even tries to make her happy by helping her date her friend Alex.

The economy of Jane's desire in the film is a perverse economy in which Jane herself paradoxically takes the central part. Holly may desire Abe, Robin the house with the picket fence, and Jane Robin, but the audience, aligned with the cinematic apparatus, the narrative "secret" of unexpressed desire, and Jane as desirer, is aligned with desiring as a mode of watching. Although it is entirely possible that viewers will desire any of the traditionally desirable characters (Robin, Holly, Abe), the film's dynamic of unrequited desire also makes Jane a hugely desirable character. Although Jane's unrequited desire for Robin is a desire for desire, this desire for desire becomes the desire to see desire, which not only aligns

Robin (Mary Louise Parker) and Jane (Whoopi Goldberg) in *Boys on the Side*

the audience with Jane (in happy compliance with the apparatus) but also becomes a desire for Jane, for her desire, or both.

Centralizing Jane's point of view as a desire for desire suggests that the reinvented secondary has become a site of desire, not only structurally or mimetically but also as an object of identification. This identification is no longer simply epistemological but has become hysterical. Offered as a centered site for identifications through the cinematic construction of her point of view and the film's sympathetic narrative, Jane's desire for desire becomes the focus of audience desire. We become like Freud's Witty Butcher's Wife, who wanted to be in the position of her desiring friend and rival.[7] The audience's own eccentric position in relation to the film has become a literal dynamic on the screen.

Although the politics of Jane's self-sacrificing love may not be too realistic or promising, the transmutation of the female comic second from wise spinster sidekick to thwarted lover, from fourth in the credits to first, suggests the commodity envaluation of the minor as a position of perpetual desiring. Just like Ida in *Mildred Pierce,* Jane has an alternative story, one that throughout the film accompanies the dying Robin. But at the end of the film, when we see Holly happily settled and Robin dead, Jane heads off to Los Angeles, her story neither complete nor predictable. The film seems to suggest that lesbians are better off unsatisfied (or that lesbian means the failure of satisfaction and tortuous longing), but Jane's embodiment of a centered marginality enacts an ethics of selfless love that has lurked with the female comic second all along. Performing the reluctant, growling, wisecracking friend has long been the role of the female comic second from *Mildred Pierce*'s Ida to *Rear Window*'s Stella; in the 1990s, as it combines with other marginal categories, such a position becomes valued in itself as a position of superior humanity. A persona such as Whoopi Goldberg, then, becomes the star in *Sister Act, Boys on the Side, Eddie,* and *The Associate,* playing the role of the marginal and perverse whose very qualities of independence, insight, strength, and tough love propel her inevitably to centrality in each.

With desiring as a commodity also comes control. Although the unrequited desirer seems to lack control, desiring is an active position (as opposed to the passivity of being an object). Jane seems to have less control over everyday occurrences than Robin, but in fact she gains increasing control as Robin gets sicker. Although one might well argue that *Boys on the Side* illustrates the cooperation of women each contributing her personality to a successful dynamic, the two straight women become increasingly dependent as the film continues, Holly going to jail and relinquishing control to the naive Abe and Robin becoming dependent on her mother and Jane. Because Jane never makes any sort of proposal or declaration to Robin, she even seems to be in control of the one thing she cannot change: her desire. One suspects that Jane prizes this perverse desire (perverse because it is for the "whitest woman on earth" who "isn't her type"), choosing to give in to it when in other areas of her life she has taken aggressive and definitive action (such as moving west). Goldberg performs a character who thus seems always in control, whose stoicism provides a site from which differences, details, inanities, and conundrums might be domesticated and exploited. Like the common-man superheroes—Mel Gibson, Bruce Willis, Arnold Schwarzenegger, and even Jackie Chan—of action films, the centered comic second has the hidden power to defeat, manage, and vanquish domestic villains with unruffled humor and aplomb. It is as if Ida could have dressed Veda down herself and at the same time told off Monte, saved Mildred from humiliation, and then disappeared into the sunset.

However, Whoopi Goldberg is uniquely mobile, moving from white culture to black, from Hollywood to space, from the working class to success with ease and verisimilitude. But her comedy represents a post-studio response to the dilemma of how to manage commodity culture bombardment—how to manage the images, roles, trivia, and differences that seem to clog contemporary existence. Incarnating racial, gendered, sexual, and class differences, Goldberg becomes the quintessential fool who is no fool, the winner who can take it or leave it with the strength to resist fads and fight for loyalty, courage, friendship, and nobility of spirit. When the center has rotted, the secondary emerges to save the day, reprising the old center while pretending the secondary exists on the side. Like the perverse, the survival of old centrist values can occur only if they seem to emanate from somewhere other than the center; it is crucial that even if centered (which Goldberg obviously is) she continue to perform as if she is still on the side. Only by maintaining a fiction of the secondary and the indirect can formerly corny centrist values become the desirable flashy wisdom of the margins.

This is perhaps nowhere more true than in *The Associate*, Goldberg's 1996 film about a genius investment counselor, Laurel Ayres, who, because of prejudice and sexist preconceptions, can never be taken seriously for the financial wizard she is. First her co-worker Frank Peterson (Tim Daly) easily takes credit for her work, garnering a promotion that makes Laurel angry enough to quit. Then as she attempts to start her own investment business, she finds that she can get nowhere without the specter of a white male boss who is to be credited with the ideas Laurel is trying to sell. Accordingly, Laurel fabricates such a figure, the fictional

Robert S. Cutty (named after a bottle of scotch), man of the world, big game hunter, and entrepreneur who "fronts" Laurel's projects (just as she seemingly fronts for him). To be successful, Laurel realizes that her race and gender damn her to being merely the associate, so the associate she becomes. Aided by another mistreated secondary character, Frank's former secretary, Sally (Dianne Wiest), Laurel takes the corporate world by storm, holding off all requests for an actual audience with Cutty by telling clients that he is reclusive, hates meetings, is a globetrotter, and dislikes the media. When the nasty Frank decides to call Laurel's bluff by reporting what appears to be insider trading to the Securities and Exchange Commission, the commission responds by issuing a subpoena for Cutty. Deciding that Cutty's appearance in the flesh is absolutely necessary, Laurel gets her friend the drag queen to disguise her as a white man and shows up at the Plaza Hotel in an appearance calculated to give everyone a covert glimpse of the unsociable Cutty. But finally Cutty gets to be too much for her, and Laurel decides that he must die. After trying vainly to take advantage of a fortuitous shipwreck, Laurel blows up her (Cutty's) Mercedes and announces that Cutty is dead, only to have the calculating Frank resurrect him as a new partner at Laurel's former employer. Cutty returned, Laurel is blamed for stock fraud and effectively put out of business, until on the advice of Sally who wisely points out that "if Frank has Cutty, he has you," Laurel decides to become Cutty one more time for his induction into the all-male Peabody club and the acceptance of their award for Businessman of the Year. Showing up by surprise (at least for Frank), Laurel as Cutty accepts the award, kisses Frank long and hard on the lips, and removes her disguise to the applause of the black waiters and the women waiting in the lobby. Unmasked as a black woman, Laurel is able finally to be the center, taking over her former company and having Sally (now an executive) fire Frank.

Though itself another fantasy-of-success-by-the-underdog film, *The Associate* makes clear both the limitations on and power wielded by the secondary. The minor, obscured by the major, must nonetheless wield the major until they are free to reveal their true identity. Only in the extreme pressures of media hype and masquerade can the minor ever be taken seriously. An allegory of how the minor finally gets its major due, the film traces Goldberg's rise to prominence and the increasing centrality of the secondary as powerful and interesting in its own right. An associate is no longer a sidekick. The question has become, rather, who is the associate: the secondary female or the white guy who has held center stage for so long? Although *The Associate* seems to suggest the latter, what it finally illustrates, I think, is that no mater how compelling the secondary is, its status is a part of a dynamic that is in part responsible for producing the power attributed to the secondary position. In other words, stars who embody characteristics associated with the secondary incarnate the paradox of what happens to the minor when it becomes major. *The Associate* plays with the balancing of places that, by sleight of hand, keeps the secondary Laurel primary while making her appear to be secondary.

In a sense this displacement of the minor into the major evacuates the category of the minor, appearing to remove finally all hierarchies, prejudices, and binary topographies. Binary structure bows to variety. But variety is merely a cover for the extant power structures that produce the illusion of variety, the power structures that market diversity while maintaining a classed status quo. If the minor is a site of imaginary power, then that power, like Robert Cutty, has dived underground, leaving the appearance of democratic enfranchisement on the surface to cover its tracks. Although this probably states too strongly some sense of intent or design, the point is that the minor has been annexed as a mask for a center that still dominates. The major has become the man behind the curtain but one who wields real fire with only the illusion of his impotency and decenteredness.

Either the formation has changed so radically that the category of the minor no longer makes sense, or it is hidden by the more spectacular minor that has taken the fore. But the minor hasn't disappeared at all; it has been displaced. If the dynamic between center and margin played out in *The Associate* typifies contemporary commodity culture and transnational corporatism's ploys, the minor and the perverse still play in relation to their coopted former selves. If the nerds can take revenge (as they did throughout the 1980s) where does the minor, the perverse, the secondary operate at the turn of the century? As in the 1930s and 1940s, it is minor, so we don't see it. The minor we do see—that has been brought into prominence—is not minor at all. Rather, the minor, as always, recedes.

One Last Word; or, So What?

If we take the female comic secondary character as a symptom of the narrative middle, then her history through the twentieth century seems to show a shift in the forms narrative takes. As the middle disappears in favor of serial variety, the perverse, which heretofore was masked as a function of the narrative middle, emerges as part of the variety possible. This economy of serial variety matches the apparent choices of commodity culture well; the serial narrative and the commodity were made for each other. Insofar as commodity culture seems to offer multiple easily accessible choices, so the metonymical narrative seems to offer multiple surface versions that are all the equivalent of one another. What this means, however, is that the bliss of the middle and its coexistent disruption seem to disappear. Although variety might appear to challenge a white straight mainstream, it is also evidence that such challenge must now occupy a different site. The extent to which the category of female comic seconds survives, and even expands to include gay men, children, and others, indicates that although the middle may have been dislocated from the middle, it still functions from some point, even if the neat dynamic that surrounded it has disappeared. If narrative itself has become more serial, the female comic second has become a guerrilla force that works far more opportunistically than before, only occasionally coming into focus in such personae as Goldberg. As always, it is difficult to analyze without turning it into exactly the major player it is not.

Tracking the fate of the female comic second shows something about the many forces that came into play at the end of the studio system and especially the growing interdependency of Hollywood film and television. However, it does not provide a very complete picture of Hollywood under the studio system because many films did not have such fully drawn secondary characters or used a different kind of minor character altogether. Although Hollywood enabled the development of the female comic second through its contractual and casting practices, it did not turn the secondary character into anything more than a convention used enough to make it familiar with audience but not so much that these figures ever became overwhelming stars or that every film had to include such a character. Thus, although the female comic second tells us something about Hollywood practice, it certainly cannot tell us everything.

Making the secondary primary is what I've done in this book, selecting only those who have stood out as stars, who have became major in some way or another. The truly minor may well be those we don't remember, but if we look we might find that they too manifest some of the same traits as characters played by Eve Arden, Thelma Ritter, Rosalind Russell, and Whoopi Goldberg. The minor, like the perverse, is never completely deviant but always contributes in some way to maintaining the values of normative society. But they nonetheless hint at something queer, some other possibility, some power, strength, wisdom, insight, and perception necessary to pleasure and desire in cinema.

If the narrative middle traditionally represents some threat, some potentially unleashed difference, does noticing and focusing on it apart from the constraints of wholeness liberate its threat? Is attending to the middle a way to escape what seem to be the dead-end trajectories of narrative, ideology, and a perpetuation of the same? The answer is yes and no. On one hand, defining structures such as narrative open up and become less secure and totalizing. The automatic assumption of closure, wholeness, and a guarantee of meaning is brought into question. There is space in narrative for something other. On the other hand, narrative still reigns, its structure pervasive and its middle matter in service of a sense that satisfies in a way different from that of the middle. The point is that the middle is there; it works, pleasures, challenges, exists. It is never entirely contained, but its operations are indirect and deviant. The middle asks us to look differently for the way to hope.

NOTES

Introduction: Some Minor Considerations

1. The history of narrative theory from Aristotle to Tsvetan Todorov, Roland Barthes, Robert Scholes, and Robert Kellogg, and innumerable others accepts this basic structure as defining narrative.

2. Many critical readings of film read the narrative dominant as aligned with dominant ideology. Some film criticism focuses on how narrative is aligned with other cinematic systems (e.g., cinematography, space, motif); other criticism analyzes failures, exceptions, or rifts in that dominant that enable counterideological discourse or finds where film narrative itself seems counterideological. In other words, narrative moors a large tradition of critical work in film.

3. For an analysis of the relations between narrative and ideology, see Fredric Jameson, *The Political Unconscious*, and my *Come As You Are*.

4. Deleuze and Guattari use this term throughout their work to represent a nonbinary, nonhierarchical relationship.

5. Some films valorize the minor for its own sake, such as *Auntie Mame, Harold and Maude, Le roi des coeurs*, and *M*A*S*H*. These are often cult films, reaping rewards from a fringe of viewers; *Auntie Mame* seems to be the exception.

6. Of course, this is not uniformly true but a generalization. It tends to be the case that secondary characters disappear before the ends of films, although they may be present at the beginning.

7. Feminizing does not always equal queering. Males can be feminized without being queered, and they can be queered without being feminized. Feminizing relates to representations of the male himself (is he in an apron, for example), whereas queering has to do with a denaturalizing of position and role—a displacement in relation to other characters of the same sex. See Alexander Doty's analysis of Jack Benny and Rochester in *Making Things Perfectly Queer* for an analysis of the complexities of this relationship.

8. The issue of gender in relation to the minor is linked to issues of gender and narrative, questions about gender and representation generally, and the politics of patriarchy. The ways male secondary characters are queered have been the subject of work by queer theorists including Richard Dyer, Steven Cohan, and Lee Edelman. Understanding the relations between genders in the minor might be one way to understand the relations between genders and

sexualities more broadly in culture. See Richard Dyer's *Now You See It*, Alexander Doty's *Making Things Perfectly Queer*, Steven Cohan's *Masked Men*, and Lee Edelman's *Homographesis*.

9. There are several additional books that work the other way around, studying overt or deliberate representations of lesbians in film, including Chris Straayer's *Deviant Eyes, Deviant Bodies*, Andrea Weiss's *Vampires and Violets*, and Judith Mayne's *Framed*. David Bordwell, Janet Staiger, and Kristin Thompson use narrative as a central organizing structure in *The Classical Hollywood Cinema*. Teresa de Lauretis examines the role of narrative in cinema in *Alice Doesn't*, as does Stephen Heath in *Questions of Cinema*.

10. In relation to the Production Code, Richard Maltby notes, "While the Code was written under the assumption that spectators were only passive receivers of texts, the texts themselves were, out of the straightforward economic logic of what Umberto Eco has called 'the heavy industry of dreams in a capitalistic society,' constructed to accommodate, rather than predetermine, their audiences' reactions. In its practical application, the Code was the mechanism by which this multiplicity of viewing positions was achieved. Once the limits of explicit 'sophistication' had been established, the production industry had to find ways of appealing to both 'innocent' and 'sophisticated' sensibilities in the same object without transgressing the boundaries of public acceptability. This involved devising systems and codes of representations in which 'innocence' was inscribed into the text while 'sophisticated' viewers were able to 'read into' movies whatever meanings they were pleased to find, so long as the producers could use the production Code to deny that they had put them there. Much of the work of self-regulation lay in the maintenance of this system of conventions, and as such, it operated, however perversely, as an enabling mechanism at the same time that it was a repressive one" (40).

Chapter 1: The Minor Made Major

1. *Auntie Mame*, which had been popular since the publication of Patrick Dennis's novel in 1955, was a filmed adaptation of the successful Broadway play. Rosalind Russell, who starred in both play and film, suggested that Warner Brothers retain the show's Broadway director, Morton (Tec) DaCosta, and some of its original Broadway cast, including Jan Handzlik (Patrick), Tony winner Peggy Cass (Agnes Gooch), and Yuki Shimoda (Ito). The rest of the cast remained in the Broadway show with Greer Garson. The part of Vera Charles was last to be cast (Vivian Vance had done a screen test for the part). DaCosta hired British actress Coral Browne, who rushed from London to Hollywood but whose hair, after being dyed platinum, fell out, giving new meaning to Mame's line, "If I kept my hair natural the way you do, I'd be bald!" Warner Brothers had been included in the original deal to stage Patrick Dennis's novel, but that deal did not initially include Russell. As Richard Jordan notes, "Eve Arden was suggested as the ideal Auntie Mame for the screen" (107). But Russell also had a large interest in the property as its prin-

cipal investor, and the success of the play made it easy to convince Warner Brothers to have her star in the film. She had been involved in writing the stage play, adding details from characters she had known in her own life. In the play version, Gooch carried part of the comedy; as Rosalind Russell remembers, "we discussed various broad comedic shoulders available to us, and finally decided on Gooch—the mousy secretary who winds up soused and pregnant—to bear the burden" (*Life* 192). This is also true in the film, although Gooch is dwarfed by the set and other business of the film. The film set was entirely too large, Russell recalls, the stairs having been changed from the stage set's narrow spiral staircase to a wide, curving stair that reaches grandly into the ceiling. The big set was a problem according to Russell: "It's difficult to play comedy in a huge set. You lose the intimacy of the looks, the takes that get the giggles" (*Life* 213).

2. According to Alexander Doty, Russell, who literally owned the part, was a lesbian/gay "culture figure" (*Making* 17). In addition, the position of aunt has been linked to the queer, as in the case of the spinster aunt (which Mame is at the outset). See Eve Sedgwick's "Tales of the Avunculate."

3. If through the performative (at least according to Judith Butler's reading of it in relation to the constitution of gender identity) a subject constantly asserts a gendered position that is in some way not entirely "normal" to it, then accompanying this performative must be the constant reestablishment of the normative. Gender is a normativizing category, and the subject of this performativity is a normativity. In *Auntie Mame*, Lindsey Woolsey constantly performs the responses of the "normal" viewer in relation to the film's legions of eccentrics. He is the normative performative. See Butler's *Gender Trouble.*

Chapter 2: Spatial Attractions

1. There has been much critical work that both links the private and domestic to the feminine and questions and critiques that distribution of space. See Friedland and Boden's *NowHere,* Keith and Pille's *Place and the Politics of Identity,* Aiken, Brigham, Marston, and Waterstone's *Making Worlds;* and Wigley's "Untitled: The Housing of Gender." In Hollywood cinema, domestic private spaces such as kitchens and bedrooms tend to be feminine realms and are presented *as if* off-screen; that is, the action that occurs in these spaces tends to be out of the stream of plot action even if it constitutes such action. In *The Woman at the Keyhole,* Judith Mayne develops the problems and meanings of public and private through a range of films and contexts.

2. David Cook includes this definition in a footnote in *A History of Narrative Film* (464), followed by another footnote a few pages later (470) in which he goes on to say that the appearance of women's films intended for female audiences came as a "result of a widespread impression among studio executives that women comprised a majority of the film-going public." The fact that this nomenclature and explanation occurs only in the footnotes attests to the eccentricity I have been claiming. It also attests to the somewhat vague

and contested definition of the term itself. For a more extended discussion of women's film as a genre, see Andrea Walsh's *Women's Film and Female Experience, 1940–1950.*

3. Patricia White examines the coded portrayal of such supporting characters as lesbian in much greater depth in *The unInvited.*

4. For an extended discussion of the production history of *Stage Door,* see Elizabeth Kendall's *The Runaway Bride.* Before this film, Hepburn had already starred in eleven films and had won an Academy Award for *Morning Glory* (1933). Her character in *Stage Door* resembles the early Hepburn who often argued with directors and was fired from plays before they were ever staged. Rogers, in tandem with Fred Astaire, was seventh on the year's Top Ten list of box office stars and had already had much experience playing wisecracking secondary characters. Ginger Rogers's addition to the cast was seen as a hedge against Katharine Hepburn's recent lack of box-office success. Rogers, who had been immensely popular as Fred Astaire's partner in the RKO hits *Top Hat* (1935) and *Swing Time* (1936), was returning to the wisecracking blonde character type she had originally played in her pre-Astaire days in Paramount's B films or Warner's *42nd Street* (1933). Capitalizing on her recent success, RKO made Rogers the film's headliner with Adolphe Menjou, despite his smaller and less significant part. Discovering her third billing, Hepburn confronted producer Pandro Berman and demanded bigger lights. The combination of Rogers and Hepburn made *Stage Door* both a box-office attraction (as the only RKO comedy of the decade to make it to the *Film Daily* Top Ten list) and a critical success (as it garnered four Oscar nominations).

Director Gregory La Cava, a notorious alcoholic, was hired without Hepburn's approval, and she did not like working with drunks, much less with improvisers such as La Cava, who made Hepburn's studied method difficult. Hepburn was not told that Rogers's part was being built up to rival her own; both stars were touchy (perhaps because they were both reportedly romantically involved with Howard Hughes), so tempers flared when Hepburn's role began to dominate Rogers's (Edwards 160). The rest of the cast watched the stars' various jealousies and modes of performance. Eve Arden remembers "how we looked at Katharine Hepburn with a certain awe. . . . Not envy, but a respect, an admiration. She was always full of advice for us. . . . I have always admired her integrity, strength and courage" (63). The one player Hepburn got close to was Constance Collier, who played the part of the aging duenna and who, as in the film, undertook to advise Hepburn on the set.

Rogers, whom La Cava called "menthol," was difficult to stimulate into any extreme reaction, especially crying on camera. At the climactic scene of the play, when the boardinghouse denizens are watching Terry Randall's touching memorial performance, they all break into tears. Director La Cava filmed Rogers separately as she watched a film of Hepburn's performance; he didn't want to take a chance that her stoicism would ruin the group take. More apocryphal accounts say that La Cava told Rogers her house had burned down to get her to cry. It is more likely that he merely told others that such a catastrophe is what it would take. But Hepburn had her own ideas about how to move Rogers; in one myth, Hepburn dumped a pail of water on Rogers's mink coat, then said, "If it is real mink, Ginger, it won't shrink" (Edwards 160).

5. La Cava selected Eve Arden when he viewed a test at Universal for another actress and saw Arden stalking in the background saying funny lines. He cast Constance Collier as an aging duenna, playing almost a caricature of herself. Lucille Ball, who had played mainly bit parts, became the comic cynical optimist, a role she played for the next forty-five years. Ann Miller, who played an aspiring dancer, was in fact an aspiring dancer who had been in only two films before *Stage Door* but who went on to become a dancing star. Andrea Leeds, who plays the true but unfortunate talent in the film (and who was nominated for an Oscar for Best Supporting Actress), married a millionaire and retired from Hollywood three years after *Stage Door.*

6. La Cava, who had directed the romping comedy *My Man Godfrey* (1936) and whom W. C. Fields thought had the best comic mind in Hollywood besides his own, was an improviser who spent the mornings rehearsing, lunch rewriting the script, and the afternoons filming. This worked admirably for the group scenes, giving them the spontaneous and slightly chaotic feel of a community. It also enabled him to alter the script to the personality of the players, a process that allowed the film to capitalize on its cast of exceptional secondary characters.

7. Kendall's excellent analysis of *Stage Door*'s production and its relation to the issue of the star personae of its leads demonstrates what happens when one focuses only on the major. In this film, the dominant doesn't quite make sense. Kendall takes little account of the rest of the film's cast except for Menjou.

8. Eve Arden reports that she herself contributed the business about the cat she wears draped over her shoulders and the fact that she had the cat's sex wrong. See her autobiography, *The Three Phases of Eve.*

9. For an analysis of this propensity to heterosexualize representations of lesbians in film, see my book *A Lure of Knowledge.*

10. In "Lesbian Looks," Judith Mayne makes an elaborate and convincing argument about several other ways Hollywood cinema can figure and problematize a lesbian erotic, including in the ambivalent site of visibility versus invisibility. Patricia White continues this argument in relation to the suggestions evinced by specifically secondary character types such as Agnes Moorehead in *The unInvited.*

11. See Richard Dyer's *Heavenly Bodies* and Jackie Stacey's *Star Gazing.* Star culture is a subspecialty of film studies, and the position of supporting actors and actresses in the star system would be an interesting sidenote to star studies because many supporting actresses and actors were quasistars with enough celebrity to make them known but not so much that they served as role models (except, notably, among gay viewers, as suggested by Doty, Dyer, White, Hollinger, and others).

12. In *Making Things Perfectly Queer,* Alexander Doty points out the queer

encodement attached to Cukor himself and the ways Cukor's own reputation is worked into the women's badinage. In his essay "Queerness, Comedy, and *The Women*," Doty analyzes the film's queer subtext formed around jokes about Cukor.

13. The order of this sequence seems to have mixed motives. The first five appear in the order in which their names appear in the first set of credits, but Phyllis Povah, who is listed third in the first set, is listed eighth in the second. The first five animals form the center of the plot around Mary's marriage, and the last five seem to be more supporting characters.

14. Crystal is haunted by her own nemesis, another salesgirl who comments comically on Crystal's shameless duplicity on the phone with Stephen. Wherever there is pretense, there is a female comic second to shatter it.

15. A certain genre of sadomasochistic erotica is almost synonymous with such all-female settings as girls' schools, women's prisons, and even convents. Although the step into whips and chains in prison seems somewhat motivated by the institutions' supposed function, there seems to be something about a segregated female space in the cultural imaginary that permits its inversion from innocent and safe into the site of torture. Perhaps such inversion is linked to the institution's strong sense of hierarchy and order, or perhaps cynical irony transforms the very innocence such institutions try to protect. There are surprisingly (or maybe not so) few spaces that are logically all female.

16. There are films about nuns who have moved out into the world ministering charitably—*The Nun's Story* (1959) or *Change of Habit* (1969), in which the sisters must choose between their vocation and marriage—but these films do not feature the safe, homogeneous space of the convent.

17. *Where Angels Go, Trouble Follows* (1968) retains Rosalind Russell as Mother Superior and Mary Wickes as Sister Clarissa, but the Hayley Mills character comes back as Stella Stevens. Instead of taking place within the convent, the sequel plays out a conflict between the socially active Mary and the retiring and conservative Mother Superior. *Sister Act II: Back in the Habit* (1993) retains almost its entire cast, but the order now works in the community, salvaging inner-city kids.

18. In *Now You See It*, his study of queer cinema, Richard Dyer points out the ways in which characters looking conveys an encoded homosexuality. This incident is different in that it avoids identity encodement to produce a desiring dynamic.

Chapter 3: Tracking Ida

1. Of course, many other actresses consistently played secondary roles, such as Patsy Kelly, Audrey Meadows, Marjorie Main, Ruth Hussey, Mary Wickes, and Charlotte Greenwood. Because an encyclopedic examination of them all would extend this volume, I've chosen Arden and Ritter as representative. Other actresses have slightly different qualities but play pretty much the same way.

2. *Mildred Pierce* has stimulated an extended discussion of the problems of patriarchy, cinematic apparatus, and social context. Other critics include Janet Walker, in her essay "Feminist Critical Practice." Both Cook and Nelson argue convincingly about the ambivalence of the film's gender politics, focusing on the figure of Mildred. But Ida is an equally ambivalent figure who is perhaps even more openly "bisexual."

3. Both Linda Williams (in "Feminist Film Theory") and Mary Beth Haralovich discuss *Mildred Pierce*'s relation to postwar gender anxieties.

4. David Bordwell and Kristin Thompson quote producer Edgar Selwyn's advice to Daniel Comstock: "The human being is the center of the drama. The face is the center of the human being. And the eyes are the center of the face. If a process is not sharp enough to show clearly the whites of a person's eyes at a reasonable distance, it isn't any good no matter what it is" (130).

5. In *From Reverence to Rape*, Molly Haskell characterizes Ida as follows: "Independent, witty, intelligent, a true friend to her own sex and of all women the most apparently 'complete' within herself, she is made to talk constantly and longingly of men, to deprecate her own powers of attraction . . . to bemoan her 'incompleteness.' . . . There is something as disheartening as it is brave in her acceptance of the status quo, for she is using her brains to deprecate their importance and downgrading her friendships with women as second-best arrangements" (180–81). This is a very straight reading and a good example of what comes from analyzing film as only a dominant narrative in very simple binary gender terms typical of the 1970s. Given such analyses' focus on the dominant and assumption of patriarchal supremacy, it cannot see the ways Ida challenges, negotiates, critiques, and undermines the status quo.

6. Such alternative narratives might include the continuation of Ida's story (including what she does when she is not with Mildred), Wally's story, Bert's story, Lottie's story, and the stories of all the customers in Mildred's restaurants.

7. Judith Mayne maps approaches to spectatorship thoroughly (but slightly differently) in *Cinema and Spectatorship*, and in "Theorizing Mainstream Female Spectatorship," Karen Hollinger provides an account slightly different from Patricia White's.

8. Although Mulvey's "Visual Pleasure and Narrative Cinema" hints at a kind of epistemophilia contained in fetishistic scopophilia, the epistemophilia I am suggesting here is linked expressly to a narrative rather than imagistic function and is linked to character positions around whom scopophilia is nearly impossible.

9. McCallum, reading Freud's various pronouncements on the fetish, argues in *Object Lessons* that the fetish actually serves as a mode of negotiating differences.

10. One tradition of criticism on *Rear Window* represents the metacinematic and voyeuristic qualities of the film. See Roberta Pearson and Robert Stam's "Hitchcock's *Rear Window*, Robin Wood's "Fear of Spying," Jeanne Allen's "Looking through *Rear Window*," R. Barton Palmer's "The Metafic-

tional Hitchcock," Elise Lemire's "Voyeurism and the Postwar Crisis of Masculinity," and Michel Chion's "Alfred Hitchcock's *Rear Window.*"

11. Hitchcock says, "Of all the pictures I have made, this to me is the most cinematic" (40).

12. The Law and the prohibitions it represents emerge as a third term in the oedipal phase, separating the infant from the mother and instituting a separation that produces desire and language. This doesn't have to be a literal father, merely an agent that effects or signifies this separation and the prohibition against rejoinder. See generally Ellie Ragland-Sullivan's *Jacques Lacan and the Philosophy of Psychoanalysis.* I cite Ragland-Sullivan here because she gathers together the disparate threads of lacanian thought about this structure.

13. Stewart is homespun at least in this film and in a tradition of films including *It's a Wonderful Life* and *Mr. Smith Goes to Washington.* But Stewart also has another, less stable side, as manifested in such films as *Vertigo.*

14. Ritter's real talent consisted in part in her ability to enact down-to-earthness. Actress Susan Hayward, with whom Ritter worked on *With a Song in My Heart*, testifies that "the real joy of making the picture [*Song*] was Thelma—Thelma Ritter, also Brooklyn. . . . She used to yell at me like this— 'Hey Sue, what're ya' doin'? C'mon over here and take your shoes off and be yourself'" (Howard Thompson, *New York Times*, April 20, 1952). Ritter came to film late in a career that was mainly spent unspectacularly on Broadway, and her lack of pretension situated her as a representative of "just plain folks" whose common sense often provided a baseline against which the extremes of other characters seemed eccentric. But in *Rear Window* she is paired with Jimmy Stewart, another actor renowned for his down-to-earth qualities; together they played out the results of a natural curiosity about one's neighbors. Joined by the warmly seductive Grace Kelly, the three solve the mystery of a neighbor's invalid wife's disappearance. Working with Hitchcock on the elaborate thirty-one-apartment set constructed on a Paramount soundstage, the cast watched Hitchcock overcome the technical problems of shooting within and from a single room. Although Hitchcock reportedly told off-color jokes and taunted his stars by calling them "cattle" and proving it by demonstrations of the Kuleshov effect (by which viewers read various emotions into an actor's neutral facial expression depending on the images with which it is juxtaposed), he did not seem to give them much direction. Ritter suggests that his direction was merely low-key: "You knew whether you were OK or not. If he liked what you did he said nothing. If he didn't he looked as though he was going to throw up" (Pickard 120).

15. In *"Rear Window"* Hitchcock says the film's MacGuffin is the wedding ring.

16. Bette Davis's first film away from Warner's, *All about Eve*, was nominated for fourteen Oscars, but unlike Crawford in her first film away from MGM, Davis didn't win in the movie that came to represent all that was camp about her career. Like Crawford, Davis was not the first choice for the film's starring role; both Gertrude Lawrence (who was dropped from the list when she disagreed with director Joseph Mankiewicz) and Marlene Dietrich, Dar-

yl Zanuck's favorite (who refused to do the film unless she could sing in the party scene), were considered for the role. Zanuck and Mankiewicz chose Claudette Colbert, who had to drop out because of a back injury. Like *Mildred Pierce* and unlike *Stage Door, All about Eve* came from fiction, Mary Orr's "The Wisdom of Eve," which appeared in *Cosmopolitan.* Mankiewicz expanded on the short story, adding the frame narrator character Addison De Witt (George Sanders).

Like that of *Stage Door, All about Eve*'s backstage drama is enclosed and a little claustrophobic; the film tracks the relationships of a small number of characters in the rarefied world of theatrical success. It elaborates on the idea of the established star being usurped by a newcomer, but its framed narratives and movement into several locales (the dressing room, the stage, Margot Channing's apartment, a car) makes its limited circle seem even more vicious and inescapable. Davis, who excelled at delivering such campy lines as "Fasten your seatbelts. It's going to be a bumpy night," complements De Witt's rather snide observations, producing together a somewhat poisonous atmosphere that was offset by kindly Karen Richards and Eve herself as she ambitiously oozed sweetness. Only Birdie seems to be able to cut through the miasma; *New York Times* critic Bosley Crowther notes that "Thelma Ritter is screamingly funny as a wised-up maid until she is summarily lopped off" (October 14, 1950). The film probably was Davis's last great cinema performance; it won the Oscar for the best picture, best director, and best supporting actor. Ritter was nominated but lost out to Josephine Hull of *Harvey* (1950).

In the *unInvited* Patricia White discusses Birdie's role briefly in her study of the lesbian connotations of supporting actresses such as Ritter but focuses most of her attention on the figure of Eve.

17. The violent and stylized "realism" of Sam Fuller's *Pickup on South Street* represents "the fullest exposition of fifties-style anticommunist paranoia of any American film" (D. Cook 505). Although *Pickup on South Street* was critically acclaimed, winning a bronze medal at the Venice Festival, its combination of gangster film, film noir, and anticommunist vehicle made it ambiguous as it conflated the mob with the communists and pressed the limits of psychological verisimilitude. Critic Bosley Crowther, always a Ritter fan, suggests that Moe's death mars *Pickup:* "There is something about the destruction of Miss Ritter that punches a hole in the film" (*New York Times* June 18, 1953). *Variety*'s reviewer is even more a Ritter proponent: Thelma Ritter is "the only halfway convincing figure in an otherwise unconvincing cast . . . proving that it takes more than a bad script to defeat real talent" (August 13, 1953).

18. Although *Pillow Talk* plays with the misunderstandings and dramatic ironies of masquerade in heterosexual romance, it also exploited rumors about Hudson's homosexuality. According to the *Variety* reviewer, its mixture of suggestiveness and innuendo was "about as broad as traffic allows these days" (August 12, 1959), but it was enough to garner an Oscar for the story and screenplay. Doris Day was also nominated for an Academy Award for Best Actress, and Tony Randall and Thelma Ritter, according to one reviewer,

"deliver with authority, contributing a hefty proportion of the laughs" (*Variety*, August 12, 1959).

Several critics have read the various levels of gay enunciation in the film. Steven Cohan has the most thorough look at the film's sexual politics in *Masked Men*. Cynthia Fuchs provides another angle in "Split Screens," and Ellen McCallum analyzes the film's telephonic propensities in "Mother Talk."

19. With its screenwriter, Arthur Miller, and star, Marilyn Monroe, on the verge of breaking up; another star, Montgomery Clift, recovering from a serious automobile accident; and another star, Clark Gable, recently married and about to become a father for the first time, the set of *The Misfits* was already full of newsworthy personalities in newsworthy circumstances. Filmed on location in Reno and the Nevada desert, *The Misfits* became a production plagued by delays as Monroe (who would not work before noon) and Clift struggled with depression, anxiety, and drug-induced uselessness. Because Huston wanted to shoot the film in order and in black and white, when Monroe was hospitalized for exhaustion, filming had to stop. Gable, who was impatient with inactivity, undertook to perform more of the stunts normally performed by stunt doubles. He died of a heart attack soon after the film was shot (and before the birth of his son). Eli Wallach and Thelma Ritter complained about Monroe's unprofessionalism, and Huston gambled compulsively in the evenings after the shooting. The resulting film cost $4 million, the most expensive black-and-white film since 1925.

20. During the filming of *Cover Girl*, Harry Cohn, who was notoriously economical, walked onto the scene just as Arden ripped the felt. He was beside himself until he realized that the table had a false top.

21. Burl Ives, a well-respected actor, was also considered for the role of the Judge in Otto Preminger's *Anatomy of a Murder*, but Preminger opted for extreme authenticity. *Anatomy* was based on the best-selling account of a murder trial written by Michigan Supreme Court Justice John Voelker (under the pseudonym Jack Traver). Wanting the greatest possible verisimilitude, Preminger decided to make the film on location in Ishpeming, on Michigan's upper peninsula, using the local courtroom and hotel as settings. He also decided to hire a real jurist as the judge, casting Joseph N. Welch, the army lawyer who stood up to McCarthy in the Senate hearings (as well as Welsh's wife, who portrayed a member of the jury).

Chapter 4: Reliant Constructions

1. African-American characters do not disappear from the screen, but they do tend to disappear from stereotyped servant roles. They begin to reappear in secondary roles, but not in the stereotyped configuration of faithful retainer. Part of this may be an awareness that the stereotype of the black servant is a problem, but if that is the case, Hollywood certainly did little to alter that stereotype until later. William Faulkner, one of the many screen writers to contribute to *Mildred Pierce*, suggested making Lottie African Amer-

ican, although he envisioned "a Dilsey type." See Albert La Valley's introduction to *Mildred Pierce* (36). Donald Bogle notes that Beavers, who was anything but domestic, was forced into playing hearty maid types. She was even required to gain weight for her parts (62–67). Butterfly McQueen, he notes, was more a "surreal" rather than stock character. Her kind of comic talent seemed to limit her to maid roles (93–94).

2. The film does include fleeting parts played by two other African-American actresses in the extended beauty salon scene at the beginning. In both cases, the parts are associated with animals, the first a lapdog sitter, the second a maid in a back room who adds the comment, "She sure do shed" to another worker's observation about the amount of hair on a client's arm.

3. See Linda Williams's "Feminist Film Theory" and Mary Beth Haralovich's "Too Much Guilt Is Never Enough" for accounts of why the film was so threatening and what anxieties it allayed in the postwar context.

4. The Breen Committee was reportedly worried about Veda's illicit love life with Monte. Original versions of the script have Veda running off with him, which is a revision from James M. Cain's novel, in which Veda is pregnant.

5. See Steven Cohan's thorough analysis of the sexual politics of *Pillow Talk* in *Masked Men*.

6. Opinions differ about who "knew" Rock Hudson's sexuality, so the joke would work differently depending on audience knowledge. If the audience was aware of even rumors of homosexuality, the joke works as an ironic commentary on the star. If Hudson is assumed to be the straight romantic hero, then the joke is about the absurdity of such a claim. Hudson himself suggested that the public didn't really want to know. See Cohan's *Masked Men*.

7. Of course, this is only a tendency rather than a rule. Certainly there are films that are both organizational and epistemological. It is a question of which pole they tend toward. However, the increasing emphasis on epistemology does accompany the increased interest and deployment of variety for its own sake. The realm of epistemology exists where knowledge is posed as a prime cause for the shape of events. In other words, narrative that organizes around issues of epistemology locates its chaos not in actual chaos but in the mismanagement of a knowledge that already has control of events. Such narrative is defensive in that it actually admits no chaos except the chaos of misdirection. Narrative organized around issues of organization (categorization, classification, identity) locates its chaos in the initial illegibility of middle elements, which appear as out-of-control haphazard elements. This kind of narrative makes sense out of this nonsense, whereas epistemological narratives try to make sense out of sense.

Chapter 5: From Sidekick to Associate

1. In *Tube of Plenty*, Eric Barnouw traces the evolution of television in the 1940s and 1950s, showing how it deployed radio stars and more minor stars from Hollywood.

2. In *The unInvited* Patricia White thoroughly analyzes Agnes Moorehead's lesbian import.

3. This follows other cultural manifestations of the same dynamic. For example, in the 1980s feminist literary critics began to turn their attention to the black women who had been marginalized both in the women's movement and in thinking about women. The same thing happened, but less zealously, about ten years later with lesbians. This centering of what is perceived from a dominant cultural perspective as marginal also enacts certain of Jacques Derrida's notions about the importance of the margins as well as its marginal status (see *Spurs*). However, there is a difference between attending to black women as a part of a scholarly endeavor whose goal it is to be universal and all-inclusive and the ascendancy of Whoopi Goldberg, a black woman who both signifies and exceeds marginal categories as they were formulated in post–World War II America. There is also a difference between margins and the secondary: Margins are a part of a centrist topography. The secondary belongs to the perverse, which is a part of a dynamic narrative interplay. The former secures a structural system of binary oppositions; the latter, though dependent on binary structures, intermingles secondary and primary as part of a chaotic middle.

4. Tania Modleski (*Feminism*) demonstrates the ways Goldberg works as the site for the embodiment of the contradictory ideas of black women as too much woman (i.e., the mammy) and not woman at all, a duplicity that may reflect racist stereotypes rather than any subversive possibility. In *Working Girls* Yvonne Tasker makes a similar point, arguing that Goldberg is often desexed. At the same time, Modleski notes that "Goldberg's powerful acting allows her frequently to transcend some of the limitations of her material or else to bring out the subversive potential buried within the text" (133). I second Modleski's estimation and add that Goldberg embodies a middle that has come to be expressed as racial, sexual, and gender variety and is, above all, desiring.

5. If, as Judith Butler argues in *Gender Trouble*, gender is performative insofar as one produces a gender by reiterating its marks, Goldberg's gender is performance—that is not at all performative (in that it doesn't make her characters one gender or another). Performance shows control rather than essence and ultimately has little to do with gender as performative.

6. In her essay on the film, Ann Pellegrini picks up a familiar argument about the need for some kind of visual difference in depicting lesbians, arguing that Jane's blackness is the visible signifier of lesbian sexuality in an economy of sameness. However, although race may be a marker of sexual difference, it also marks other differences (Jane's independence, her patience, her strength), and other attributes mark her as lesbian (her clothing, manner, walk).

In *A Lure of Knowledge*, I hypothesize that lesbian desire often is represented as a desire for desire. In *The Practice of Love*, Teresa de Lauretis comes to a similar conclusion.

7. In *The Interpretation of Dreams*, Freud analyzes the case of a butcher's wife who identifies with her friend as someone who desires an unrequitable desire. She desires desire.

WORKS CITED

Aiken, Susan, Ann Brigham, Sallie Marston, and Penny Waterstone, eds. *Making Worlds: Gender, Metaphor, Materiality.* Tucson: University of Arizona Press, 1998.

Allen, Jeanne. "Looking through *Rear Window:* Hitchcock's Traps and Lures of Heterosexual Romance." In *Female Spectators: Looking at Film and Television.* Ed. E. Deidre Pribram. London: Verso, 1988. 31–44.

Arden, Eve. *Three Phases of Eve: An Autobiography.* New York: St. Martin's, 1985.

Aumont, Jacques, Alain Bergala, Michel Marie, and Marc Vernet. *Aesthetics of Film.* Trans. Richard Neupert. Austin: University of Texas Press, 1992.

Balio, Tino. *Grand Design: Hollywood as a Modern Business Enterprise, 1930–1939.* Volume 5 of *History of the American Cinema.* Berkeley: University of California Press, 1993.

Barnouw, Erik. *Tube of Plenty: The Evolution of American Television.* 2d rev. ed. New York: Oxford University Press, 1990.

Barthes, Roland. *The Pleasure of the Text.* Trans. Richard Miller. New York: Hill & Wang, 1975.

Baxter, John. *Hollywood in the Thirties.* New York: Paperback Library, 1970.

———. *Sixty Years of Hollywood.* South Brunswick, N.J.: A. S. Barnes, 1973.

Berenstein, Rhona. *Attack of the Leading Ladies: Gender, Sexuality, and Spectatorship in Classic Horror Cinema.* New York: Columbia University Press, 1996.

Bogle, Donald. *Toms, Coons, Mulattoes, Mammies, and Bucks: An Interpretive History of Blacks in American Films.* 3d ed. New York: Continuum, 1994.

Bordwell, David, Janet Staiger, and Kristin Thompson. *The Classical Hollywood Cinema: Film Style and Mode of Production to 1960.* London: Routledge & Kegan Paul, 1985.

Bordwell, David, and Kristin Thompson. "Technological Change and Classical Film Style." In *Grand Design: Hollywood as a Modern Business Enterprise, 1930–1939.* Ed. Tino Balio. Volume 5 of *History of the American Cinema.* Berkeley: University of California Press, 1993. 109–41.

Bronski, Michael. *Culture Clash: The Making of Gay Sensibility.* Boston: South End Press, 1984.

Brooks, Peter. "Freud's Masterplot." In *Literature and Psychoanalysis: The*

Question of Reading Otherwise. Ed. Shoshana Felman. Baltimore: Johns Hopkins University Press, 1982. 280–300.

Butler, Judith. *Gender Trouble.* New York: Routledge, 1991.

Chion, Michel. "Alfred Hitchcock's *Rear Window:* The Fourth Side." In *Alfred Hitchcock's Rear Window.* Ed. John Belton. Cambridge, England: Cambridge University Press, 2000. 110–17.

Cohan, Steven. *Masked Men: Masculinity and the Movies in the Fifties.* Bloomington: Indiana University Press, 1997.

Cook, David. *A History of Narrative Film.* New York: W. W. Norton, 1990.

Cook, Pamela. "Duplicity in *Mildred Pierce.*" In *Women in Film Noir.* Ed. E. Ann Kaplan. London: British Film Institute, 1980. 68–82.

de Lauretis, Teresa. *Alice Doesn't: Feminism, Semiotics, Cinema.* Bloomington: Indiana University Press, 1984.

———. *The Practice of Love: Lesbian Sexuality and Perverse Desire.* Bloomington: Indiana University Press, 1994.

———. "Rethinking Women's Cinema: Aesthetics and Feminist Theory." In *Multiple Voices in Feminist Film Criticism.* Ed. Diane Carson, Linda Dittmar, and Janice R. Welsch. Minneapolis: University of Minnesota Press, 1994. 140–61.

Deleuze, Gilles, and Felix Guattari. *Kafka: Toward a Minor Literature.* Trans. Dana Polan. Minneapolis: University of Minnesota Press, 1986.

Derrida, Jacques. "Différance." In *Speech and Phenomena.* Trans. David Allison. Evanston, Ill.: Northwestern University Press, 1973. 129–60.

———. *Limited, Inc.* Evanston, Ill.: Northwestern University Press, 1990.

———. *Spurs.* Trans. Barbara Harlow. Chicago: University of Chicago Press, 1979.

Doane, Mary Ann. *Femmes Fatales: Feminism, Film Theory, Psychoanalysis.* New York: Routledge, 1991.

———. "Film and the Masquerade; Theorizing the Female Spectator." *Screen* 23 (1982): 74–88.

Doty, Alexander. *Making Things Perfectly Queer.* Minneapolis: University of Minnesota Press, 1993.

———. "Queerness, Comedy, and *The Women.*" In *Classical Hollywood Comedy.* Ed. Kristine Karnick and Henry Jenkins. New York: Routledge, 1994. 380–97.

Dyer, Richard. *Heavenly Bodies: Film Stars and Society.* New York: St. Martin's, 1986.

———. *The Matter of Images: Essays on Representations.* London: Routledge, 1993.

———. *Now You See It: Studies on Lesbian and Gay Film.* London: Routledge, 1990.

Edelman, Lee. *Homographesis: Essays in Gay Literary and Cultural Theory.* New York: Routledge, 1994.

Edwards, Anne. *A Remarkable Woman: A Biography of Katharine Hepburn.* New York: William Morrow, 1985.

Eisenstein, Sergei. "Through Theater to Cinema." In *Film Form.* Ed. and trans. Jay Leyda. Cleveland: World Publishing, 1957. 3–17.

Freud, Sigmund. *Beyond the Pleasure Principle.* Ed. and trans. James Strachey. New York: W. W. Norton, 1961.

———. *The Interpretation of Dreams* (1900). In *The Standard Edition of the Complete Psychological Works of Sigmund Freud.* Trans. James Strachey. London: Hogarth, 1953. Vols. 4–5.

———. "Three Essays on the Theory of Sexuality" (1905). In *The Standard Edition of the Complete Psychological Works of Sigmund Freud.* Trans. James Strachey. London: Hogarth, 1953. 7:125–246.

Friedland, Roger, and Deirdre Boden, eds. *NowHere: Space, Time, and Modernity.* Berkeley: University of California Press, 1994.

Fuchs, Cynthia. "Split Screens: Framing and Passing in *Pillow Talk.*" In *The Other Fifties: Interrogating Midcentury American Icons.* Urbana: University of Illinois Press, 1997. 224–51.

Hansen, Miriam. "Pleasure, Ambivalence, Identification: Valentino and Female Spectatorship." In *Film Theory and Criticism.* Ed. Leo Braudy and Marshall Cohen. New York: Oxford University Press, 1999. 584–601.

Haralovich, Mary Beth. "Too Much Guilt Is Never Enough for Working Mothers: Joan Crawford, *Mildred Pierce,* and *Mommie Dearest.*" *The Velvet Light Trap* 29 (Spring 1992): 43–52.

Haskell, Molly. *From Reverence to Rape: The Treatment of Women in the Movies.* New York: Holt, Rinehart & Winston, 1974.

Heath, Stephen. *Questions of Cinema.* Bloomington: Indiana University Press, 1981.

Higham, Charles, and Joel Greenberg. *Hollywood in the Forties.* New York: A. S. Barnes, 1968.

Hitchcock, Alfred. "*Rear Window.*" In *Focus on Hitchcock.* Ed. Albert LaValley. Englewood Cliffs, N.J.: Prentice Hall, 1972. 40–46.

Hollinger, Karen. "Theorizing Mainstream Female Spectatorship: The Case of Popular Lesbian Film." *Cinema Journal* 37.2 (Winter 1998): 3–17.

Jameson, Fredric. *The Political Unconscious: Narrative as a Socially Symbolic Act.* Ithaca, N.Y.: Cornell University Press, 1981.

Jordan, Richard Tyler. *But Darling, I'm Your Auntie Mame!: The Amazing History of the World's Favorite Madcap Aunt.* Santa Barbara, Calif.: Capra Press, 1998.

Katz, Ephraim. *The Film Encyclopedia.* New York: Harper & Row, 1990.

Keith, Michael, and Steve Pille. *Place and the Politics of Identity.* London: Routledge, 1993.

Kendall, Elizabeth. *The Runaway Bride: Hollywood Romantic Comedy of the 1930s.* New York: Alfred E. Knopf, 1990.

LaValley, Albert, ed. *Mildred Pierce.* Madison: University of Wisconsin Press, 1997.

Lemire, Elise. "Voyeurism and the Postwar Crisis of Masculinity in *Rear Window.*" In *Alfred Hitchcock's Rear Window.* Ed. John Belton. Cambridge, England: Cambridge University Press, 2000. 57–90.

Maltby, Richard. "The Production Code and the Hays Office." In *Grand Design: Hollywood as a Modern Business Enterprise, 1930–1939.* Ed. Tino Balio. Volume 5 of *History of the American Cinema.* Berkeley: University of California Press, 1993. 37–72.

Mast, Gerald. *The Comic Mind: Comedy and the Movies.* Chicago: University of Chicago Press, 1979.

Mayne, Judith. *Cinema and Spectatorship.* London: Routledge, 1993.

———. *Framed: Lesbians, Feminists, and Media Culture.* Minneapolis: University of Minnesota Press, 2000.

———. "Lesbian Looks: Dorothy Arzner and Female Authorship." In *How Do I Look?: Queer Film and Video.* Ed. Bad Object-Choices. Seattle: Bay Press, 1991. 104–43.

———. *The Woman at the Keyhole: Feminism and Women's Cinema.* Bloomington: Indiana University Press, 1991.

McCallum, Ellen. "Mother Talk: Maternal Masquerade and the Problem of the Single Girl." *Camera Obscura* 42 (Sept. 1999): 71–94.

———. *Object Lessons: How to Do Things with Fetishism.* New York: SUNY Press, 1998.

Modleski, Tania. *Feminism without Women: Culture and Criticism in a Postfeminist Age.* New York: Routledge, 1991.

———. *The Woman Who Knew Too Much.* New York: Methuen, 1988.

Mulvey, Laura. "Afterthoughts on 'Visual Pleasure and Narrative Cinema' Inspired by *Duel in the Sun* (King Vidor, 1946)." *Framework* 15–17 (1981): 12–15.

———. "Visual Pleasure and Narrative Cinema." *Screen* 16 (1975): 6–18.

Naremore, James. *Acting in the Cinema.* Berkeley: University of California Press, 1988.

Nelson, Joyce. "*Mildred Pierce* Reconsidered." *Film Reader* 2 (1977): 65–70.

Newquist, Roy. *Conversations with Joan Crawford.* Seacaucus, N.J.: Citadel Press, 1980.

Palmer, R. Barton. "The Metafictional Hitchcock: The Experience of Viewing the Viewing of Experience in *Rear Window* and *Psycho*." *Cinema Journal* 25.2 (Winter 1986): 4–19.

Pearson, Roberta, and Robert Stam. "Hitchcock's *Rear Window*: Reflexivity and the Critique of Voyeurism." *Enclitic* 7 (Spring 1983): 136–45.

Pellegrini, Ann. "Women on Top, Boys on the Side, but Some of Us Are Brave: Blackness, Lesbianism, and the Visible." *College Literature* 24.1 (Feb. 1997): 83–97.

Pickard, Roy. *James Stewart: The Hollywood Years.* London: Robert Hale, 1992.

Ragland-Sullivan, Ellie. *Jacques Lacan and the Philosophy of Psychoanalysis.* Urbana: University of Illinois Press, 1986.

Robertson, Pamela. "Structural Irony in *Mildred Pierce*; or, How Mildred Lost Her Tongue." *Cinema Journal* 30.1 (Fall 1990): 42–54.

Roof, Judith. *Come As You Are: Narrative and Sexuality.* New York: Columbia University Press, 1996.

———. *A Lure of Knowledge: Lesbian Sexuality and Theory.* New York: Columbia University Press, 1991.

Rowe, Kathleen. *The Unruly Woman: Gender and the Genres of Laughter.* Austin: University of Texas Press, 1995.

Rudlin, John. *Commedia Dell-arte: An Actor's Handbook.* London: Routledge, 1994.

Russell, Rosalind, and Chris Chase. *Life Is a Banquet.* New York: Grosset & Dunlap, 1977.

Schatz, Thomas. *The Genius of the System: Hollywood Filmmaking in the Studio Era.* New York: Henry Holt, 1988.

———. *Old Hollywood/New Hollywood: Ritual, Art, and Industry.* Ann Arbor, Mich.: UMI Research Press, 1983.

Sedgwick, Eve. "Tales of the Avunculate: Queer Tutelage in *The Importance of Being Earnest.*" In *Professions of Desire: Lesbian and Gay Studies in Literature.* Ed. Bonnie Zimmerman and George Haggerty. New York: Modern Language Association, 1995. 191–209.

Siegel, Scott, and Barbara Siegel. *American Film Comedy.* New York: Prentice Hall, 1994.

Stacey, Jackie. *Star Gazing: Hollywood Cinema and Female Spectatorship.* London: Routledge, 1994.

Staiger, Janet. *Interpreting Films: Studies in the Historical Reception of American Cinema.* Princeton, N.J.: Princeton University Press, 1992.

Stoddard, Karen. *Saints and Shrews: Women and Aging in American Popular Film.* Westport, Conn.: Greenwood Press, 1983.

Straayer, Chris. *Deviant Eyes, Deviant Bodies: Sexual Re-orientations in Film and Video.* New York: Columbia University Press, 1996.

Tasker, Yvonne. *Working Girls: Gender and Sexuality in Popular Cinema.* London: Routledge, 1998.

Walker, Janet. "Feminist Critical Practice: Female Discourse in *Mildred Pierce.*" *Film Reader* 5 (1982): 164–72.

Walsh, Andrea S. *Women's Film and Female Experience, 1940–1950.* New York: Praeger, 1984.

Weiss, Andrea. "'A Queer Feeling When I Look at You': Hollywood Stars and Lesbian Spectatorship in the 1930s." In *Multiple Voices in Feminist Film Criticism.* Ed. Diane Carson, Linda Dittmar, and Janice R. Welsch. Minneapolis: University of Minnesota Press, 1994. 330–42.

———. *Vampires and Violets: Lesbians in the Cinema.* London: J. Cape, 1992.

White, Patricia. *The unInvited: Classical Hollywood Cinema and Lesbian Representability.* Bloomington: Indiana University Press, 1999.

Wigley, Mark. "Untitled: The Housing of Gender." In *Sexuality and Space.* Ed. Beatriz Colomina. Princeton, N.J.: Princeton University Press, 1992. 327–89.

Willeford, William. *The Fool and His Scepter: A Study in Clowns and Jesters, and Their Audience.* Evanston, Ill.: Northwestern University Press, 1969.

Williams, Linda. "Feminist Film Theory: *Mildred Pierce* and the Second

World War." In *Female Spectators: Looking at Film and Television.* Ed.
E. Deirdre Pribam. London: Verso, 1988. 12–30.
———. "When the Woman Looks." In *The Dread of Difference.* Ed. Barry
Grant. Austin: University of Texas Press, 1996. 15–34.
Willis, Sharon. "Race on the Road: Crossover Dreams." In *The Road Movie
Book.* Ed. Steven Cohan and Ina Rae Hark. New York: Routledge, 1997.
287–306.
Wilton, Tamsin, ed. *Immortal, Invisible: Lesbians and the Moving Image.*
London: Routledge, 1995.
Wood, Robin. "Fear of Spying." *American Film* 9.2 (Nov. 1983): 28–35.

INDEX

JUDITH ROOF is a professor of English and codirector of the Film Studies Program at Michigan State University. She is the author of *A Lure of Knowledge: Lesbian Sexuality and Theory* (1991), *Come as You Are: Narrative and Sexuality* (1996), and *Reproductions of Reproduction: Imagining Symbolic Change* (1996) and the coeditor of *Feminism and Psychoanalysis* (1989), *Who Can Speak?: Authority and Critical Identity* (1995), and *Staging the Rage: The Web of Misogyny in Modern Drama* (1998).

*The University of Illinois Press
is a founding member of the
Association of American University Presses.*

---

*Composed in 9.5/12.5 Trump Mediaeval
at the University of Illinois Press
Manufactured by Thomson-Shore, Inc.*

*University of Illinois Press
1325 South Oak Street
Champaign, IL 61820-6903
www.press.uillinois.edu*